T0072434

"[Ifill] makes it clear that Barack Obama's breakthrough has a back-story as old and complicated as America." —*New York Daily News*

"Ifill offers considerable insight into this pivotal moment."
—*The Globe and Mail* (Toronto)

"Gwen Ifill adds depth and perspective to a political narrative we thought we already understood. . . . Ifill's fine book is the first to put the Obama phenomenon in the larger context of African-American political empowerment." —*The Root*

GWEN IFILL

THE BREAKTHROUGH

Gwen Ifill is moderator and managing editor of *Washington Week* and senior correspondent of *The NewsHour with Jim Lehrer*. Before coming to PBS, she was chief congressional and political correspondent for NBC News, and had been a reporter for *The New York Times*, *The Washington Post*, *The Baltimore Sun*, and *The Boston Herald American*. She lives in Washington, D.C.

www.pbs.org/weta/washingtonweek
www.pbs.org/newshour

THE BREAKTHROUGH

THE
BREAKTHROUGH

*Politics and Race
in the Age of Obama*

GWEN IFILL

ANCHOR BOOKS

A DIVISION OF RANDOM HOUSE, INC.

NEW YORK

⚓

FIRST ANCHOR BOOKS EDITION, OCTOBER 2009

Copyright © 2009 by Gwen Ifill

All rights reserved. Published in the United States by Anchor Books,
a division of Random House, Inc., New York, and in Canada by Random House
of Canada Limited, Toronto. Originally published in slightly different form
in hardcover in the United States by Doubleday, a division
of Random House, Inc., New York.

Anchor Books and colophon are registered trademarks of Random House, Inc.

The Library of Congress has cataloged the Doubleday edition as follows:
Ifill, Gwen.
The breakthrough : politics and race in the age of Obama / by Gwen Ifill.—1st ed.
p. cm.
1. African American politicians—History.   2. United States—Race relations.
3. Obama, Barack—Influence.   4. African Americans—Politics and government.
5. United States—Politics and government.   6. Presidents—United States—
Election—2008.   I. Title.
E185.615.I34 2009
973.932092—dc22
2008051074

Anchor ISBN: 978-0-7679-2890-8

Book design by Lovedog Studio

www.anchorbooks.com

146122990

For my parents, Oliver and Eleanor Ifill,
who did not live to see the day

CONTENTS

THE BREAKTHROUGH

INTRODUCTION

I LEARNED HOW TO COVER RACE RIOTS BY TELEPHONE. THEY DIDN'T pay me enough at my first newspaper job to venture onto the grounds of South Boston High School when bricks were being thrown. Instead, I would telephone the headmaster and ask him to relay to me the number of broken chairs in the cafeteria each day. A white colleague dispatched to the scene would fill in the details for me.

I've spent thirty years in journalism since then chronicling stories like that—places where truth and consequences collide, rub up against each other, and shift history's course. None of that prepared me for 2008 and the astonishing rise of Barack Obama.

It is true that he accomplished what no black man had before, but it went further than that. Simply as an exercise in efficient politics, Obama '08 rewrote the textbook. His accomplishment was historic and one that transformed how race and politics intersect in our society. Obama is the leading edge of this change, but his success is merely the ripple in a pond that grows deeper every day.

"When people do something that they've never done before, I think that makes it easier to do it a second time," David Axelrod, the Obama campaign's chief strategist, told me just days after Obama won. "So when people vote for an African American candidate, I think it makes it easier for the next African American candidate."

The next African American candidates (and a fair share of those already in office) subscribe to a formula driven as much by demographics as by destiny. When population shifts occur—brought about by fair housing laws, affirmative action, and landmark school desegregation rulings—political power is challenged as well. It happened in Boston, New York, Chicago, and every other big city reshaped by an influx of European immigration. It is happening again now in Miami and Los Angeles, in suburban Virginia and rural North Carolina, where the political calculus is being reshaped by Latino immigrants. With African Americans, freighted with the legacy of slavery and the pushback from whites who refuse to feel guilty for the sins of their ancestors, the shift has been more scattered and sporadic, yet no less profound.

When I began my journalism career at the *Boston Herald American* in 1977, Boston was awash in the sort of racial drama that foreshadows dramatic change. While I was attending Simmons College, the federal courts demanded that the city's very political school committee fix the city's racially unbalanced education system.

The solution, imposed by U.S. District Court judge W. Arthur Garrity in 1974, seemed pretty straightforward: send white children to schools in black neighborhoods and black children to schools in white neighborhoods. It came to be known as forced busing. The idea was to impose balance where it no longer existed. The optimistic reasoning was that the resources—teachers, textbooks, shared experience— would follow. But history now shows us that busing—moving twenty thousand students to and fro in search of quality education—was, in fact, a far more radical notion than originally envisioned.[1] It struck at the heart of neighborhood and racial identity in cities all over the nation, most memorably so in Irish South Boston and black Roxbury. White residents of insular neighborhoods railed—sometimes violently—against the incursion into their neighborhood schools. Black residents in Roxbury railed right back.

As I walked to my college classes in Boston's Fenway neighborhood that fall, I saw the result with my own eyes—Boston's finest in riot gear stepping in to prevent clashes at English High School. It was a scene that played out again and again all over the city, all over the country.

"The white kids don't like black kids and black kids don't like white kids," a white student said after one of the melees I covered by phone. "All of it is prejudice. All I know is that no one's getting any education."[2]

"It's a perfect example that forced desegregation and forced busing does not work," Elvira "Pixie" Palladino, an anti-busing member of the school committee, told me at the time.

White students fled the city schools during those years, so many that the majority-white city's education system became majority-black within a decade. By 2000, only a quarter of the city's children were white, and white children accounted for under 14 percent of enrollments in the city's elementary schools.[3]

It took some years, and a more sophisticated understanding of how race and poverty intersect, for me to begin to understand that what I saw in Boston was about more than just black and white kids not liking each other. It was the beginning of a power shift that was defined by, but not limited to, race.

I moved to Baltimore in 1981, where the tipping point I had witnessed taking shape in Boston was a little further along. When I arrived, the city's leaders were still mostly white, but 56 percent of the city's residents were already nonwhite, a number that grew to 64 percent by 2000.[4]

On the surface, Baltimore's political vibe was less charged than Boston's, but the power shifts were no less significant. The city's paternalistic mayor, William Donald Schaefer, had revived downtown with a national aquarium and a Disney-like harbor development that brought tourists in droves. Twin baseball and football stadiums were poised to sprout on downtown's southern edge. Gleaming condominiums and hotels replaced what had been run-down waterfront docks. Schaefer was hailed in national magazines as an urban savior. Howard Cosell told a *Monday Night Football* audience that Schaefer was "the genius mayor."[5]

But not far from the glittering downtown development most convention visitors saw, the picture was more complicated. Crime was climbing. The schools were sliding. And change was in the offing.

Schaefer, an unmarried curmudgeon used to getting his own way, was suspicious of change. And he was doubly suspicious of any call for change that seemed rooted in racial claims. That meant that he would also be suspicious of me, a black woman whose job it was to ask him questions he did not like. As he growled and snapped at me—and, honestly, at most other reporters too—I came to realize what I was witnessing: the friction that is a necessary by-product of sandpaper change.

In 1983, Billy Murphy, a black judge and scion of a prominent local family, decided to use the sandpaper. Schaefer was still immensely popular, but he was also aware that new minority majorities had recently swept black mayors into office for the first time in cities such as Atlanta, and that the barrier was about to fall that year in Philadelphia as well.

In the end, Murphy turned out to be a pretty inadequate Democratic primary candidate, disorganized and unfocused. Even though Andrew Young (then mayor of Atlanta), Martin Luther King III, and comedian and activist Dick Gregory came to town to campaign for Murphy, Schaefer still managed to snare fully half of the black vote in a majority-black city.[6]

In defeat, though, Murphy's challenge was enough to open some eyes to the possibility that the "mayor for life," as Schaefer had been dubbed, might be displaced. Perhaps it was time for a candidate who looked like most of the people who lived in the city. Schaefer hated this line of reasoning, openly detested Murphy, and refused to speak his name aloud. Still, he saw the handwriting on the wall.[7]

Four years later, Baltimore did get its black mayor when, after sixteen years in charge, Schaefer was elected governor and selected a successor to fill his unexpired term. Clarence "Du" Burns, the affable city council president who had risen to that position from humble beginnings as a locker room attendant, was only too happy to claim a job he might never have been able to win outright. "I got standing ovations at churches," Burns marveled years later. "I hadn't done anything for them, but I was the first black mayor, y'understand?"[8]

Burns, who learned the ways of city politics behind every closed door at city hall, ended up spending seventeen years there, but only eleven months as mayor. The first time he ran for the job outright, Burns was defeated by a younger, politically unanointed Yale- and Harvard-educated attorney, a black man with the unlikely name of Kurt Schmoke. Schmoke had abandoned a prestigious post in the Carter White House to return home to Baltimore. "I thought, why did he give up working in the White House?" said his former White House colleague Christopher Edley Jr. "What's going on? And he said, 'I'm going to indict a few bad guys, make some connections in the corporate world, and run for office.'"

That is exactly what Schmoke did, first winning election as state's attorney before making the run for city hall. Even though he was up against the well-oiled Schaefer machine, Schmoke defeated Burns by five thousand votes by capturing the imagination of Baltimore voters, black and white, in a way that neither Murphy nor Burns, with their old-school ties and backroom ways, could.

"I was kind of the beneficiary in a way of a change sparked by the latter end of the civil rights movement," said Schmoke, who is now the dean of the Howard University School of Law, which produced Thurgood Marshall, L. Douglas Wilder, and Vernon Jordan. "The Voting Rights Act, which opened up so many opportunities throughout the country, started to hit its stride by 1980, and people built on that."

That trend was also in evidence about forty minutes down the interstate highway in Prince George's County, Maryland. By 1984, I had taken my unintentional road trip through sandpaper politics to this Washington suburb, where between 1980 and 1990 the African American population spurted from 37 percent to 50 percent. During that same period, nearly seventy-seven thousand whites moved elsewhere—a loss of nearly 20 percent of the county's white population.[9]

The county's power structure was in the midst of a corresponding shift from mostly white to mostly black when I was covering it for the *Washington Post*. As occurred with Schmoke in Baltimore, the resulting friction provided for a memorable foreshadowing of what was later to be revealed on the national stage.

Wayne Curry was Prince George's County's version of Kurt Schmoke—but with a little backroom dealing experience thrown in for good measure. Smooth and politically astute, he learned early on to navigate the shoals of the backwater politics that had defined this collection of poor and middle-class black and white suburbs and tobacco-growing rural communities.

Middle-class blacks were thronging to Prince George's, replacing farmland with cul-de-sacs and even gated golf course communities. Between 1979 and 1989, the county's median household income, once adjusted for inflation, rose by 15 percent.[10] As a result, PG, as it was still derisively called by people who did not live there, had become the home of the most prosperous population of African Americans in the nation. By 2005, 66 percent of the county was black.[11]

Curry, who made his mark as a real estate development lawyer, parlayed his business connections into two terms as county executive from 1994 to 2002. Over the years, he managed to establish close ties to both the existing white political establishment and the emerging black one.

In his salad days, Curry was considered a rabble-rouser, a smooth talker who could speak the language of the moneyed developers and old-time pols who were together plotting the county's future. In short, he was the kind of guy who made white and black people nervous. Fifty-eight years old and watching from the sidelines those following in his footsteps, Curry has mixed feelings about the generation of black politicians now rising. "I don't automatically see it as a good thing," he told me. "I think it could be a very, very discouraging moment, in fact, if once guys get in those positions they don't have an idea or theory about who to help or why—just to become figureheads that aren't doing much of anything to make it better for people across the board." Elected as a Hillary Clinton delegate to the 2008 Democratic National Convention, Curry endorsed Obama only after Clinton dropped out in June.

Curry's concerns echo throughout any discussion of black politics today. What is the point of electing African Americans to high office if their ties to the black community do not bind them tightly enough to black causes? Is a black candidate who, for instance, opposes affirmative action a breakthrough worth having? Or as Georgetown sociology professor Michael Eric Dyson put it to me: "If this is the price we pay for that kind of access, we'd rather not have it."

By the time the *Post* assigned me to cover the Reverend Jesse Jackson's second presidential race in 1988, I had grown familiar with variations on this argument, which usually cropped up whenever a new black face intruded on a previously all-white, and sometimes all-black, political landscape. The toughest tests often played out from within the black community itself, where in most cases political achievement and the conflict that came with it were only a generation old.

In 1984, Jackson ran for president, doubled the number of black voters casting ballots in that year's New York primary, and startled the political world with his powerful "I am somebody" imagery and his unabashedly racial appeals. It did not bother him one bit to use the assassination of Martin Luther King Jr. as part of that imagery, in part because he had been a witness to it.

"On April 4, 1968, there was a crucifixion in Memphis," he would say while campaigning. "In New York this week, we began to roll the stone away. The crucifixion of April 1968 will become the resurrection of April 1984."

Jackson scared people, and he was perfectly aware of it. The headline in that week's *Time* magazine reflected the nervous political zeitgeist of the moment: "What Does Jesse Really Want?"[12]

Jackson's 1988 run was different from his more quixotic 1984 candidacy. By then, white faces had joined the black faces on the Jackson bandwagon. His campaign manager, Gerald Austin, was a white man. And some of his most influential supporters—including Democratic operatives Harold Ickes and Ann Lewis—would go on four years later to help get Bill Clinton elected. Jackson had worked energetically to reach beyond his black church base to establish himself as a force to be reckoned with.

"My friend Gary is out of the race," he told a crowd at a predominantly Hispanic Denver Roman Catholic parish where former senator Gary Hart sat in the front pew. "That makes me Colorado's favorite son."[13]

Jackson's ability to enlarge his base continued to rattle the political establishment. He emerged the victor of the 1988 Michigan primary. This time, the *Time* magazine cover line shrieked: "Jesse!?"[14] Writers began to speculate that he would sweep lily-white Wisconsin too.

I interviewed the mayor of Sheboygan, Wisconsin, during that period.[15] Upon meeting me, he anxiously pointed out the framed pictures he had on his wall of boxers and other athletes, to prove that some of his best friends were black. I was surprised only that he actually said this to my face, and the exchange convinced me that maybe this was not Jackson country. The following week, Michael Dukakis trounced Jackson in the Democratic primary, not only in Sheboygan but in all the rest of Wisconsin as well.

Still, there was something happening here. Jackson's supporters were made up of far more than the traditional civil rights constituency. They were, in fact, the left-wing version of the very same people who flocked to rallies that year for another man of the cloth, Pat Robertson.

Everywhere he went, Jackson preached a now-familiar sermon—the power of hope. Obama would appropriate that powerful theme decades later. Jackson's effort eventually crumbled amid intraparty acrimony, but by the time the August convention rolled around he had won in more than a dozen contests, and there were a breathless few months where much seemed possible.

That spring, Jackson frequently told a story on the stump about a white man who had approached him in Beaumont, Texas, to tell him that he too had attended the famous Selma-to-Montgomery civil rights march in Alabama in 1965. But, the man told Jackson, he'd been there with the Ku Klux Klan. Time had passed, priorities had changed, and now, the man said, he was supporting him.[16]

"Even extremes learn to come together to survive," Jackson preached.

The more possible the nomination seemed, the more Jackson attempted to broaden his appeal. He kissed a lot of white babies for photographers that spring and suddenly started eschewing talk of storming the gates in favor of more mainstream rhetoric.[17] "I don't understand boundless liberalism," he told the Women's Economic Club of Detroit. "Neither do I understand static conservatism."

"We opened up an exclusive club and turned the mainstream into a flowing river," he told me at the time. "By broadening the stream, my views are now in the center."[18]

These voters felt disenfranchised. Their conviction that no one was listening or speaking to them was about more than race. It was about shared grievance too. Even before Michael S. Dukakis captured the Democratic nomination, Willie Brown, the canny San Francisco mayor who served as Jackson's national campaign chairman, correctly began calling the campaign the "Jackson movement."[19]

The political part of the movement stuttered to a halt after Dukakis refused to pick Jackson as his running mate. But as the Democrats prepared to convene in Atlanta to nominate their ticket, the resourceful Chicago preacher did not immediately leave the stage. He took his entourage by bus from Illinois to Georgia. Along the way, the vanquished candidate stopped at a rally at Jefferson Street Baptist Church in Nashville, where he spoke in front of a large banner strung behind the pulpit. JESSE YOU'RE A WINNER, it read.

But even that would not work out as planned. As Jackson spoke, the banner behind his head began to sag and peel. Organizers struggled to right the banner, then remove it. But as it fell, its weight ripped a second banner almost in half. That one read: WHERE DO WE GO FROM HERE?

Still, Jackson managed a breakthrough of sorts, one that went beyond politics. Everywhere, the terrain was changing. Black politicians were going mainstream. Twenty years later, network cameras would capture Jackson standing in Chicago's Grant Park, tears streaming down his face, as Obama walked onstage to accept the presidency.

In 1990, L. Douglas Wilder, a Korean War veteran who was raised in Richmond, Virginia, and attended that city's segregated schools, was elected the commonwealth's sixty-sixth governor—and the nation's first African American state leader ever. But he won the election by a lead far narrower than preelection polls had predicted. This came to be known as the "Bradley effect," after former Los Angeles mayor Tom Bradley, an African American who lost the 1982 race for California governor to a white man, George Deukmejian, even though polls had shown him winning by as much as twenty-two points.[20]

"People lied!" Wilder told me years later, but months before Obama would be elected. "And they will continue to lie. Racism is never going to go away, and we shouldn't convince ourselves that it could."

There has, however, been considerable debate about the Bradley effect. One Deukmejian pollster said the conclusion was based entirely on the speculation of respected California pollster Mervin Field, who had no other way to explain why his preelection polling was off the mark. "The Bradley Effect was born amidst some major polling errors and a confusing array of mixed predictions, hardly a firm foundation to construct a theory," pollster V. Lance Tarrance Jr. wrote twenty-six years later.[21] Obama himself called the theory "outdated and overstated."[22]

In fact, the question of how voters behaved in secret when faced with a racial choice increasingly cut the opposite way. In the 2006 midterm elections, African Americans lost four out of five statewide races. But in those cases, their losses were foreshadowed—accurately—in preelection polling.[23] Harold Ford Jr., who ran and lost a race for U.S. Senate, actually drew more votes overall, not just white votes, on Election Day than the last polls had predicted he would.

Obama continued that trend. Exit polls showed not only that he outperformed 2004 nominee John Kerry among white voters but also that those who made up their minds within the last few days—theoretically the secret, lying racists of the Bradley effect—voted for him as well. RIP, the Bradley effect.

Once again, Obama became the most famous example of a trend that was already taking hold largely out of the public eye. Other African Americans have also successfully attracted white support over the years, many of them in local and state government. In 1996, environmentalist and county council member Ron Sims, who marched in civil rights protests with his parents while he was growing up in Spokane, Washington, was appointed to the top executive's job in Seattle's overwhelmingly white King County and has since been re-elected twice.[24] By 2007, there were 622 black state legislators, 30 percent of them from predominantly white districts. In 2001, only about 16 percent of the black legislators represented majority-white areas.[25]

The evolution that has brought us to our latest sandpaper crossroads has been as much generational as racial. Black mayors have been elected, with significant white support, in Cincinnati, Ohio; Buffalo, New York; and even Iowa City—part of a wave of more than forty African Americans now running American cities.

Barack Obama's historic 2008 presidential campaign touched on all the themes I have covered throughout my career and all of the layers of meaning that run through black politics. Ambition, aspiration, fear, folly—all were on display as Obama boarded the roller coaster that ultimately led to the White House. And as he took on that ultimate political challenge, America's conflicts about race were laid bare, again and again.

Edward W. Brooke, who was elected Massachusetts attorney general in 1962 and four years later became the nation's first post-Reconstruction black U.S. senator, believes that if his state was ready four decades ago, the rest of the country might be now.

"I would love to see a lot of things happen between now and the time I lay me down to rest," said Brooke, now retired and living in

Florida, where he is encouraged by the rise of a new generation of black politicians. "All I'm saying is that you can't win unless you run. You've got to have that fire in the belly, that desire to achieve, to win that position, and to do something with it when you do win."

Obama sent Brooke a copy of one of his books, inscribed "Thank you for paving the way." Brooke responded with a signed copy of his own autobiography, in which he called Obama "a worthy bearer of the torch."[26] But the passing of the torch has been fraught with all of the insecurities and rivalries that can be brought on by consequential change. Hovering over every conflict for these breakthrough candidates has always been the question of race.

A career spent watching politicians of every gender, color, and creed trying to sort their way through the abrasions of political change has taught me much. I've witnessed the uneasy transition from the civil rights struggle to direct engagement in electoral politics. As black politicians have broken through, I've documented the friction that has resulted when new realities, demographic as well as political, confront established customs and institutions.

So it should have come as no surprise to me when I was briefly caught up in the crosswinds of the very conflict I'd spent the past years documenting. But it did. Barely twenty-four hours before I was to moderate the season's only vice presidential debate, John McCain supporters decided to stir the pot (and, they imagined, throw me off balance) by suggesting that they had just discovered that this book was to be a piece of pro-Obama puffery.

It was easy enough to discover that this was not true. The book and its true topic had been hiding in plain sight for more than a year as I interviewed dozens of subjects and wrote on the topic for more than one national magazine. But I was a hard target to resist—an African American journalist writing about race could not possibly be capable of thinking bigger thoughts, could she?

In retrospect, this was a small distraction that blew over the second the debate ended. And I quickly came to realize that my brush with sandpaper politics was a mere scratch compared to the struggles of African American politicians who had been fighting to establish a political beachhead for decades before I—or Barack Obama, for that matter—ever came along.

The difference now is that in the twenty-first century, the breakthrough generation of black politicians is aiming to capture much bigger territory. Obama's relentless and disciplined giant-slaying campaign is by no means the only story. This book will tell the rest.

CHAPTER ONE

BREAKING THROUGH

So the first generation comes through, and they say great, you get your law degree and you go out and you be a trou-blemaker in the black community. Second wave comes through, and aha, now I've got opportunities in business. Third wave comes through, and maybe we've gotten to the point where we can get somewhere with mainstream poli-tics, not protest politics. It becomes a viable choice in ways that it might not have . . . in more places than it might have been.

—CHRISTOPHER EDLEY JR.

IT IS EASY TO OVERLOOK CHANGE WHEN IT HAPPENS, EVEN WHEN it is as dramatic and historic as this year's breakthrough presidential election. But as I stood at Denver's Invesco Field on the night Barack Obama accepted his party's nomination for president, I swear I could feel the rumbling under my feet.

The Reverend Jesse Jackson strode through the crowd remember-ing how different this night was from the day twenty-four years before when he'd had his own star turn at a Democratic National Convention. "I'm excited beyond measure," he told me. His son, Illinois congressman Jesse Jackson Jr., held court at a purposeful distance from his father.

Cory Booker, the mayor of Newark, New Jersey, and Deval Patrick, the governor of Massachusetts, grinned and backslapped and owned the night as the rising stars they are. Artur Davis, the Alabama congressman with designs on the governor's office, sorted through a crowded dance card of public appearances. Benjamin Jealous, newly elected to lead the venerable NAACP, choked up. He was thirty-five years old.

Each in his own way was basking in the political glow of the night. They were not interlopers or token black invitees at this particular party. They did not necessarily even know each other particularly well. But they were the stars of the evening. For one night, all of the friction and below-the-radar political positioning each had endured—much of it obscured by Obama's meteoric rise—was on display. It was a rare lightning-stroke moment that finally illuminated the dramatic shift in tone, message, and leadership that has forced a redefinition of black politics and of black politicians. It was the Age of Obama, in full effect.

On television, that sparkling night in Denver appeared to be all about a presidential nomination. But in the stadium itself, it was about so much more. It was about the past, about progress, and about race—the most divisive issue in the nation's history. And it provided a convenient yardstick with which to measure what the change Obama talked so much about could really mean. Before my eyes, I was able to witness the romance and achievement of 1960s civil rights marches bearing fruit, as the lions of the movement mingled with the up-and-comers. Some had been slow to embrace Barack Obama. Some had been quick. But this night, all wanted to bear witness.

The 2008 election forced Americans unused to talking about race to confront their own biases or their own naiveté. Civil rights heroes had to learn to relate to a generation of excited new voters—black, white, and brown—who had not yet been born when they scored their last legislative victories. Newcomers pondered how to push their elders off the stage without being disrespectful. It was a sandpaper moment for everyone as Americans struggled with the kind of friction that forces self-examination, conflict, and finally actual change.

There were many ways to measure this race-based change. In 1958, more than half of Americans responding to a Gallup poll said they would not vote for a black candidate.[1] By 1984, that number had dropped to 16 percent. By 2007, only 4 percent told *Newsweek* they would not.[2] In 2008, 43 percent of white Americans cast their votes for Obama. That sounds unimpressive until you notice that John Kerry, a white candidate, got only 41 percent of the white vote in 2004.[3]

The nation had moved a long way even from the 1970s, where the prospect of black mayors taking over from white mayors spawned slogans like "Atlanta's too young to die" and, in Los Angeles, "Will your city be safe with this man?"[4]

Obama's unexpected breakthrough made it blazingly clear that we had reached a place we had not been before. John Lewis, the Georgia congressman who was twenty-three years old when he appeared on the steps of the Lincoln Memorial with Martin Luther King Jr. at the 1963 March on Washington, said 2008 was unlike anything he had ever experienced.

"I think it's something new, it's different, it's exciting," said Lewis, who had his own breakthrough when he was elected to Congress in 1986 at the age of forty-six. "It is almost like the dreams, the hopes, the aspirations are being realized."

To be clear right off the bat, I do not believe this to be a "postracial" moment, as so many have claimed. After talking to scores of people for this book, I am still not even entirely sure what that term means. My well-reported suspicion is that it is the type of code language that conveniently means different things to different people. For those interested in resisting any discussion of racial difference, it is an easy way to embrace the mythic notion of color blindness. For civil rights veterans, it is a term that sparks outrage. (Why is "getting past" race considered to be a good thing? Does that make race a bad thing?) For some up-and-coming politicians hoping to build their success on erasing rather than maintaining lines of difference, the idea has some appeal.

Those are the fault lines. Can insiders effect real change, or do they become change's worst enemy once they're inside? This is when the friction kicks in, that sandpaper place where change happens and the nerve endings of ambition become exposed and frayed. Sometimes sparks fly, and often—for a while at least—it is difficult to discern the good. The protest marchers find themselves picketing black elected officials. The officials—so recently inside the door—find it necessary to push back. In politics, this usually signals that a painful and challenging power shift is under way. And seldom are all of the parties involved happy about it.

That is what happens with a breakthrough. The first ones through the door often get bruised, if not broken. Eventually, with a little political acumen and racial sensitivity and a lot of hard work, a smooth new place can emerge.

"There has never been a change in the condition of blacks that has been as dramatic and consequential as the change from the time I was born to now," Roger Wilkins, a seventy-six-year-old historian, journalist, and veteran activist, told me. "Never. Never. And as the country changes, as the opportunity structure for black people changes, we're going to get different leaders."

The breakthrough has not occurred overnight, although it sometimes seems as if it did. There were critical moments along the way. In 2006, *five* black men ran for governor or U.S. Senate in Ohio, Maryland, Tennessee, Pennsylvania, and Massachusetts. Three were Republicans. That was a breakthrough. In the end, however, only one—Patrick—won.

But how quickly things shifted. When the Massachusetts governor went to Boston Common two years later to endorse Obama, ten thousand people gathered to cheer the two black men, who stood, hands clasped, on the same bandstand used by segregationist George Wallace as he campaigned for president in 1968.[5] That was another breakthrough.

Similar signs of racial progress have been popping up everywhere, and many optimistic Americans seem ready to embrace it. In mid-2007, 71 percent of all voters assessed relations between blacks and whites as "very" or "somewhat" good.[6] The pessimists, interestingly enough, were African Americans. Only 55 percent were willing to offer a similarly positive response.

Americans have come a great distance, as the 2008 election results and the multiracial euphoria that followed demonstrated. But when it comes to any issue, debate, or ambition shaded by race, we have not yet come to a common place. Discussions are coded, and politicians often stumble unaware into definitional chasms. How was Delaware senator Joe Biden to know the uproar he would ignite when he called Obama "clean" and "articulate"? And should Bill Clinton—famous for being simpatico with African Americans—have realized that referring to Obama's record as a "fairy tale" or comparing his electoral victories to Jesse Jackson's would sound racially dismissive? John McCain stumbled into the same minefield when he caustically referred to Obama as "that one" during a presidential debate. Whites I talked to considered it dismissive but not insulting. Blacks I talked to were outraged.

It can be consequential when intention diverges so sharply from meaning, and race is involved. Throughout our nation's history, the most eventful change has often been driven by racial conflict. Wars have been fought, marches have been led, and movements have been nurtured from the pain and discovery of our evolving debate over the politics of difference.

"Segregation made us all alike. It made us think alike," Julian Bond told me over coffee in a Washington, D.C., bakery where—integration aside—we were the only black customers. "We lived together. We read the same newspapers, our own newspapers, so we had a group consciousness that has been dissipated to some degree by the demise of segregation. So we are a different kind of people now than we would have been, say, thirty, forty, fifty years ago. And it has its upsides, and it has its downsides."

Many of us—no matter what race—are content to remain perched on the sidelines of our great political debates. For the better part of the 1990s, most Americans, and certainly the news media, appeared more preoccupied with televised murder trials and helicopter chases than with elections and voting. We seemed capable of being roused from our spectator's pose only when something truly spectacular was at stake: war, terror, global economic crises that threatened our 401(k)s.

Obama's 2008 run proved an exception to this trend. While overall voter turnout remained roughly the same from 2004, more Democrats, propelled by the Obama candidacy, did go to the polls. It was the Republicans who stayed home.[7]

Politics affects every decision we make, as well as every decision taken out of our hands. It defines our past and dictates our future. When politics intersects with our lives, history books must be rewritten. This has been especially true for African Americans making their way in the United States, seizing first equality and then power in fits and starts.

Abolitionist Frederick Douglass was correct in 1857 when he said, "Power concedes nothing without a demand."[8] As the demands have grown more urgent, the history of blacks in politics has always been inextricably linked to the progress of the civil rights movement.

Rosa Parks did not just happen to be on that bus in Montgomery. She signed up for civil rights training first.[9] Fannie Lou Hamer did not just happen to integrate Mississippi's (unseated) delegation to the 1964 Democratic National Convention. She began trying to register to vote in 1962.[10] And Martin Luther King Jr. did not limit his agitations to marches and pulpits. Civil rights historians have chronicled how exhaustively he also pulled the levers of politics and power to maneuver the passage of civil and voting rights legislation. Demand—some of it overt, some of it leavened with political nuance—has long been the key to black political advancement in America.

Now that this demand has forced laws onto the books and black politicians have been elected, what has become of that movement? Who has inherited the King legacy? And as the 1960s leaders age and fade, a new generation is asking a different question: Does this century even require another King—a single leader?

Tony West, a forty-two-year-old African American lawyer in San Francisco who raised money and knocked on doors for Obama in 2008, is the picture of upper-middle-class success in his downtown high-rise office. Pictures of Malcolm X, Martin Luther King Jr., and Michael Dukakis—the former Massachusetts governor who gave him his first job in politics—line the walls. He is enough of a political junkie that he studied for the bar exam while on the Democratic National Convention floor in 1992, and he worked the floor for Obama again in 2008. Activism, he said, has taken on a different tone from the days when an older generation had to risk violence and arrest to make a difference.

He tried—once—to run for office on his own and got a taste of what happens when you step out of line. He was defeated resoundingly. "The lesson I learned is how angry people get with you when you don't go through the traditional channels," he says now, "when you don't wait your turn, when you don't kiss the ring, when you don't do all the things that you're supposed to do in order to get there."

West says he learned how to take risks from his parents, who grew up, met, and were educated in the South. But his experience has been different. "Their day-to-day life experience in dealing with discrimination, dealing with segregation, Jim Crow, is just something that at best I've read about or know the stories of as told to me," he said. "But it is not something that I have had to confront on a daily basis."

Superlawyer Vernon Jordan has more in common with West's parents. He earned his civil rights bona fides running the Urban League and the United Negro College Fund, but he learned the ropes of the movement chauffeuring NAACP pioneer Roy Wilkins to and from meetings in Georgia in the 1960s. He identifies five distinct brands of black leadership: the grassroots activist, the corporate titan, the traditional civil rights organizer, the self-made entrepreneur, and the elected official. These leaders range from CEOs to hip-hop artists to mayors, and they do not necessarily represent a single worldview.

"When we went across the Edmund Pettus Bridge, there was no guarantee we were all going to come out the same on the other side," Jordan told me over lunch, figuratively invoking the lessons of the 1965 Selma-to-Montgomery march. "Clarence Thomas went across the Edmund Pettus Bridge too, but there was no guarantee we all would be alike. Because there have always been divisions in the community."

There is yet a tougher question: Do all African Americans even want the same things? It is lazy and simple to lump them all together as a group that harbors the same grievances and aspirations. In fact, as a 2007 National Public Radio/Pew Research Center poll of more than a thousand African Americans showed, African Americans are no monolith. Sixty-one percent said they saw more differences than similarities between the values of middle-class and poor blacks. The same Pew report also found that more than one-third of African Americans believe that blacks are too diverse to be thought of as a single race.[11]

The gulf, the report concluded, existed between middle-class and poor blacks. Interestingly enough, it was not a case of the bourgeoisie looking down its nose at the underclass. The survey showed poorer blacks were the ones more likely to see the existence of a gap between the poor and the middle class in what had come to be branded "family values."[12] (Although conservatives had appropriated a term that came to be a politically loaded one, it turns out poor folks own the term too.)

Perhaps African Americans have already reached a turning point, at least in theory. After all, Bill Cosby can sell Jell-O, Oprah Winfrey can sell books, and Michael Jordan can sell Hanes underwear. Denzel Washington outranks Tom Hanks as America's favorite movie star.[13] Why shouldn't black politicians be equally acceptable to the majority?

One of the things all these well-known names have in common is the ability to short-circuit white guilt. None of these popular figures seems to be pointing the finger of blame. How could race still be a problem in America if white people could now identify with black entertainers and athletes, if Bill Cosby was welcome in their homes? No less a political figure than Republican Karl Rove made just such a point during Fox News' election night coverage in 2008.

David Bositis, senior research associate at the Joint Center for Political and Economic Studies in Washington, senses the mood has been shifting for decades, as access to the education afforded by civil rights advances—including desegregation and affirmative action—has created a new breed of black politician able to straddle the racial divide.

"You started seeing younger black elected officials who more and more had the profile of what more prominent white elected officials had," he says. "If you look at a lot of the candidates for president, they went to Ivy League schools or law schools or business schools, and you started seeing that in black candidates. And those are the kind of credentials that white voters expect in the kind of people they are going to support for statewide office."

Beginning in the early 1990s, Bositis' Joint Center polling also began documenting a generational divide among black Americans that eventually began to drive a shift in political priorities. One-quarter of young black voters now describe themselves as conservatives, and nearly a third say they are moderates. The remaining group, 48 percent, describe themselves as liberal. Fully two-thirds of them support arm's-length solutions such as school choice and the partial privatization of Social Security. Blacks over the age of forty, by contrast, oppose school vouchers.[14]

Wasn't this, after all, what Whitney Young, John Lewis, and Barbara Jordan were reaching for? Is this not true diversity of thought as well as action?

Colin Powell was, for a time, the prototype of a nontraditional political figure. He was already fifty-eight years old and a much-decorated and admired retired general—years before the second Iraq war sullied his reputation—when he was lured into a deep and serious flirtation with the presidency in 1995. His mulling gripped the political world—including many white assignment editors who were convinced Powell would be the breakthrough. Reporters like me were sent on long-term political stakeout to divine his interest and intentions. While working for NBC that fall, I traveled all the way to London just to corner Powell in a BBC greenroom while he was on a book tour.

The general, whom I then knew only slightly, was startled to see me, but not so caught off guard that he declared his candidacy to me. Powell wrote later that he was "desperately torn" about his decision, swayed alternately by pressure from Republicans, Democrats, and independents.[15] Everyone took turns trying to convince him he could be the candidate to transcend race and party. He had, after all, been the first black four-star general, the first black chairman of the Joint Chiefs of Staff. Why not be the black Eisenhower as well?

That decision was left to his wife, Alma, a sweet-natured but tough-minded military wife who possessed a will of steel and a sharp instinct. That instinct told her it was not safe for her husband, or for any other black man, to run for president. Not yet. When Powell ultimately announced his decision not to run at a packed news conference in a Washington hotel ballroom only months after the Powell-for-president frenzy began, Alma, standing by his side, looked only relieved.

Powell declared that running for president would require "a calling that I do not yet hear."[16] But even as he stepped away, he seemed to sense the change in the air.

"In one generation," he declared, "we have moved from denying a black man service at a lunch counter, to elevating one to the highest military office in the nation and to being a serious contender for the Presidency."[17] But in deciding not to run, Powell never tested the idea of whether the nation was, at that time, truly ready for a black commander in chief.

"The question lingered as to whether or not that would have been a serious problem," he told me a dozen years later as we chatted in his postretirement office in Alexandria, Virginia. "Many of my close friends and relatives said, 'Colin, don't believe it. When they go in that booth, they're not going to vote for a colored man.'"

Plus, Powell was not that impressed by all the "first black" stuff. When people marveled to him that he was the first, say, black secretary of state, he thought: "Is there a [first] white one somewhere?" This is not to say that Powell is not proud of his accomplishments; he's just weary (in the way so many "firsts" are) of being given primary credit for the life factor he had the least control over—his race.

Powell's decision to remove himself from electoral politics was also a blow to the Republican Party, and one from which it has never quite recovered. When Oklahoma congressman J. C. Watts left Congress in 2002, he was the last of the black Republicans there. By the time 2008 arrived, not a single credible black Republican candidate was running for the House, for the Senate, or for governor in any of the fifty states.[18]

Powell would not have been the first black candidate for president. That distinction belongs to Shirley Chisholm, the tart and bespectacled immigrants' daughter who, in 1968, was the first African American woman elected to Congress. Chisholm was ahead of her time, and—aside from their shared West Indian ancestry—unlike Powell in almost every way. She had chosen politics, not the military, as her path to public service. And she took pride in her reputation as a maverick, both in her Brooklyn district and on Capitol Hill.

Mavericks were not exactly welcome in the early years of black political power on Capitol Hill. When she decided to run for the Democratic nomination in 1972, other black elected officials, including members of Congress, were among her fiercest critics. In his book on the history of the Congressional Black Caucus, former representative William L. Clay Sr. called her candidacy "grandiose." Ohio's Louis Stokes called it an "ego trip." Both men were elected to Congress on the same day in 1968 Chisholm was, but they were not close.

"No matter how unrealistic, she was entitled to her hallucinations," Clay wrote. Ronald V. Dellums, who initially endorsed Chisholm, switched to George McGovern, the eventual nominee.[19] Chisholm's candidacy appealed to some feminists and some African Americans, but she ultimately earned only 5 percent of the vote in the Democratic primaries.

L. Douglas Wilder, the former Virginia governor who is now the mayor of Richmond, launched his own almost unnoticed nine-month run for the nomination in 1992. His effort was short-lived and marked by what turned into an unseemly feud with the Reverend Jesse Jackson, who himself had run for president twice. Jackson did not feel Wilder was giving him his due; Wilder simply did not like Jackson.

But Jackson ran the most serious national campaign prior to Obama's. In 1988, his second presidential campaign, he managed to win thirteen primary contests and seven million votes.[20]

The Jackson-Wilder feud is but one example of a more perilous straddle for black politics—negotiating the friction within the black community itself. It is one of the delicately untold stories of our time. The problem? No one wants to air the dirty laundry. When popular talk show host Tavis Smiley dared to voice his doubts of Obama early on in the presidential race, many of his African American viewers and listeners turned on him in force.

Still, this type of intraracial political friction is not as unusual as it may seem. When there are only so many ladders available to climb, the struggle to maintain one's hold on any one rung can become intense. When thousands of activists descended on Jena, Louisiana, in 2007 to protest the imprisonment of six black teenagers, Jackson made head-lines by criticizing Obama for not joining the march. Obama, Jackson told a reporter, was "acting white." He later said he did not recall us-ing those words, and released a statement reiterating his support for the Obama candidacy. But Jackson's diffidence about Obama became a recurring theme, one he later said he came to regret even as he ac-knowledged the strain that began to build between the two Illinois politicians.

"It's not a hostile tension necessarily, though it can be at times," he told me months later. "There's a creative tension that makes for change. You reshape iron when it's hot."

Al Sharpton—another political lightning rod—played the 2008 presidential race card differently. For a time, he served as closet adviser to both Hillary Clinton and Barack Obama, even saving their pleading calls on his cell phone to play back for reporters. He laughs when people tell him the success of civil rights outsiders such as Obama renders insiders such as himself obsolete. That, he has said, would be like expecting soul singer James Brown to have made crooner Sammy Davis Jr. obsolete.

"I think white America wants to make us all one dimension," he told me one morning over breakfast. "Okay, we've got one black at a time. Jesse had his day, Al was there, and then now Barack. But that ain't how it is."

Indeed, Sharpton is less troubled by Obama's rise than some who believe the black community can sustain only one leader at a time might expect. The two held one very public meeting over fried shrimp at Sylvia's, the famous Harlem soul food emporium, but Sharpton had enough self-awareness about his political radioactivity to stay mostly behind the scenes after that.

"I don't think that white media gives white folks credit for having good sense," Sharpton said. "They understand that a Barack Obama's got to deal with me at some level. They just don't want to see I'm controlling it. White folk ain't crazy now."

Sharpton acknowledges the difference between his approach and strategies developed by the new generation of black politicians banging their heads against the ceiling of power politics. They are almost all middle-class, college-educated, and comfortable in multiracial situations. They are not the 1960s stereotype of a civil rights leader.

When it comes to ambition, they take much from the Doug Wilders, the Jesse Jacksons, and the Colin Powells. But they reject much as well. Like a ship maneuvering its way through a narrow channel, they embrace civil rights politics when it helps, and move past it when it does not.

"We are in the aftermath of a black freedom struggle that culminated, it ended in 1980 with the election of Ronald Reagan," Eddie Glaude Jr., a professor of religion and African American studies at Princeton, told me. "We're talking about a period post–mass struggle. We're talking about different conditions under which young people come of age politically."

And there are the shape-shifters. Harold Ford Jr., a Democrat who lost his U.S. Senate race in 2006, is a card-carrying member of the National Rifle Association and uses his platform as chairman of the moderate Democratic Leadership Council to argue for a more conservative brand of Democratic politics. Michael Steele, a Republican who missed his chance to be elected to the U.S. Senate from Maryland that same year, is trying to do much the same for his party as chairman of GOPAC, a Republican think tank. Neither man adheres to the traditional orthodoxies of black politics. Each is more impressed by what he sees in the business world than by what he sees in politics.

During the 2007 celebration honoring the fiftieth anniversary of the integration of Little Rock Central High School, Ford—now a vice chairman at Merrill Lynch—told an audience how he walked into a dinner meeting of black CEOs in New York, sat down, and thought, "This is the America that Dr. King was talking about."

Likewise, Steele argues for the need to move beyond the traditional civil rights paradigm. "This generation is less interested in having a seat at the lunch counter and more interested in owning the diner," says Steele. "That is the difference between those who marched and those who now follow behind that march."

Indeed, there have always been different routes to progress. Powell did not take part in civil rights marches. He was serving in the Army. "I thought that my job, since I wasn't going to march, was to take advantage of what those who had marched had created," Powell says. "But I never had any illusions that it was all over."

In his autobiography, Powell described the Army as a natural destination for a young black man in the 1960s because it harbored "less discrimination, a truer merit system, and leveler playing fields" than any "Southern city hall or Northern corporation."

"The Army, therefore, made it easier for me to love my country, with all its flaws, and to serve her with all my heart," Powell wrote.[21]

In that respect, Powell, now seventy-one, has something in common with the generation currently rising to power. Only 9 percent of the black elected officials eighteen to forty years old were active in the civil rights movement, as opposed to 68 percent of the politicians who came before them. As institutional barriers fell—especially with the 1965 enactment of the Voting Rights Act—politics became more integrated.[22]

"These guys have taken an unprecedented leap into the Grand Canyon of history," said Wayne Curry, the former executive of Maryland's majority-black Prince George's County. "There's no precedent for it, there's no road map. They're pioneers, and like all explorers and pioneers, some will make it to the ultimate destination. Some won't. But somebody behind them will come along, and follow as close as they could—and of course if they can find the map, maybe get a little further."

But maps are not that dependable when the roads are still under construction. As Michael Steele notes, integrating lunch counters is now an antiquated and unnecessary concept. Has anyone born in the drive-through age ever even eaten at a lunch counter?

"We don't go out and march," Julius L. Chambers, legendary civil rights attorney and former president of the NAACP Legal Defense Fund, told me prior to Obama's election. "We don't have the protests that we had before. Today we can run for Congress and the Senate, and we can have some clout in venues other than the court. The one thing that is still missing is our ability to use all three of those areas—the executive, the legislative, the courts."

"Overall, I don't see the young folks coming along as being threats," said Joe Reed, a longtime black Democratic leader in Alabama. "The only thing I see as being a threat, in my opinion, is that they want so bad to get there that they forget who they are. That's what we have to watch."

Former congressman Dellums has shuttled through each of these political worlds, returning to his hometown of Oakland, California, to run for mayor after decades in Washington.

"Forty years ago we tried to change the world," Dellums told me. "Civil rights movements were very important, and then suddenly, somewhere along the way, people said, 'Okay, integrating at the lunch counter is cool, but you've got to have a job. Integrating the college and the university is okay, that's fine, but you've got to have the resources to be able to get there. Integrating a neighborhood is fine, but you've got to have a job to buy a home, pay the mortgage.' So suddenly it was not just about civil rights in the abstract and about the law, it was justice, economic justice, social justice, and it expanded to environmental justice."

Until very recently, whatever group protest that was to be found in the black community sprang from the churches, the only organizations blacks truly controlled. Now it finds its home on the Internet, and most of today's marches are more a form of nostalgia or solidarity than a forum for demands. At practically every level, black politics has been transformed. Not everyone agrees it is all for the good.

"There is a twenty-first-century black politician, and then there are twenty-first-century black politics," said Dianne Wilkerson, who recently lost her seat as the first and so far only African American in the Massachusetts State Senate. "Not necessarily always the same thing."

If that's true, it's because black *politicians* have been transformed— many of them a step ahead of the communities they represent. Increasingly, they are a generation who have reaped the fruits of the civil rights movement and are applying—investing—those benefits in different ways. "That generational leadership is occurring at a time when a number of other forces are converging, which make the challenge of this new generation of politicians in many respects even more difficult than the challenges that faced the previous generation," said

Wade Henderson, the executive director of the Leadership Conference on Civil Rights.

The forces, which include competing ambitions and disagreements over how to define true progress, are not only converging. They are colliding. As young people began graduating from the schools that would not have accepted their parents and taking jobs at the companies that would not have employed them, the political landscape began shifting as well.

Henderson sees only potential in all this. There is room, he says, for bridge building that goes beyond threat of protest, backroom deal making, and moral outrage preached from a pulpit. Plus, he says, there are new challenges—and opportunities—on the horizon for politicians of every stripe in a nation where nearly one in five Americans speaks something other than English at home.

"Coalition politics is the politics of the twenty-first century," said Henderson, who was impressed when he saw Newark's Cory Booker slide effortlessly into Spanish at a news conference. "Politicians who ignore that do so at their own peril. They either will not be elected or they won't be elected long if they are not within the realm of transition. And transition is happening all over the country." Indeed, Obama beat John McCain in part because he attracted more than two-thirds of the Latino vote.[23]

With that transition comes some risk. There is not a black politician, businessperson, or academic in existence who has not grappled with the dilemma of making sure he or she is heard in a majority environment unused to African Americans' presence.

Kendrick Meek, an African American member of Congress from Florida, told me that on Capitol Hill, some of his best friends—as they say—are white. And he is keenly aware that many of those colleagues have put him in a racial box.

"America outside of black America is looking at us and saying, 'Can I trust them?'" he told me. "'Do they carry that anger?'"

One feature of the "Obama effect," as I have come to label it, is that whites are more comfortable with black candidates who do not seem to carry that anger, while blacks are often more suspicious. For every rising star, there is a cautionary tale. In this book I will focus on Obama's story, and also on the stories of three other such ambitious young men, who are redefining the future of black politics as beneficiaries of the Obama effect.

"There's no doubt there are some white voters that find an African American candidate exciting, that find a Latino candidate exciting, or an Asian candidate exciting," said David Plouffe, who managed Obama's presidential campaign and also worked to elect Deval Patrick in Massachusetts. "But I think for the most part it's more about the message, and that the people you're looking at—certainly Booker, Patrick, Obama—have a message that we really need to turn the page here."

Few of these successful black politicians claim to have pulled off success on their own. But those who marched back then often turn out to be the biggest critics of those who are poised to take over now. This debate, largely invisible to mainstream eyes, continues to play out with no small amount of ferocity in church basements, black think tanks, and anywhere civil rights leaders meet.

Former congressman Floyd Flake, until recently president of historically black Wilberforce University and pastor of a twenty-three-thousand-member African Methodist Episcopal congregation in Queens, New York, believes the key is for the next generation of leaders to step beyond the politically liberal confines of the traditional civil rights movement. "I think what is happening is, you're seeing the first step away from the traditional civil rights kind of leader," he told me. "I think the upside is great, but I don't think you can say we're there yet."

Vernon Jordan, the Washington attorney, moved on from his civil rights roots to a lucrative and high-octane career in law, on Wall Street, and on corporate boards. Nearly any Democrat who aspires to power has made his or her way to Jordan's northwest Washington home. The same was true for Obama, but Jordan remained a staunch Clinton supporter throughout the 2008 primaries, rallying to Obama's side only after his old friend lost.

What he sees missing is the mentoring he remembers receiving from his elders when he was rising through the movement. "I think that's one of the differences," he told me. "There is not much laying on of hands now."

So, I asked him, is it that the laying on of hands from the elders is being withheld from the new generation? "I'm not sure if they're not asking or not listening," he replied.

Sandpaper politics. Friction. These are the consequences when power shifts along race, gender, or generational lines. We saw it all play out in the remarkable 2008 election. But when the dust from the breakthrough settles, will the Obama effect have exposed new strengths or new weaknesses?

I argue that, at the very least, it will reveal a healthy new vision of what breaking through looks like. While the nation's race generals were fighting the old wars, an explosion of black political activism has taken root that now straddles generations, legacies, race and gender identity, and even partisanship.

CHAPTER TWO

THE GENERATIONAL DIVIDE

In the beginning, we thought all we needed to do is get into the mainstream. We were too naive to understand that the mainstream was polluted. And that when you get in there, you also have to purify the stream so the whole body politic can survive.

—THE REVEREND JOSEPH LOWERY

ANDREW YOUNG WAS SITTING BEHIND A LITTLE ROUND TABLE IN a sports coat and open-necked black shirt in Atlanta on the evening of September 5, 2007, more than a year before Barack Obama was elected president. Seated comfortably across from him in front of the audience was Maynard Eaton, host of a popular Atlanta interview show. Eaton held a microphone in his right hand while, in the back of the room, a camera rolled.

Then a Sunday school teacher in the audience posed an open-ended question: What did Young, the former Atlanta mayor, UN ambassador, and civil rights icon, think about Barack Obama?

"I'd like Barack Obama to be president," Young replied, to a burst of applause from the audience.

"In 2016," he added. The applauders were caught up short. A few booed.

Young continued, and his line of reasoning—coming from a man who had linked arms with Martin Luther King Jr. to march for voting rights when he was decades younger than Obama—was nothing short of amazing. Black men who reach too far too fast, he said, die early.

Maynard Jackson, the first black mayor of Atlanta, would have been alive today, Young said, if he had been older when he ran for mayor. Another former Atlanta mayor, Bill Campbell, who recently completed a two-year prison sentence for tax evasion, would not have been sent to jail, he said.[1] Even Martin Luther King Jr., who died at the age of thirty-nine, would still be alive today if he had not achieved so much so soon.

"Martin's home got bombed the first year," Young said as the room grew quiet. "They took all of his money the second year and sued for income tax evasion. He got stabbed the third year. The fourth year they took him.

"It's not a matter of being of being inexperienced," Young said of Obama in a matter-of-fact tone. "It is a matter of being young." Young said he was supporting Hillary Clinton, essentially because of Bill Clinton. And Bill Clinton, he said, "is every bit as black" as Barack Obama. This, he said, was because he'd once seen Bill Clinton do a Michael Jackson moonwalk—an image it is hard to conjure.

More important, Young's comments revealed—in an unusually candid and naked manner—how little he knew about someone he essentially considered a whippersnapper. He insisted, for instance, that Obama's stepfather was Chinese, although he was Indonesian. He basically did not know this young man who had the temerity to aspire to the presidency.

When I asked Young about his comments after it was clear Obama would become president, he attributed his pessimism to a combination of political loyalty to Clinton and deep suspicion about what America would allow.

"I had a hard time believing the Obama phenomena," he admitted. "And it was not that I didn't trust him or that I didn't like him. I liked everything about him. It's just that my experience in American politics has been, well, somewhat treacherous."

Young, an ordained minister, often reaches for biblical references to explain himself. "I had too many scars from Egypt and wandering in the wilderness to see clearly into the Promised Land," he said of Obama.

The rift between black politicians born in the 1930s and 1940s and those born in the 1960s and 1970s is a deep one that is often papered over. The worldview of the older politicians, many of them preachers like Young, was defined by limitation. They could not eat at lunch counters. They could not sit where they liked on buses or vote how and for whom they liked. They could not attend the schools they preferred or aspire to the jobs they believed they were qualified to hold. Every time one of those barriers fell, it was power seized, not given. They marched, they preached, and they protested.

Their children, who walked freely down the streets where their parents marched, were raised to believe they could do anything. Their schools were integrated, and Ivy League colleges came looking for them. "They're idealistic enough not to be carrying the luggage of the older generation," said Dayton, Ohio, mayor Rhine McLin, sixty, who was lobbied by an impressive series of young Obama aides during the primary campaign.[2]

These true believers did not grow up with Jim Crow laws or lynching trials, and they lived in a world shaped by access instead of denial. "The prior generation that they replaced defined their position, their mission, their program, in opposition to whites," said Christopher Edley Jr., a former Carter and Clinton administration official. "And in that sense, the new generation defined their position, their vision, their program in a way that is—again that word we're looking for; it's not *nonracial*, it's not *postracial*—*supraracial*."

Whatever the correct label, it set them up for sandpaper conflict, essentially, with their own parents. When Chicago pastor Jeremiah Wright's angry preaching and fiery, edited videos threatened to unbalance Obama's strained efforts to get past race, the nominee relied on this supraracial identity to try to bridge the divide. The key, Obama knew, was to find a way to bury the old resentments, not inflame them.

"The older people have to work very diligently not to allow themselves to get into a time warp," said seventy-two-year-old Ron Dellums. "Each generation carries its own baggage, but the challenge of life is to be able to move beyond the baggage, to continue to update and refine, to stay in the moment, to stay in the time, to stay focused on the future, to stay focused. That allows you to move beyond generation. And I think too many of our older people continue to view the world through the same old lens."

Shannon Reeves, an outreach adviser for the Republican National Committee and one of the few African Americans in GOP party leadership, puts it more succinctly. "These are the leaders," he told me, "who take the gavel to the grave." But Reeves has a tough job. At the same time as the new leaders are coming of age, the number of African Americans who seem to think the Republican Party is a reasonable alternative is shrinking. Less than 2 percent of the twenty-three hundred delegates to the 2008 Republican National Convention were black, down from nearly 7 percent in 2004; Obama garnered 95 percent of the black vote, and 66 percent of the ballots of voters under the age of thirty.[3] "It's embarrassing," said Republican Michael Steele, the former lieutenant governor who was one of the few African American officials to speak at the GOP convention.[4]

Young, the movement patriarch, stumbled right into this clash with his off-the-cuff remarks about Obama. Like so many of the mini-explosions that were the hallmark of the 2008 presidential campaign, his outburst faded quickly but left marks all over the place. "His post-political life has become a cautionary tale about the assumption that wisdom comes with age," columnist Deborah Mathis wrote caustically on BlackAmericaWeb.com. "Alas, it isn't necessarily so, and Young is proof."

Music is as good a place as any to chart this divide. Obama's iPod included the rapper Jay-Z. Only people under the age of thirty grasped what Obama was doing when he responded to campaign criticism by making a motion as if brushing off his shoulder. (Turns out that's a Jay-Z dance move.)[5]

By contrast, I watched seventy-six-year-old Andrew Young truly get down at a black-tie dinner in New York when the jazz combo swung into a version of the durable George Jackson hit "Down Home Blues." Their musical psyches are at least forty years apart.

After it became clear Obama would become his party's nominee, University of Chicago political science professor Michael Dawson noted that criticism from Young, and later from millionaire Black Entertainment Television founder and Clinton supporter Robert Johnson, may have, in fact, helped Obama. "Closing ranks around an African American leader perceived to be unfairly under attack has been a long and honorable tradition since the 19th century," he wrote.[6]

But if you followed the trail their critical footprints left, it was impossible to miss the generational divide. Young Obama voters were the leading edge in enthusiasm and engagement. As the 2008 primary campaign caught fire, participation among voters under thirty quadrupled in Tennessee and tripled in Iowa, Georgia, Missouri, Mississippi, Oklahoma, and Texas.[7] In the general election, Obama improved on 2004 nominee John Kerry's performance with voters under thirty by 12 percent. (John McCain bested Obama only among voters age sixty-five and older.)[8] "You had probably a little over thirteen million new voters jumping into the process," Obama pollster Cornell Belcher told me. "And among those new voters, Barack Obama won close to 70 percent of them. Part of his strategy from the beginning was [to] change the face of the electorate."

The distinction between how the old guard gained power and how the newcomers are breaking through is significant. The elders sprang up from a civil rights movement that helped create artfully drawn majority-black districts. Once inside the circle, officials elected from these districts—especially in Congress—acquired a power of incumbency that virtually guaranteed reelection, year after year after year. The white political power structure, happy with separate but equal, generally looked the other way to protect their own politically safe preserves.

But a gulf began to develop as the second and third generations of ambitious black leaders began to come of age at the same time as the venerable leaders began to age out. The big names—the Reverend Jesse Jackson, Vernon Jordan, and Colin Powell—are in their sixties and seventies. Obama and his cohorts are, for the most part, in their thirties, forties, or at most fifties, with their own networks and ideas about the best way to seize power. Changing the face of the electorate is a brand-new political concept for black politicians.

Jackson, who staged his own breakthrough in the 1960s, describes his generation as the "demolition crew" that got bloodied in order for the latest generation of leaders to walk through the rubble to power. Shifting leadership, he said, reaching for another analogy, is like shifting kitchen personnel without changing the recipe.

"If you change cooks but don't change the formula, the biscuit won't rise," he told me. "There is a lot of media focus on 'new cooks'! But you go in the inner city, nothing has changed."

The straddle proved especially difficult for Georgia congressman John Lewis, a civil rights movement icon who spent the better part of a year torn between Clinton and Obama. On one hand, Lewis remembered keenly what it was like to negotiate the internal growing pains of a nascent movement when he led the Student Non-Violent Coordinating Committee. Lewis spent critical years attempting to bridge the gaps in philosophy and execution between blacks and whites, as well as with the more moderate Southern Christian Leadership Conference. Those fights—which featured disputes between historic figures such as King and Stokely Carmichael—made the 2008 disputes seem tame.[9]

Plus, the Clintons were his old friends. Shortly before the South Carolina primary, Lewis was out shopping for groceries in Atlanta when the cell phone in his pocket started ringing. It was Bill Clinton on the phone, imploring him to come to the Palmetto State the following day to help him campaign for Hillary in black churches. "You don't say no to the president," he reasoned, and boarded a plane for South Carolina.

But Lewis made yet another leap across the generational divide after his own Atlanta district went three to one for Obama during the Georgia primary. He switched to Obama. In a politician less admired, it would have been called a flip-flop, but with Lewis the shift seemed genuinely painful. The process, he told NBC correspondent Andrea Mitchell, was more difficult than getting his head bashed in as he crossed Selma's Edmund Pettus Bridge in 1965.

"You do have would-be black elected officials or black candidates that have moved far beyond the civil rights rhetoric of my generation," he told me, sitting in a congressional office where every wall is covered in civil rights memorabilia. "And they are able to deal with issues that are human issues. It's not just affirmative action, not just a matter of social justice. These guys and girls believe in social justice and affirmative action and all of that, but something else is out there."

Before Lewis abandoned Clinton for Obama, he wrestled quite publicly with the fear that he might end up on the wrong side of history. He was all too keenly aware of the generational chasms opening up around him.

"I saw it in Atlanta with some of the old guard, towards some of the young people—you hear, 'They haven't paid their dues,' 'It's not their time, they need to get in line,'" he told me. "I think some of the old-line black leaders during the sixties, the late fifties and the sixties, wanted us to stay in our places, not get out of line, that we were going too fast, that we were pushing too fast. And they didn't understand this new, young degree of militancy."

Other members of the Congressional Black Caucus reported they were threatened or harassed for choosing to support Clinton over Obama. The late congresswoman Stephanie Tubbs Jones of Ohio, a staunch Hillary Clinton supporter, called it "Harvard arrogance."

The split ran hard and deep among a collection of elected officials who typically walked in lockstep on most issues. "You do see the clash because it's generational," said Representative William Lacy Clay Jr., a fifty-two-year-old black Missouri Democrat who supported Obama. "They have a way of doing things in their generation and they don't really like the way some of us approach issues."

But the pressure went deeper than that. Eugene R. Miller, a state lawmaker from Cleveland, said his support for Clinton got him tagged as an "Uncle Tom" sellout in some areas of his district. "There's a lot of pressure to switch sides," he said in the week leading up to the March Ohio primary. "There's a lot of emotion. All I can say is, thank God it's winter and no one is outside, because there would be more than angry words on the street."[10]

Even those who tried to straddle the divide came in for their share of reprobation. Democratic National Committee member Donna Brazile remained neutral throughout the primary campaign but discovered that this did not satisfy her old friends in the Clinton campaign, who built loyalties in the black community the old-fashioned way—through selected elected officials and church-based leaders. Many owed their success to the Clinton organization. "You assumed that the traditional black organizers and the black leaders were going to be for you because you birthed us," Brazile said she told her Clinton friends. "And I wanted off that plantation."

The bad feelings endured on many levels. Both Brazile and another neutral Democrat, South Carolina representative William Clyburn, the highest-ranking black lawmaker in the House of Representatives, reported finding themselves on the receiving end of Bill Clinton tongue-lashings.

"The figureheads are not actually gatekeepers to the black vote. No disrespect, but they don't speak for us," William Jelani Cobb, a history professor at Spelman College, said as this unfolded. Just a short time earlier he had written, "Positioned as he is between the boomers and the hip-hop generation, Obama is indebted, but not beholden, to the civil rights gerontocracy. A successful Obama candidacy would simultaneously represent a huge leap forward for black America and the death knell for the reign of the civil rights–era leadership—or at least the illusion of their influence."[11]

Lewis' early support for Clinton earned him not one but two black challengers when he ran for reelection, the first time in sixteen years that he faced any kind of primary challenge. Both of them—State Representative "Able" Mabel Thomas and the Reverend Markel Hutchins, a thirty-one-year-old activist—were black.

"This kind of loyalism and political indebtedness has stifled our communities," Hutchins said. "And we're going to see next-generation civic-minded leaders rise to the occasion and heed Senator Obama's call for change."[12] Hutchins posted his announcement to his MySpace page and attempted to link himself to Obama.

But Lewis trounced all comers, winning 69 percent of the votes cast in the Fifth District and, as is customary, drawing no Republican general election challenger. He won, in part, by reminding his constituents of his past glories. "Some people talk about change," he said. "I am change."[13] Like many, he cried the night Obama was elected president, telling ABC News: "If someone had told me in 1961 or in marching across the bridge in Selma . . . that I would be witnessing this unbelievable transformation in American politics, I would have said you're crazy, you're out of your mind, you don't know what you're talking about."[14]

The generational story line—and the resentment the divide created—spread throughout the community with a fury that seemed to feed on itself. Spike Lee, the fifty-one-year-old film director, was one of those whose anger spilled over into mainstream discussion. "These old black politicians say, 'Ooh, Massuh Clinton was good to us, massuh hired a lot of us, massuh was good!' Hoo!" the filmmaker told *New York* magazine. "Charlie Rangel, David Dinkins—they have to understand this is a new day. People ain't feelin' that stuff. It's like a tide, and the people who get in the way are just gonna get swept out into the ocean."[15]

Established black politicians got the message once it became clear Obama was about to wrap up the Democratic nomination. Some of Clinton's last remaining loyal black supporters began anxiously sidling over to Obama. When the senator did a victory lap of sorts on the House floor in the spring—making a rare appearance in the opposite chamber—he received big hugs from Representatives Gregory Meeks and Alcee Hastings, who had spurned his advances earlier in the year. And Representative Yvette Clarke of New York rushed to get him to autograph a copy of that day's New York *Daily News*. Its headline: "It's His Party."[16]

Here's one rough measure of how quickly the generational game changed. South Carolina state representative Bakari T. Sellers was twenty-one years old when he defeated a twenty-six-year incumbent. The first thing he hung on his Columbia office wall was a photo of himself at the age of four in the arms of the Reverend Jesse Jackson. By twenty-three, he was an outspoken supporter of Barack Obama. Young Bakari, the son of another noted civil rights leader, Cleveland Sellers Jr., embodied the notion that waiting was a dated concept that has less and less to do with race.

"The struggle has changed," Bakari Sellers told me. "If you're poor and black in South Carolina or poor and white in South Carolina, you face basically the same issues."

This idea is emblematic of the thinking of the new generation of young black leaders. Midway through the election year, the NAACP, the nation's oldest civil rights organization, elected a thirty-five-year-old president, Benjamin Jealous—nearly splitting itself in two in the process in eight hours of contentious closed-door debate.

Jealous, the president of a San Francisco Bay area foundation, is the organization's seventeenth leader and its youngest ever, but he had spent a decade cutting his teeth working for organizations such as the

National Newspaper Publishers Association and Amnesty International. At the age of fourteen he began registering people to vote.

Unlike previous NAACP heads, Jealous was neither an ordained minister nor an elected official, so his selection represented a drastic break. The NAACP, about to celebrate its one hundredth anniversary, has nevertheless spent the past two decades struggling with internal debate over money, mission, and leadership—just the sort of conflict that can result in wholesale change, or wholesale collapse.

"Ultimately, politics is war without bloodshed," Jealous told me. "Just like in war, you have to fight for the opportunity to lead."

His rise at the NAACP seemed to come out of the blue, and not everyone was happy about it. Several members of the board complained of the tactics they said Jealous used to win the post. The dispute, which spilled into the newspapers, exposed yet another generational rift. Columnist George Curry wrote that "Jealous got up before the board and dissed Jesse Jackson and Al Sharpton."[17]

Jealous says he did no such thing. But he freely admits that he subscribes to the notion that power must be seized, not passively inherited.

"Look at the average age of people who led," he said, citing civil rights icons of years past. "I look at the fact that Malcolm and Martin were dead by thirty-nine and Medgar was dead by thirty-seven. And they all had been involved in the struggle for over a decade at the leadership level by the time they died."

Jealous was not alone in rethinking the mission of the nation's oldest civil rights organization. Eddie Glaude Jr., an influential forty-year-old professor of religion and African American studies at Princeton University, is an outspoken critic of an old guard he said was ruining the NAACP. He argues that older leaders were "caught in a time warp"[18] and tended to "fetishize" dated forms of dissent.[19]

"We live in a post-civil-rights age," he told me. "And we don't mean by that, that civil rights is no longer important. That's where people get that kind of twisted."

Glaude, who was born in 1968, at the height of the protest movements, published an article calling for rethinking the NAACP, and
says he received a harsh letter in reply from one of its elders: civil rights
icon Julian Bond. Glaude remembers meeting Bond at Morehouse
College when Glaude taught there. "I remember asking him, 'How did
you guys do this? How did you get the older generation to pass the
torch?'" Glaude told me. "He said, 'They didn't pass it, we took it.'"
And now that it's being taken from them, Glaude added, "they're crying foul." It should be noted, however, that two weeks after the 2008
presidential election, Bond announced he was relinquishing his chair-
manship of the NAACP.

Many of the surviving lions of the movement were among the most
tardy to climb aboard the Obama bandwagon. Not so the Reverend
Joseph Lowery, eighty-two, cofounder of the Southern Christian
Leadership Conference, who supported Obama early and enthusiastically. At the same time, he vigorously rejects the idea that the nation
has moved past civil rights.

"We've been calling this, almost ever since Martin died, a post-
civil-rights era," Lowery said as we sat in his Atlanta office. "And that's
always given me problems. Because I don't think we're in a post-civil-
rights era. I think we're in a post-media-top-priority era." Electing a
black president, he said, is an "exciting, traumatic, dramatic turning
point in the struggle—but it won't be the end. We'll still have many,
many problems."

Much of this debate boiled down to a conflict that Obama's success
could never quite quell. On one hand, there was immense pride over
the prospect of the election of a black president. "I wouldn't be where
I am if I waited on the people who told me it couldn't be," talk show
host Oprah Winfrey told twenty-nine thousand voters crowded into a
South Carolina stadium. "The moment is now."

On the other hand, there was widespread, scarcely concealed worry
that in order to succeed, anyone who became the first black president
would have to strain to escape the confines of race. Obama's African

American critics, the Reverend Jesse Jackson said before the election, "want him to win, and know that the price may be some tension. But if it does not work, that same group will be quick to say, 'We knew it was high-risk.'"

Obama somehow managed to escape one rite of passage for black politicians—the need to explain or distance himself from well-known but divisive leaders such as Sharpton, Jackson, and Louis Farrakhan.

"That comparison is one that isn't appropriate," Obama told the *New York Times*, referring to the tendency to compare him to other, more controversial leaders such as Jackson and Sharpton. "Because neither Reverend Jackson nor Reverend Sharpton is running for president of the United States. They are serving an important role as activists and catalysts but they're not trying to build a coalition to actually govern."

It is a challenge no white candidate ever has to deal with. Former North Carolina senator John Edwards was never asked why he wasn't Jesse Helms. And Arizona senator John McCain was allowed to accept the backing of controversial white supporters time and again, with comparatively little blowback.

Not so for black candidates. The shadows, links, and political equations to leaders of previous generations never went away. A sneaky, funny, and largely overlooked animated sketch on a campaign-year episode of *Saturday Night Live* captured the tension perfectly. In it, Obama met with Jackson in a broom closet for "secret strategy sessions," dispatching him as an envoy to imaginary African countries. Sharpton, meanwhile, was fitted with a collar that jolted him with an electric shock whenever he got too close to an Obama event.

Sharpton insists he was playing an insider's game all along, often dialing up the presidential candidate for quiet chats that neither he nor the campaign was interested in publicizing. "Blacks understand we got to march *and* vote," he told me. "In the black areas, where he needs 90 percent of the vote, but 90 percent of four million votes rather than just two, it will help, especially with Jesse saying he ain't really helping,"

Sharpton said, adding up the value of increased black turnout in his head and relating his conversation with Obama. "The balance the whites don't understand is he needs maximum black turnout while he tries to work on the percentage of whites. If he had me and Jesse lukewarm at the same time, that hurts his turnout."

Jackson's grumbling from the sidelines attracted considerably more attention—including the famous occasion when he mumbled into an open microphone that he would like to cut Obama's "nuts" off for "talking down to black people." To top it all off, Jackson casually dropped the *n*-word, not to describe Obama, but in a colloquial manner that still did not help. He swiftly apologized and told me on the night Obama accepted the party's nomination that he was only trying to broaden the breakthrough candidate's message. "It is my job as a kind of force of conscience to say: Let's focus on the working poor."[20]

All around the country entrenched and emerging politicians have spent the better part of the last decade trying to master the hat trick Obama pulled off this year. Former Birmingham mayor Richard Arrington Jr., now seventy-four, reflected on the shift that was occurring before his eyes in 2002 when he watched Representative Earl Hilliard, a five-term incumbent, go down to defeat at the hands of Artur Davis, a man decades younger.

"The people who vote and support endorsements of political organizations are my generation and maybe a generation behind me," Arrington said. "It may also be a commentary on how blacks feel or how secure blacks are in our society today. I grew up in a time and served in office for a time that we felt like we had to unite. It was in our interest to bloc-vote. With some of our blacks, many are doing better. They don't feel they need to maintain that herd instinct. You get outside the herd, you don't need to worry about the wolf getting to them."[21]

Eddie Glaude Jr. has a different take on the differences in worldview that drive the conflict between older black leaders who lit the torch and younger ones who now want to relieve them of it.

"My generation struggles to find its political voice because we've come of age in the shadow of racism," said Glaude, who was born in 1968. "What's interesting is we know the languages of that moment don't quite capture our own and we are groping. We look different, we sound different, and what's so striking about the way in which the old guard responds to us is that they don't know what to do with us. And what's so striking to me as well is, we don't quite know what to do with ourselves either."

The pushback, however, has been predictable and insistent. When the Reverend Calvin O. Butts III, the legendary pastor of the historic Abyssinian Baptist Church in Harlem, endorsed Clinton on the eve of the 2008 King holiday, he stressed the importance of experience over the excitement generated by Obama, the younger candidate. "Experience is not synonymous with status quo nor should it be vilified for the sake of campaign sound bites," he said, reading from a prepared statement in Harlem's winter cold while Clinton stood nearby. "With experience, comes the value of lessons learned. . . . In our quest for change, it's time that we returned to the fundamentals—experience, ability, respect, character."[22]

The SCLC's Lowery rejected every bit of that. As one of the few members of the so-called old guard who opted to support Obama over Clinton early on, he dismissed the dissension that sprang up among the civil rights leaders who once marched with King. Some of that generation, he says now, claimed the first wave of leadership and then dropped the ball.

"In the beginning, we thought all we needed to do is get into the mainstream. We were too naive to understand that the mainstream was polluted," he told me. "We haven't been there long. We're going to make mistakes. Look how long white folks been holding on, and they're still corrupt and ignorant and dumb. So we've got to expect our folks to go through that as well."

Watching the rise and fall of some of those who stumbled—Marion Barry in Washington, D.C., and Kwame Kilpatrick in Detroit come to mind—some talented young black leaders have opted out of seeking elected office entirely. But that pendulum appears to be swinging, and political veterans believe elected officials who planned to retire in office should now be watching their backs.

"Either you're going to pull yourself through the political ladder or you're going to stay in place and somebody's going to run right over you," said Donna Brazile, the Democratic strategist who ran Al Gore's 2000 campaign. "That is what the Obama effect will actually come down to. Our folks are not going to sit down and wait for somebody to come and recruit them. They're going to recruit themselves to run for office."

Ron Rice Jr., a forty-year-old city councilman in Newark, New Jersey, who is considering running for Congress, is one of the self-recruiters. "The folks who would consider themselves the classic black consensus would like to spin it that we are all stalking horses, Trojan horses," he told me. "But it's that we understand we're going to be judged not by being the first, or not being the first people of color who occupied seats. We're going to be judged, and rightly so, by the results that we bring to the table. I think that's fair. If we're going to tout new ideas and ways of looking at things, and new paradigms of governance, I think we should be held responsible for results."

But Obama's success, in the end, might undercut the very idea that diverse representation can be achieved only through the crafting of "majority minority" districts—political affirmative action. A pair of husband-and-wife academics, Abigail and Stephan Thernstrom— she with the conservative Manhattan Institute, he a history professor at Harvard, both among the nation's most vigorous opponents of affirmative action and racial preference—argued in a *Los Angeles Times* opinion piece well before the general election that the white support Obama received proved that racial preferences are no longer needed.

"Today, it is even clearer that race has become less of a factor in voting," they wrote. "The high level of white votes for Obama strongly suggests that other black candidates facing overwhelmingly white constituencies can do well. . . . Whites refusing to vote for black candidates has finally gone the way of segregated water fountains."[23]

Others quickly embraced that argument, including Ward Connerly, the black champion of race-blind government. Campaigning in Denver on behalf of a state initiative that would outlaw granting special hiring preferences to women or minorities, he declared Obama a "postracial candidate." "I applaud as an American his effort to keep race out of the equation," Connerly said, instantly confirming the worst political fears of many liberal black leaders. "He is not a black candidate." Connerly even wrote the Obama campaign a $500 check, but his Colorado initiative failed.[24]

Obama did not argue that he was not a black candidate, but the generational split did in some ways transcend race. Many of Obama's big endorsers—including Pennsylvania senator Robert P. Casey Jr.—were white politicians who said they were urged into the Obama camp by the entreaties of their children. Some of the generational tilt appeared to cross party lines as well. Former secretary of state Colin Powell, a Republican, endorsed Obama just before the election. At least one of his daughters was a supporter of Obama, while his son, Michael Powell, a former Bush appointee, supported John McCain.[25]

Ron Dellums, who has come full circle from doorbuster in the 1960s through congressional insider in the 1970s and 1980s to hands-on municipal leader now, says black leaders have got to stop treating change as a threat. "You have to update your analysis, update the nature of your politics," he says. "You can't be 1958, you can't be 1968, you have to be 2008, but you build on those realities."

Dellums' conclusion—at least during the primaries—was that Hillary Clinton was better suited to build on those realities. But he was, by far, the exception to the rule in his age cohort. Roger Wilkins, who was an assistant attorney general under Lyndon B. Johnson, is a big Obama fan.

"I love this transition, because my generation has done its work," says Wilkins, seventy-six. "Whatever one thinks of the result of that work, it was consequential work, and it did help change the nation. But now we're old. And there are people whose path we made possible who see the country very, very differently than we did." Seeing the world differently, he believes, is the key to breakthrough politics.

Still, Andrew Young, who by Election Day was a full Obama convert, offers this caution to a generation of young leaders he sees pursuing future opportunities at the expense of lessons from the past. "It's not sour grapes," he said of his hesitation. "When you get to the Promised Land—and we're with you when you go all the way—don't forget how you got there. Don't forget that it was God who parted the Red Sea, who fed you in the wilderness when you were hungry."

In other words, don't leave the past entirely behind.

CHAPTER THREE

BARACK OBAMA

*If you were to get a handbook on what's the path to the
presidency, I don't think that the handbook would start by
saying, "Be an African American named Barack Obama."*

—BARACK OBAMA

TWO EVENTS IN THE COURSE OF BARACK OBAMA'S TUMULTUOUS
twenty-one-month campaign for president stand as testament to the
clashing impulses of race and politics. One occurred on a bitterly cold
morning in Atlanta, Georgia, the other on a perfect balmy evening in
Denver, Colorado.

A light snow dusted rooftops and a thin sheen of ice coated the
reflecting pool at the Martin Luther King Jr. National Historic Site
on Auburn Avenue the January day Obama arrived. This was unusual
weather in the Deep South, and all across town, churches canceled
Sunday morning services. But not at Ebenezer Baptist Church. Not on
the King holiday weekend.

Obama, who almost exactly one year later would be sworn in as
the nation's first African American president, had an appointment

that day in Dr. King's pulpit—or at least in the new version of it. The congregation at Ebenezer now worshiped in a soaring, modern sanctuary directly across the street from the old red brick church, which still stands. The future president laid a wreath on the graves of Martin and his wife, Coretta, who are buried next door.

Obama had come to Atlanta, a city where every other downtown street seems to be named after peaches or 1960s civil rights leaders, to pay his respects. Just the night before, Hillary Clinton had beaten him like a drum in the Nevada Democratic caucuses, and he was in need of reassurance. The warm and welcoming Sunday morning crowd was eager to supply it.

Two thousand worshipers filled the sanctuary to the rafters. Hundreds more who could not get in braved the frigid weather outside to listen via loudspeakers. Here was the familiar: an African American candidate for office entering a sanctuary while a choir sang James Weldon Johnson's "Lift Every Voice and Sing," known as the Negro national anthem. (Bill Clinton famously knew every word of every verse.) Next the candidate and the ministers clasped hands as the congregation swayed and joined in the full-throated singing of "We Shall Overcome." The choir, surrounding the candidate on three sides and draped in kente cloth, broke into the rollicking gospel song "Victory Is Mine": *I told Satan, get thee behind; victory today is mine.*

"We don't take this pulpit lightly," the Reverend Raphael G. Warnock said as he introduced Obama. "We invited this brother because he's committed, he's brilliant. He has a spiritual foundation. And he is the embodiment of the American dream. Regardless of whether you are a Democrat, a Republican, or an independent, when you think about the long history of America, Barack Obama makes us proud."

Congregants, crammed into every seat on the floor and the balcony, all but willed the young senator to bring them to their feet. But the candidate had other things in mind. This sermon would not be about race. Not exactly.

"Unity is the great need of the hour," he told the worshipers. "It is the great need of this hour as well. Not because it sounds pleasant or because it makes us feel good, but because it's the only way we can overcome the essential deficit that exists in this country."

Then Obama slipped into what would become a running theme when he addressed black audiences: spreading the blame around. "All of us understand intimately the insidious role that race still sometimes plays—on the job, in the schools, in our health care system, and in our criminal justice system," he said. "And yet, if we are honest with ourselves, we must admit that none of our hands are entirely clean. If we're honest with ourselves, we'll acknowledge that our own community has not always been true to King's vision of a beloved community."

This was classic Obama. When given the chance to talk about race in the ways most expected to hear, he resisted. Race was worth talking about, he thought, but only in the context of broader issues. You would never catch this black man with his fist in the air.

Obama accepted the Democratic nomination for president at Invesco Field in Denver on the forty-fifth anniversary of King's "I Have a Dream" speech. Once again—this time in front of eighty thousand cheering supporters and thirty-eight million television viewers—he was presented with a tailor-made opportunity to talk about the nation's racial history. Again he sidestepped, although there was blackness all around him. Stevie Wonder, Jennifer Hudson, Will.i.am, and John Legend performed. Black politicians spoke. In the stands and on the field, black people danced, cried, and celebrated. But in the nearly ten-minute biographical video the campaign played on the stadium's gigantic screens, there was no acknowledgment that black history was about to turn a new page. Oscar-winning director Davis Guggenheim, who assembled the film, chose instead to emphasize Obama's Kansas roots, his white grandparents, and his white mother, alluding only briefly to his Kenyan father and his ties to the African nation where some of his relatives still live. Similarly, the film raced past his multicultural upbringing in Hawaii and Indonesia.

The nominee that night offered policy prescriptions and ritual attacks on the Republican nominee, but got to the final paragraphs of his speech before he alluded to the words of "a young preacher from Georgia," never mentioning King by name.

"The men and women who gathered there could've heard many things," he said, referring to the March on Washington. "They could've heard words of anger and discord. They could've been told to succumb to the fear and frustrations of so many dreams deferred. But what the people heard instead—people of every creed and color, from every walk of life—is that, in America, our destiny is inextricably linked, that together our dreams can be one."

This too was classic Obama. He did not deny his race, but he generally didn't bring it up either. You had to look in the pages of his acclaimed autobiography, *Dreams from My Father,* to learn about his admiration for Malcolm X and his collegiate flirtation with black activism. But the book also held these words: "My identity might begin with the fact of my race," he wrote. "But it didn't, couldn't end there."[1]

Obama and his advisers decided early that he was not going to win the presidency by playing up his race. Those who would be drawn to that aspect of his biography would vote for him in any case, they reasoned. The toughest votes to win would come from those who might overlook or distrust him because of something he could not control—the color of his skin.

"The thing is, a *black man* can't be president of America, given the racial aversion and history that's still out there," Cornell Belcher, an Obama pollster who is himself African American, told me after the election. "A *black man* can't be president of America. However, an extraordinary, gifted, and talented young man who happens to be black can be president."

So Obama was to become the world's most famous black man not by denying his biracial identity but by embracing parts of it selectively. On the podium at the Democratic National Convention, we saw his Indonesian half sister Maya Soetoro-Ng, but not his Kenyan half sister

Auma Obama. And the omissions in his biography were not limited to race: There was just passing reference made to Michelle and Barack Obama's elite educations at Princeton and Harvard and to their law degrees.

"He appreciates and embraces his blackness," observed Michael Eric Dyson, the Georgetown professor and author who climbed aboard the Obama presidential campaign bandwagon early. "But he doesn't want that to exhaust his agenda, or determine what his vocational trajectory will be. What he will say, what he will do, how he will behave, how he will act."

It was a fairly perilous tightrope Obama walked, and one that had never been managed at this level before. He had to integrate the tactical with the strategic, reaching out to some voters without alienating others, and change the face of black politics altogether. He did this in part by crafting his persona and his speeches to appeal to all listeners. On the night he won the Iowa caucuses, he was making history, but he allowed others to interpret his meaning when he bellowed, "They said this day would never come!" "I knew that it would have multiple meanings to multiple people," Obama's twenty-seven-year-old white speechwriter, Jon Favreau, acknowledged later.[2] Obama's caution continued even after he won the presidency. Steve Kroft of *60 Minutes* asked him after the election what he thought of his racial breakthrough, and Obama once again spoke of other people's reactions—the faces in the crowd, his mother-in-law—not his own.

But it became clear early on that this would be no color-blind campaign. During the heated and competitive primary season, an edgy and alarming debate took place between Hillary Clinton and Obama about race, gender, and even the legacy of Bill Clinton. The former president had famously deemed Obama's plan for Iraq a "fairy tale," and compared Obama's South Carolina victory to Jesse Jackson's twenty years before. Then Hillary Clinton credited Lyndon B. Johnson rather than King, it seemed to critics, with getting the Civil Rights Act passed. "It took a president to get it done," she said. "That dream became a reality, the power of that dream became real in people's lives, because we had a president who said were going to do it and actually got it done."

Obama called her remarks "ill-advised." Senator John Edwards told a black church audience he was "troubled" by the comment.[3]

The Clintons were furious at being accused of playing the race card. There was "not one shred of truth" to suggestions that she was trying to exploit racial tension in the campaign, Hillary Clinton said indignantly on *Meet the Press*. "I don't think this campaign is about gender, and I certainly hope it is not about race."[4]

"She started this campaign saying that she wanted to make history, and lately she has been spending a lot of time rewriting it," Obama responded tartly.[5]

But most of the time, Obama left it to his surrogates to defend him when it came to race. In narrowing the differences between Obama and the majority-white nation he was appealing to, the campaign simply set out to erase race as a negative. This was no accident. The formula counted on white voters to be comforted by this approach, and for black voters to be willing to look the other way.

"The story of this race is that race didn't play the decisive role people thought it would," David Axelrod, the campaign's chief strategist, told me shortly after the campaign ended. "During the campaign [voters] came to judge him as something other than just potentially the first African American president. People very much came to judge him on his merits."

In some quarters, however, Obama came across as a scold for repeatedly calling on the black community to lift itself up rather than asking others to do it for them. "We need fathers to realize that responsibility doesn't just end at conception," he told a gathering at the Apostolic Church of God on Chicago's South Side. "That doesn't just make you a father. What makes you a man is not the ability to have a child. Any fool can have a child. It's the courage to raise a child that makes you a father."

Obama would point out that he liked hip-hop music but not its often misogynistic lyrics. He told MTV he thought it was a waste of time for jurisdictions to pass laws banning young men from wearing fashionably sagging pants, but added, "Having said that, brothers should pull up their pants. You are walking by your mother, your grandmother, your underwear is showing. . . . Come on."[6]

And in a widely noted address to the National Association for the Advancement of Colored People—the nation's oldest civil rights organization—Obama admitted he was aware of the sensitivity his comments stirred. "I know some say I've been too tough on folks, talking about responsibility," he said to the three thousand members gathered in Cincinnati. "At the NAACP, I'm here to report, I'm not going to stop talking about it."

Later in that speech he added, "When we are taking care of our own stuff, then a lot of other folks are going to be interested in joining up and working with us and taking care of America's stuff."[7]

Many conservative black churchgoers applauded this approach, rising to their feet in venue after venue to cheer him on. But some black leaders wondered if something wasn't missing. Why wasn't Obama speaking as a champion for black people instead of pointing out their shortcomings? Why wasn't he talking specifically about racial disparities when he discussed issues such as education, health care, and criminal justice? Or, as Jesse Jackson famously whispered into an open microphone, was Obama "talking down to black people"?

Obama was not in this to prove he could lead or speak only to black people. The goal here was to romance the entire country. When I asked Obama in the summer of 2007 about whether the prospect of electing a black president was affecting how people viewed him, he recounted a conversation he'd had with Jackson.

"He said something that's very accurate," Obama told me. "He said, 'Barack, we had to break the door down, which means sometimes you're not polite. You get bloodied up a little bit. You get some scars. You haven't had to go through that, and that's a good thing. That's part of what we went through. I don't expect you to have the same battle scars that I did.'"

Obama made his most overt attempt to acknowledge the racial debt in March 2007, when every living member of civil rights royalty gathered in Selma, Alabama, to observe and reenact the 1965 "Bloody Sunday" march across the city's Edmund Pettus Bridge. Georgia congressman John Lewis, who'd had his head bashed in with a brick during the original protest forty-two years before, spent part of the day attempting to get Obama and Hillary Clinton to link arms for the photographers. It did not work, but Obama was there with another goal in mind anyway. He needed to silence the naysayers within his own community, many of whom had known the Clintons long before they had ever heard Obama's name.

"I'm here because somebody marched," he said from the pulpit of Brown Chapel African Methodist Episcopal Church. "I'm here because you all sacrificed for me. I stand on the shoulders of giants. I thank the Moses generation; but we've got to remember, now, that Joshua still had a job to do. . . .

"The previous generation, the Moses generation, pointed the way. They took us 90 percent of the way there. We still got that 10 percent in order to cross over to the other side," he said. "So the question, I guess, that I have today is: What's called of us in this Joshua generation? What do we do in order to fulfill that legacy, to fulfill the obligations and the debt that we owe to those who allowed us to be here today?"[8]

In invoking the notion that the baton should now be handed to a new generation of Joshuas, Obama was speaking for a cohort of young, accomplished African Americans who were also battling doubters within their own communities. Weeks later, Michelle Obama expanded on the theme to me, remarking that nothing worth having was ever going to come easy. "You know, this is what we were taught by the Moses generation," she said. "Short-term sacrifice—suck it up. Isn't that what we went to all these schools for? I tell myself all the time, we're *supposed* to be the ones that take the risk. What do we have to lose? And I don't mean it lightly. But in the end, who can take these risks? Who can do it?"

The risks were many. Obama received Secret Service protection earlier than any other candidate in history. In the days after he won the November election, law enforcement agencies reported that threats directed at the newly elected president spiked dramatically. Such serious safety concerns made some of the racial gibes aimed at Obama during the campaign seem juvenile, but they acted as reminders that not all of America was buying into the notion of racial transcendence.

It's hard to pick a favorite outrage. There were the men who wore monkey shirts to Obama's rallies, and elected officials who called him "uppity." There was the Kentucky Republican, Representative Geoff Davis, who referred to Obama as "that boy" during a GOP dinner in Frankfort.[9] There was the GOP vendor in Texas who marketed buttons that read, "If Obama is president . . . will we still call it the White House?"[10] And there was the ten-dollar box of "Obama Waffles" sold at a conservative political convention, complete with a picture of a black man with pop eyes and big lips, smiling at a plate of waffles.[11] There was the newsletter distributed by a California Republican club that featured an Obama caricature surrounded by ribs, watermelon, and fried chicken—all on a fake food stamp.[12] I could go on.

The taunts did not come only from white Republicans. During the heated primary campaign, Robert Johnson, the founder of Black Entertainment Television and a prominent Clinton supporter, managed to allude to Obama's teenage drug use. "Obama was doing something in the neighborhood," he said, as if steering around a confidence. "I won't say what he was doing, but he said it in his book." He also suggested Obama was a sellout, comparing him to Sidney Poitier's character in the interracial romance drama *Guess Who's Coming to Dinner.* This earned a rebuke even from the conservative columnist George Will. "For the uninitiated," Will wrote, "that is how you call someone an Uncle Tom in an age that has not read 'Uncle Tom's Cabin.'"[13]

"We're letting other people pick our leaders," Johnson later complained to the *Washington Post*.[14]

"I think we looked like we were going to win, and I think that an element of overt race awareness kicked in," campaign manager David Plouffe told me in the spring. "Which is really, 'Should it be this easy for this guy? Is he getting a break because he's an African American political superstar?' Each time he's looked like he could secure this thing, there's been a backlash."

Most of the time, Obama refused to be drawn into the racial dramas. Whenever he did, as when he suggested mildly that he did not look like other presidents seen on U.S. dollar bills, he was accused—as John McCain's campaign manager once said—of playing "the race card . . . from the bottom of the deck."[15]

Axelrod and Plouffe had worked for black candidates before, notably Massachusetts governor Deval Patrick, and they were convinced talking about race was not going to get their candidate elected. Axelrod said it was a "function of math." "It was obvious that if you were going to play in a larger venue and not just a majority-black one, you needed a candidate who could appeal" to nonblack voters, he said.

This worked for Patrick when he was elected governor in 2006. "I don't care whether the next president is the first black president or the first woman president or the first whatever, to tell you the truth," the governor told a Boston Common crowd early in the Obama campaign. "I care that the next president has moral courage, a political backbone, the humility to admit what he doesn't know, and the wisdom to learn from others."

This approach, however, was thrown spectacularly off track in spring 2008, when Obama's pastor, the Reverend Jeremiah Wright Jr., almost derailed the Obama candidacy. The campaign had worried about Wright enough to yank him from the program at Obama's February 2007 announcement of his candidacy. But that was before snippets of videotape surfaced featuring Wright at his most incendiary.

It was a controversy, which we explore at greater length in Chapter 8, ultimately kept alive by the resentful and unhelpful Wright himself. The association with a church that characterized itself as "unashamedly black and unapologetically Christian" immediately undercut Obama's labored efforts to portray himself as race neutral. Even sympathetic Obama supporters asked how he could not have known about Wright.

The future president had little choice but to attempt to calm the waters his old friend had roiled. Only then did he finally decide to talk about race. Obama, wearing an ice-blue tie on St. Patrick's Day, strode into an interview with me in the midst of the Wright storm. He was subdued, clearly troubled, and laboring under the weight of too little sleep and too much controversy.

I asked him if all this had been inevitable—this blowup about race, politics, and grievance. "It would have been naive for me to think that I could run and end up with quasi-front-runner status in a presidential election, as potentially the first African American president, and that issues of race wouldn't come up, any more than Senator Clinton could expect that gender issues might not come up," he mused. "But, ultimately, I don't think it's useful. I think we've got to talk about it. I think we've got to process it. But we've got to remind ourselves that what we have in common is far more important than what's different."

His pastor's comments, Obama said, lapsing into the harshest language he would use all week, were "stupid." "We benefit from that past," he told me. "We benefit from the difficult battles that were taking place. But I'm not sure that we benefit from continuing to perpetuate the anger and the bitterness that I think, at this point, serves to divide rather than bring us together."[16]

The next day, Obama channeled this thinking into a speech that decried the nation's "racial stalemate" and returned to his campaign's most uplifting themes—change and hope.

"The profound mistake of Reverend Wright's sermons is not that he spoke about racism in our society," Obama said. "It's that he spoke as if our society was static; as if no progress has been made; as if this country—a country that has made it possible for one of his own members to run for the highest office in the land and build a coalition of white and black, Latino and Asian, rich and poor, young and old—is still irrevocably bound to a tragic past."

Wright himself suggested that Obama was ducking a race debate: "I do what pastors do. He does what politicians do. I am not running for office."[17] But by then, Obama was not much listening to Wright anymore.

Plouffe told me the campaign and the candidate had hoped never to have to give a "race speech." "The Wright thing made it more than necessary, and he needed to put that in context," he said. "He's obviously running to do big things domestically and internationally. And if the campaign gets defined by 'Are we going to have racial reconciliation or not?' I think a lot of that gets crowded out.

"The issues he raised in that speech are not essential to his candidacy," Plouffe added. "They are essential, they're important problems we're dealing with in this country, but it's not like in August and September and October he's going to keep reprising his speech and offering his candidacy as a way to heal the country."

Indeed, just as Plouffe, Axelrod, and the candidate himself planned, Obama never gave a speech exclusively about race again. "Barack's candidacy, while he spoke to those issues, it was pitched in a much broader way," Axelrod said after Election Day. "He came to this not primarily as the black candidate, but as a candidate for president who happened to be black."

It is impossible to overstate how complicated a feat this was to pull off in a nation where the races worship and socialize separately, listen to different music, and watch different television shows. Somehow, instead of becoming a dominant feature of a historic campaign, the divisive issue of race—in Obama's words, "a part of our union that we have yet to perfect"—was ultimately reduced to the occasional eruption.

Part of the reason this happened is the temperament of the candidate himself. Obama was convinced that focusing the conversation on race in and of itself was a losing argument for a crossover black politician. "I'm sympathetic to efforts to have a racial conversation in this country," he told the National Association of Black Journalists at their summer 2007 convention. "But I find that generally there's a lot of breast-beating and hand-wringing and then not much follow-through. The kind of conversation I'm interested in having about race is very concrete. Do we have a criminal justice system that is color-blind? If we do not, how do we fix it? . . .

"My belief is that African Americans, like other racial minorities in this country, are much more interested in deeds than words," he continued. "And that's the kind of leadership that I want to show as president of the United States."

Obama campaigned in much the same way as he talked to us that day. On one occasion in South Carolina, a black woman stepped forward to tell him that her elderly father was not convinced a black man could win. "If I came to you and I had polka dots," he responded, "but you were convinced that I was going to put more money in your pockets, and help you pay for college and help keep America safe, you'd say, 'OK. You know, I wish you didn't have polka dots, but I'm still voting for him.'"[18]

This was sort of revolutionary in the defined world of black politics—appealing to black voters with the same arguments used to convince white ones. This meant setting aside certain articles of faith. For decades, speaking to black voters meant going to Harlem, South Central, the South Side, and Liberty City—touchstone black communities—climbing into black pulpits and speaking before black fraternal organizations, saying essentially the same thing over and over again. Obama went to these places, but not as often and with little fanfare.

"In the past, the way we got out the black vote, it was always through the grapevine," said Donna Brazile. "We knew who had the biggest megaphone. We built them up to talk for us. Now with Obama, it's almost the opposite. We've built ourselves up to speak for ourselves. It's transformational."

But under the radar, Obama was careful not to completely reject more traditional methods. He devoted a fair share of his time to courting black radio, dialing up influential deejays such as Tom Joyner, Steve Harvey, and Michael Baisden, who in turn filled the airwaves with unabashed Obama cheerleading. Most of this was invisible to larger white audiences and the larger white media. This was no accident. Before he gave a version of his tough-love speech to an African Methodist Episcopal church conference in St. Louis last July, he prayed with the denomination's leaders, but backstage. No media allowed.

"To think clearly about race . . . requires us to see the world on a split screen," Obama wrote after he was elected to the Senate. "To maintain in our sight the kind of America that we want while looking squarely at America as it is."[19]

"I would always get the question, 'What is Barack Obama's agenda for black America?'" Corey Ealons, who directed campaign outreach to African American media outlets, told me. "I would respond by saying, 'It's the same as Barack Obama's agenda for all America.'"

Obama's star turn at the 2004 Democratic National Convention arose out of the efforts of a trio of black Democrats—Brazile, Minyon Moore, and Alexis Herman—to lobby for black speakers in prime speaking spots. They called their plan the "Barbara Jordan Project," an homage to the Texas congresswoman who delivered a memorable convention keynote in 1976. Obama was just fifteen years old at the time, but Jordan's words sounded the themes he would utter from that podium twenty-eight years later. "Are we to be one people bound together by common spirit, sharing in a common endeavor, or will we become a divided nation?" she thundered. "For all of its uncertainty, we cannot flee the future."[20]

It was little noted how much Obama's words in 2004 echoed Jordan's. "There is not a liberal America and a conservative America," he said. "There is the United States of America. There is not a black America and white America and Latino America and Asian America—there's the United States of America."

The future, Obama was convinced, could not be painted in black and white. "I did not travel around this state over the last year and see a white South Carolina or a black South Carolina," he said in 2008 after trouncing Clinton in the Palmetto State's primary. "I saw crumbling schools that are stealing the future of black children and white children."[21]

Erasing race had another side benefit. Before he could be taken seriously as a national candidate, Obama had to get conventional wisdom on his side. Since white opinion leaders rarely engaged in race-specific conversations and largely found them uncomfortable, color blindness was considered a good thing. They were willing to embrace a black man who did not make them feel guilty about race.

This conventional wisdom about Barack Obama began forming, as it so often does about rising stars, in Washington—at Georgetown dinner parties and in fussy ballrooms all over the nation's capital, where the city's most self-referentially powerful lawmakers, government officials, and journalists meet to socialize.

Membership organizations such as Washington's Gridiron Club are almost entirely white. (Until 1974, the journalists' group was entirely male as well.) How white? The first time I attended one of their annual spring dinners, in the mid-1990s, Donna Brazile and I were greeting each other amid the sea of white ties and white skin, happy to discover at least one other African American in the room. Suddenly, we felt our elbows encased in a firm grasp, and Vernon Jordan leaned in. He was grinning, his teeth very white against his very black skin. "This isn't what they expected at all," he chortled. We laughed too. When these clubs were created we were expected to be serving, not dining. Even now, I'd bet most people in that room possessed not a single black friend. And if they did, it was likely to be Vernon or Donna or me.

So it was that much more remarkable when Obama strode onto the dais at the annual dinner in March 2006. It could have been an intimidating evening. The room was filled with movers and shakers of the first order. But Obama, who had spent a lifetime challenging preconceptions about race, politics, and political timing, seemed entirely at home. He made fun of himself, poked light fun at President Bush and Vice President Cheney, and even sang a little. He was a hit.

At some basic, well-concealed level, most politicians and the people who cover politics are idealists, so for that crowd, the idea of Obama was deeply appealing. To white people who considered themselves to be forward-thinking, he was a black man (but not too black). To black people, he was a source of pride—like Tiger Woods, only with a less murky racial identity.

Washington, a town that appreciates a good straddle, ate him up with a spoon. That was the night the whispering officially began that he might one day be president. Two years later, when he was indeed running, Obama made a return visit, this time in absentia, portrayed in one of the evening's mocking skits by an actor dressed like a knight in shining armor.

This racial straddle set the stage for what Obama would later accomplish as he hopscotched from the covers of *Ebony, Jet, Essence,* and *Vibe* to *GQ, Men's Vogue,* and *Fast Company* (cover line: "The Brand Called Obama"). The key, Michael Eric Dyson said, was for Obama to figure out "how to wink at black America while speaking to white America."

That is tougher than it sounds. Obama may have won over many liberal whites—at least those not already aligned with Hillary Clinton—but black voters remained skeptical for months, in part because Obama refused to demand support based solely on his breakthrough potential.

Roger Wilkins found Obama's racial straddle to be shrewd politics "that effectively calls on Americans to get serious about their nation's founding ideals, including we don't torture people, we don't get involved in wars of choice, we don't get wildly into debt as if the future doesn't count, and we don't ignore global warming because we think scientists are stupid. The racial issue gets subsumed in what he's doing—and that's a good thing. It's very sophisticated and it's very complex and sensitive; but right now he is pulling it off."[22]

But Obama was not naive. He was well aware there were voters who would never support him—the ones who bought the waffles and laughed. "I don't believe it is possible to transcend race in this country," Obama told me one day while he was on the campaign trail in New Hampshire. "The notion that if we just ignore race, somehow our racial problems are solved, is the kind of unfortunate thinking the Supreme Court recently engaged in on the Seattle schools case." Obama was referring to a Supreme Court decision that limited the Seattle school district's ability to use race as a factor in promoting integration.

"Race is a factor in this society," he said. "The legacy of Jim Crow and slavery has not gone away. It is not an accident that African Americans experience high crime rates, are poor, and have less wealth. It is a direct result of our racial history. We have never fully come to grips with that history."

"You just don't walk away from the past," Michelle Obama told me separately. "You bring it along with you. It is always a part of the tradition. You don't move to the next phase without understanding what happened in the civil rights movement."

Like many people of their generation, the Obamas operate at something of a remove from that movement—speaking of it with respect but not with the passion expressed by their elders. Michelle did more of this than her husband did, and even then much was under the conventional political radar. While campaigning in South Carolina, where the black vote was crucial, she would invoke the names of Coretta Scott King, Harriet Tubman, and Rosa Parks. "These were all women who cast aside the voices of doubt and fear that said, 'Wait, you can't do that. It's not your turn. The timing's not right. The country's not ready,'" she told an Orangeburg audience in a speech the campaign circulated to black voters online and on DVDs. "That gnawing sense of self-doubt that is so common in all of us, is a lie—it's a lie," she said, breaking into a preacher's cadence that belied her Princeton and Harvard education. "It's just in our heads. See, nine times out of ten, we are *more* ready. We are more prepared than we could ever know."

Obama saw himself as the bridge between those fears and the possibilities his candidacy represented. "Part of what happened in the sixties after the initial civil rights era was we lost some balance and we started thinking in terms of either-or," Obama told me during the campaign. "Either you were picking yourself up by your own bootstraps, you were an integrationist, you were Sidney Poitier, or you were burning down the house."

Some of the potholes along the way to the nomination were easily predictable. At a debate with Senator Clinton, *Meet the Press* moderator Tim Russert asked Obama to denounce Louis Farrakhan. This had become a rite of passage for black politicians because Farrakhan had had unsavory things to say about Jews and white people. Obama toed the mark, denouncing Farrakhan. And when Clinton pressed him to reject Farrakhan as well, Obama shrugged and did that too.

"There's no formal offer of help from Minister Farrakhan that would involve me rejecting it," he said with ill-concealed disdain. "But if the word *reject,* Senator Clinton feels, is stronger than the word *denounce,* then I'm happy to concede the point, and I would reject and denounce."

Significantly, Farrakhan allowed Obama his straddle. Instead of chastising the candidate for the stiff arm, Farrakhan scolded the questioner for "mischief making."

Other black leaders were not as charitable, worrying that the compromises were a red flag about what an Obama presidency would be. "Someone said, 'Well, maybe the black candidate can't say that,'" Oakland mayor Ron Dellums told me. "And I said, 'I cannot tell you over the last forty years how many rooms I've been in with white male candidates who said, "You know I love you, but don't make me have to speak to your issues right now. I've got to go get white votes, but once I win you know I care about you. Trust me—when my hands are under the levers of power, things will change."'" If a black man was saying this now, Dellums worried, maybe African Americans had not come so far after all.

Obama's fiercest critics often came from the left. Princeton's Glaude, who early on was one of Obama's most prominent black skeptics, said he was frustrated with the way the nation's first black presidential nominee was handling race.

"He's supposed to be a transformative figure," Glaude told me. "Why is it the case that he can't simply say, when we talk about health care, we know it disproportionately affects poor people and black people? Why can't he begin to talk about these issues in ways that identify black communities, without trying to sound like Reverend Jesse Jackson and Reverend Al Sharpton? The thing is, the very way that Jesse and Al have exploited the theater of racial politics, he's doing it from a different vantage point. We haven't changed the game. That's what makes me so angry. He hasn't stepped outside of the game."

Perhaps he hadn't. But an NBC News/*Wall Street Journal* poll taken one month before Election Day pointed to the reason. Forty percent of whites, and an equal percentage of self-described swing voters, declared themselves bothered that "Barack Obama has been supported by African American leaders such as Reverend Jeremiah Wright and Al Sharpton."[23] This was the backlash risk the Obama campaign had been worried about.

In the end, nothing succeeds like success, and most of Obama's black critics were muted, some because they believed political sacrifice was a necessary ingredient for victory. "We inherently believe that what he's doing he has to do," Kevin Wardally, a New York political consultant, said. "He has to not be in Harlem to get those white votes."[24]

Others, however, are playing wait-and-see. Will the nation's first African American president deliver? And what does delivering mean anymore if the normal corridors to power are not more readily available to African Americans by virtue of the fact that the man in the Oval Office is black?

There is every chance the Moses generation, in ceding the next round to the Joshua generation, may have to adapt to a new definition of success. There is also every evidence that Barack Obama has not transcended race. But his election has provided new proof that he has redefined what racial politics is.

CHAPTER FOUR

THE RACE-GENDER CLASH

I've been a woman my whole life, and every part of me believes in the empowerment of women—but the truth is, I'm a free woman. And being free means you get to think for yourself.

—OPRAH WINFREY

IN RETROSPECT, IT SHOULD HAVE BEEN OBVIOUS WHAT WAS COMING. History demanded it. With an African American man and a woman feuding for the Democratic nomination, the clash between gender and race was as inevitable as it was bound to be messy. Then, shockingly, a woman was added to the Republican ticket late in the process, creating fresh possibilities for making history.

Hillary Clinton and Sarah Palin had little in common other than their race and gender, but at different periods during the 2008 campaign, their gender appeal managed to present a huge potential challenge for Barack Obama. And during those periods, in the spring and the fall, the white men in the race—various Democrats in the spring, John McCain and Joe Biden later on—were thrust to the sidelines.

The 2008 presidential campaign, with its potential for breakthrough change in race and gender, was destined to provide the backdrop for unpalatable choices, and Oprah Winfrey turned out to be the test case. No sooner had she announced her public endorsement of Barack Obama early in the year than her Web site—usually a repository of fawning fandom—exploded with angry recrimination. How could she insert herself into politics? Choose to back a man over a woman? Choose to support a *black* man over any woman?

Winfrey was dismayed, but she should not have been surprised. Disadvantaged groups—women, racial and religious minorities—often see their causes in common only when no one is forced to choose among them. This can be tough if one's identity has many roots. When she appeared at UCLA's Pauley Pavilion in the company of Caroline Kennedy, California First Lady Maria Shriver, Stevie Wonder, and Michelle Obama just before the California primary, Winfrey felt compelled to own up to her choice. "I'm not a traitor," she told a cheering crowd, with real emotion in her voice. "No, I'm not a traitor, I am just following my own truth, and that truth has led me to Barack Obama."

As America's foremost talk show host discovered, the collision of race and gender is a dangerous place. "In the closing months of the campaign, it was so disheartening to see the campaign come down to race versus gender, as if who has the greatest disadvantage?" said the political activist Donna Brazile. "I felt as a black woman I was invisible again. I was either black or I was a female. I thought, Jesus, can't I be for both of them?"

"We spent precious time debating race versus gender," Brazile told an autumn audience at St. John's University in New York. "As if racism and sexism are not both toxic."[1]

Resentments and suspicions long kept under wraps in polite company burst to the surface with alarming regularity throughout this particularly historic campaign. And as Hillary Clinton, the nation's best chance ever to elect a woman president, began to lose ground to Barack Obama, the nation's best chance ever to elect a black president, the corrosive split came into view. But the Reverend Jesse Jackson, who knocked down barriers during the 1980s in races that paved the way for both Clinton and Obama, said he was delighted about what the clash exposed. "Now Barack and Hillary are open-field runners," he said. "A healthier, more secure, more mature America is emerging from race and gender shock."[2]

Jackson's delight was, in general, the exception.

"Women's liberation didn't lift up black women," wrote Annette John-Hall, an African American columnist for the *Philadelphia Inquirer*. "It helped keep them down."[3] Her reasoning—that white women profited disproportionately even from race-conscious remedies such as affirmative action—is a commonly held resentment. After all, though women earn less than men, black women earn the least of all.

Lani Guinier, the Harvard Law professor most famous for being selected—then summarily dropped—as a Justice Department nominee in 1993, knows a thing or two about that conflict. What many observers failed to see, she told me, was that a good number of African American women had long hesitated to link their plight to the gender concerns voiced by white women.

"You're talking about a group of people who feel very entitled," she said of the white feminists. "They are comparing themselves to white men. And they feel they deserve to be on parity with white men, and they're not. And that's absolutely true. But they're not realizing that black men and black women are so far from parity with white men."

Gloria Steinem, the feminist icon, ignited those embers of resentment when she took to the opinion pages of the *New York Times* just before the New Hampshire primary to declare gender the "most restrictive force in American life." "Black men were given the vote a half-century before women of any race were allowed to mark a ballot, and generally have ascended to positions of power, from the military to the boardroom, before any women (with the possible exception of obedient family members in the latter)," she wrote.

To Steinem and an entire generation of feminists who came of political age in the 1960s and 1970s, Obama seemed to be yet another man cutting the line. Her *Times* article caused an uproar. Who was Steinem to tell folks what side they had to choose? some raged. Finally, others cheered, *someone* said it. Just as America seemed poised to follow Great Britain, Pakistan, India, Germany, Argentina, Israel, and the Philippines into the ranks of great nations with female leaders, along came this upstart, ready to ruin everything.

Steinem even went on to belittle John McCain, the Republican nominee, who spent five and a half years as a prisoner of war in Vietnam. "Suppose John McCain had been Joan McCain and Joan McCain had got captured, shot down and been a POW for eight years," she said to an Austin, Texas, audience while campaigning for Clinton. Reporters, she said, would ask the woman, "'What did you do wrong to get captured? What terrible things did you do while you were there as a captive for eight years?'"[4]

The Clinton campaign distanced themselves from Steinem on this one, but not from the overall point being made by surrogates speaking on Clinton's behalf all over the country. Geraldine Ferraro described herself as "lunatic" over the notion that anyone—especially liberals like herself—would consider Obama a better choice than Clinton. Speaking on the radio with conservative talk show host John Gibson, she was out of breath and clearly angry. "John, between me and you and your millions of listeners," she raged, "if Barack Obama were a white man, would we be talking about [him] as a potential, real problem for Hillary?"

"You mean if he were [fellow candidate] John Edwards?" Gibson interjected.

"If he were a woman of any color, would he be in this position?" she queried, then answered her own question. "Absolutely not."[5] Ferraro returned to the sentiment throughout the campaign, ratcheting up her accusations each time. At one point she even told a small Torrance, California, newspaper that Obama was lucky to be black, because

America was "caught up in the concept." Obama branded the assertion "ridiculous," and the Clinton campaign had Ferraro step down from her official campaign role.

Such arguments echoed more loudly as Clinton's once inevitable march to the Democratic nomination began to falter. Voters anxious to make history, it seemed, had a choice of the kind of history they would make in 2008. Alice Echols, a gender studies professor at the University of Southern California, described the explosion of support for Obama as the "Prius factor." "Obama supporters can feel self-congratulatory about striking a blow against racism, in the way that Prius drivers can feel they're striking a blow for energy responsibility and independence," she said. "Striking a blow against sexism and feeling good about it has not figured nearly as much in this campaign."[6]

Robin Morgan, the author of the 1970 feminist manifesto *Sisterhood Is Powerful,* sounded another battle cry in an e-mail that whipped around the pro-Hillary feminist community. "Not since suffrage have two communities—joint conscience-keepers of this country—been so set in competition," she wrote, her words laced with outrage. In a complaint that would become common among Clinton supporters as Obama started winning, she decried the "toxic viciousness," "news-coverage target practices," and ageism she saw all around her. "Goodbye to turning him into a shining knight when actually he's an astute, smooth pol," she wrote.[7] Obama, she and others declaimed, was poised to win the nomination for no other reason than that he was a man.

The backlash—turning Obama from a shining knight into a greedy male—worked for Clinton among some segments of women voters. Even after Obama sealed up the nomination and moved toward the general election, resentments festered. Republicans watched closely, and even Sarah Palin moved quickly to exploit some of the lingering hurt feelings. "I can't begin this great effort without honoring the achievements of Geraldine Ferraro, back in 1984, and, of course, Senator Hillary Clinton, who did show determination and grace in her presidential campaign," she said on the day McCain selected her as his running mate. When Palin appeared on the scene, white women were among the first to jump off the Obama bandwagon in a shocking twenty-point swing from the Obama-Biden ticket to the McCain-Palin ticket within days after the Republican convention.[8] Within forty-eight hours of Palin's surprise pick, all high-profile Republican women were dispatched to call attention to what they saw as a double standard in news coverage. Carly Fiorina, the former chairman and CEO of Hewlett-Packard and a senior adviser to John McCain, went on Sunday morning television to declare Obama had made a "critical strategic error" in not selecting Hillary Clinton as his running mate.[9]

"There are a whole host of women in the Democratic Party who believe the Democratic Party does not understand what sexism is, routinely underestimates the impact of women," she told George Stephanopoulos. "And they are coming in droves to the Republican Party because they think the party and John McCain get it." The shock, we now know, did not last. By early October, Palin's gains among women and independent voters had almost entirely disappeared.

Claiming a double standard soon fizzled. Palin complained that the news media held her to a double standard on matters of wardrobe and conduct. But exit polls showed women either had little sympathy for that argument or had little sympathy for John McCain. Obama won among women voters 56 percent to 43 percent.[10]

During the Democratic primary campaign, the Obama-Clinton conflict morphed from rough competition to brutal political death match. Clinton learned how to periodically tap into the anger expressed by the feminists as well as the discomfort bubbling under the surface among women who did not consider themselves particularly radical. She won the New Hampshire primary, for instance, on the strength of the female vote after she grew misty-eyed when asked a sympathetic question the day before voters went to the polls. But the Clinton campaign also targeted female voters with effective direct-mail appeals as well. By the time Obama wrapped up the Democratic nomination in late spring, white women viewed him unfavorably, 49 to 43 percent.[11] Republicans noted that too.

There was indeed plenty of anecdotal evidence to support the notion that gender, not race, was the greater disadvantage in this campaign. Noisy protesters at one Clinton event in New Hampshire interrupted the candidate, shouting, "Iron my shirt!" Airport gift shops tastelessly stocked Hillary Clinton nutcrackers with what appeared to be stainless-steel thighs. And one unusually candid blue-collar worker in Youngstown, Ohio, told a white male reporter for the *Wall Street Journal* that while no one wanted to attack Obama for fear of being called a racist, "it's easier to say you want to keep a woman barefoot and pregnant. You can call a woman anything."[12] And this was a Clinton *supporter.*

Even Elton John, who raised $2.5 million for Clinton at a New York fund-raiser when she was scraping to pay the health care costs of her campaign workers, railed against sexism in politics, saying he was "amazed by the misogynistic attitudes of some of the people in this country."[13]

This created something of a straitjacket for Clinton, who, much like Obama, hoped to benefit from her history-making potential without necessarily having to call overt attention to it herself. But as Clinton began to grasp for every remaining vote in states she had to win, she was happy to declare that sexism—not racism—had the more debilitating effect.

But which really helped or hurt more, race or gender? In exit poll after exit poll during the primaries, voters who said race mattered voted *against* Obama, while voters who said gender mattered voted *for* Clinton. In a conservative state such as Kentucky, where Clinton hoped to do well, more than one in five voters in the preelection survey viewed Obama's race as a negative. When asked about gender, however, 63 percent said it didn't matter, and 11 percent said they viewed it as a positive.[14]

Remarkably, Obama lost primaries in states like this, but overcame the drag his race would have been expected to present in many others. Still, many of Clinton's most fervent female supporters grew convinced over time that misogyny—not a mismanaged campaign or Obama's appeal—was at the root of their candidate's failure. Some women seized on a moment when Obama, speaking to a female reporter backstage after a speech in Detroit, referred to her in an offhand fashion as "sweetie." He called the reporter later that day to apologize, and granted her a formal interview a few weeks later.[15]

Like many other successful politicians, Clinton often blamed the news media, telling one sympathetic female *Washington Post* reporter that it was clearly more acceptable to take potshots based on gender. "It does seem as though the press at least is not as bothered by the incredible vitriol that has been engendered by the comments by people who are nothing but misogynists," she said.[16]

As the campaign wore on, another chasm opened. Clinton retained her edge with white women, while black women continued shifting to Obama, giving him in many states the majority overall of the female vote. In South Carolina, white women voted for Clinton by nearly two to one, while black women chose Obama at nearly twice that rate.[17] In Pennsylvania, 19 percent of those who voted said the gender of the candidate helped determine their vote. Of those, a whopping 71 percent voted for Clinton. (It should be noted that an equal number cited race as a factor, but most of *them* voted *against* Obama.)[18] Within weeks, Clinton's supporters were buying full-page newspaper ads and staging noisy protests outside Democratic Party meetings to declare that sexism was driving Clinton from the race. They were incensed again when NARAL, the National Abortion Rights Action League, broke ranks to endorse Obama.

Clinton's campaign was run by longtime aides Patti Solis Doyle, a Latina, and then by Maggie Williams, who is black. For months they resisted playing the race-versus-gender card. Early polls, in fact, showed Clinton beating Obama among black women, 47 percent to 37 percent.

But once Obama began winning, black women flipped, and as the over-all gender chasm grew, old wounds between black women and white women surged back into view.

Writing for the black affairs Web site TheRoot.com, Princeton professor and Obama supporter Melissa Harris-Lacewell declared that black women were ready to reject what she called "Hillary's Scarlett O'Hara act." "Throughout history, privileged white women, attached at the hip to their husband's power and influence, have been complicit in black women's oppression," she wrote tartly. "Many African American women are simply refusing to play Mammy to Hillary."[19]

The truth is, black women have always resented being asked to choose allegiance between gender and race. Alice Walker, the Pulitzer Prize–winning author of *The Color Purple,* also chose the cyberpages of TheRoot.com to write of her disappointment at the growing conflict, her "deep sadness . . . that many of my feminist white women friends cannot see" Obama. "That they can believe that millions of Americans—black, white, yellow, red and brown—choose Obama over Clinton only because he is a man, and black, feels tragic to me.

"Imagine, if he wins the presidency, we will have not one but three black women in the White House," she said, referring to Michelle Obama and the couple's daughters, Malia and Sasha. "One tall, two somewhat shorter; none of them carrying the washing in and out of the back door."[20]

The flip side of the argument came from an older white woman, an expert in the field of gender politics, who bemoaned to me as Clinton's campaign was winding down that Obama's success meant she would never get to dance at the inauguration of a female president. This proved to be an enduring grievance that dogged Obama throughout the campaign and that, for a time, turned the Democratic nominating convention into as much a celebration of Clinton's gender breakthrough as of Obama's racial one.

After Clinton was defeated, it took some time for her most ardent supporters to embrace Obama. In another widely circulated e-mail making the rounds shortly after Obama clinched the nomination, Tim Wise, a liberal white writer, penned an "open letter to white women." Among other things, he asserted that white female Democrats contemplating a vote for Republican John McCain were engaging in "white racial bonding."

"Needless to say it is high irony, bordering on the outright farcical, to believe that electorally bonding with white men, so as to elect McCain, is a rational strategy for promoting feminism and challenging patriarchy," he wrote. "You are not thinking and acting as women, but as white people. So here's the first question: What the hell is that about?"[21]

What it was about, some academics pointed out, was a struggle for two historically disadvantaged groups to grab for the same brass ring at precisely the same moment.

"What we are seeing now is a new racial regime where blacks can play on any stage, and women can play on any stage," said john a. powell, the executive director of the Kirwan Institute for the Study of Race and Ethnicity at Ohio State University (who prefers his name in all lowercase letters). "It's just not going to be on the same stage."[22]

Democratic men, meanwhile, were slowly moving toward Obama. His edge among men of all races increased by forty points during the primary season, while Clinton's male support dropped from 42 percent to 28 percent between December and February.[23]

Clinton's most steadfast support came from white female and working-class voters, so she and her husband, Bill, created a survival strategy that required her to deftly negotiate a minefield of racial politics. But their effort often came across as divisive at worst, condescending at best. When a deadlocked election seemed to threaten her nomination chances, she began telling audiences in Obama-leaning Mississippi that they might be able to vote for him—as vice president on her ticket.[24] This was a particularly bold prediction, since at the time she was trailing him in popular votes *and* pledged delegates.

"Blacks aren't going to sit back while the winning candidate is told to sit at the back of the bus," the Reverend Eugene Rivers of Boston's Azusa Christian Community Church said.[25]

All of these feints conspired to drive the race-gender wedge even deeper. Betsy Reed, the executive editor of the liberal magazine *The Nation,* wrote that the race-versus-gender debate was "a clarifying moment as well as a wrenching one," in part because while sexism was often on more open display, "racism, which is often coded, is more insidious and trickier to confront."[26]

Reed's contention was backed by an unpublished study on unconscious bias in elections that concluded "gender matters in politics" but "it matters less than race."[27] But, the study authors noted, implicit bias—the kind most people do not admit to—made running for president a tough hill to climb for both Obama and Clinton. Each struggled to create a path through that obstacle course.

"Every so often I just wish that it were a little more of an even playing field," Clinton told ABC's Cynthia McFadden, invoking an analogy often employed in debates about affirmative action. "But, you know, I play on whatever field is out there."[28]

Clinton was uncommonly good at turning her gender into an advantage whenever it helped, once laughing off a Rush Limbaugh criticism by suggesting he'd always had a "crush" on her. But she also never hesitated to complain about gender's disadvantages, a claim Palin was later quick to embrace as well.

Dianne Bystrom, director of the Carrie Chapman Catt Center for Women and Politics at Iowa State University, says many women were troubled when Obama's shooting star eclipsed Clinton's, especially since Clinton had taken him under her wing when he arrived in the U.S. Senate. "Here you are, the bright intelligent person in the workplace, and you basically train this new young man, and he gets promoted over you," Bystrom said.

Bystrom and others also see echoes of past resentments in the recurring race-gender clash. When the Fifteenth Amendment to the U.S.

Constitution was ratified in 1870, black men were granted the right to vote, but women were not. That did not happen until the Nineteenth Amendment was ratified in 1920, after seventy-two years of agitation.[29] "There was also this sort of racial undertone in the women's suffrage movement," Bystrom said. "I kind of wonder sometimes, are we seeing the same types of issues in this current campaign?" Left unexplored were some of the hard facts: White women never had any problem exercising their hard-won franchise. Black men certainly did.

Sharon Sayles Belton, an Obama supporter and former mayor of Minneapolis, watched the gender clash carefully from the sidelines. Although she was her city's first black mayor, she got the job after she was recruited to run by women's activists, most of them white. This year, she said, she was astonished when Clinton supporters she knew would tell her they might support McCain instead.

"I told them, 'You're crazy, you're out of your mind,'" she said to me. "'Excuse me. How dense are you?' I had to hit them on the head."

The politics of gender especially caught fire whenever powerful men began to apply political pressure. When Obama supporters such as Vermont senator Patrick Leahy and New Mexico governor Bill Richardson began to call for Clinton to abandon her campaign, many of her supporters—including her husband, Bill—began accusing the "boys" of bullying the "girl" to drop out. *Boston Globe* columnist Joan Vennochi even complained that "the media" were characterizing Clinton's female supporters "as cranks who refuse to accept defeat."[30] And when Joe Biden prepared to debate Palin, all anyone wanted to know was whether he would be able to face her down without giving off an odor of condescension.

Some of this gender-based analysis ignored a home truth that undercut both Clinton's and Palin's core appeal. "Women do not operate as a voting bloc," Carol Hardy-Fanta, the director of the Center for Women in Politics and Public Policy at the University of Massachusetts in Boston, told me. "Women—feminist movement people—would like to see women unify around a woman candidate, because a woman should be elected. That doesn't exist. Despite the op-eds that have been written, and Gloria Steinem and all these other people, it doesn't exist." This election year was no exception. After about a week of widely covered bitterness in the wake of Clinton's defeat in the primaries, pollsters from NBC News and the *Wall Street Journal* discovered Obama had opened a nineteen-point lead among all women over Republican John McCain.[31] In 2004, John Kerry beat George W. Bush among women by only three points, so Obama's performance among women—after having defeated a historic female candidate—was actually an improvement.[32] And in the end, Palin's appearance on the GOP ticket did not help close the Democrats' post-Hillary advantage. So much for the enduring gender divide.

Another critical factor was often overlooked in the race-versus-gender analysis. The generational split may have played a larger role in exacerbating—or, Obama backers might argue, erasing—the race-gender divide. Dianne Bystrom at Iowa State noticed that young women, in particular, did not necessarily consider it a test of sisterhood to embrace sixty-year-old Hillary Clinton. "As one of my students said, 'I really like Hillary Clinton but she reminds me of my mother.'"

For every aggrieved white woman for Hillary, there popped up a famous white (or black, or Latina) woman who opted for the black man—including women such as Caroline Kennedy and Senator Claire McCaskill, who said their children talked them into supporting Obama.

I asked Obama about all this during a spring 2007 conversation. Was Senator Clinton right when she said her victory would be "shattering the highest and hardest glass ceiling"?

He smiled as if acknowledging the understatement to come. "Oh, you know, I would say it would be pretty significant if we had an African American president." The smile turned into a chuckle, but he backed away from the rhetorical trap I'd laid. "You know, I don't want to get into a contest in terms of which would be more significant. I think that either one would be significant. So, ultimately,. the question for the

American people is, who do they think is best equipped to actually solve the problems that we face right now? And if you as a voter, regardless of your race or gender, decide that it's Senator Clinton, then you should vote for Senator Clinton. If it's me, you should vote for me."

Perhaps Obama's rhetorical ten-foot pole kept him safely out of the middle of the race-gender debate that particular day, but it raged all around him. Only in the voting booth does the public get to exercise any latent bias they harbor in complete privacy and with complete impunity. That makes the stakes especially high.

Shirley Chisholm, the first black woman to run for president, always maintained gender was the higher hurdle. In a speech she delivered in 1970, she sketched out her dilemma. "The harshest discrimination I have encountered in the political arena is anti-feminism, both from males and brain-washed, Uncle Tom females," she said at a conference on women's employment in Washington. "When I first announced I was running for Congress, both males and females advised me, as they had when I ran for the New York State legislature, to go back to teaching—a women's vocation—and leave the politics to the men."[33]

Certainly for African American women, the ceiling has been especially high. There are eleven African American women in the U.S. House of Representatives, none in the U.S. Senate, and only one serving in a statewide office—Connecticut treasurer Denise Nappier. Illinois's Carol Moseley Braun, in fact, is the only black woman ever to have served in the Senate. The numbers are better in the nation's state legislatures, where in 2008 African American women occupied 237 of the 1,748 seats women held nationwide.[34]

But the number of black women holding statewide elective office is on the decline, and although none of the black women in Congress arrived prior to 1991, in the year Barack Obama ran for president, only two were younger than forty-five.

The barriers to higher office are varied and complicated. But sometimes the simplest episodes illustrate the problem. When Moseley

Braun ran for president in 2004, she frequently arrived onstage at candidates' debates wearing her trademark tailored skirt suits only to discover she was expected to climb onto high stools and perch there throughout, her knees clamped awkwardly together, while her male competitors sprawled comfortably. "Gender," she later told former Vermont governor Madeleine Kunin, "is more intractable than race."[35] No wonder Hillary Clinton has spent her entire political career in slacks. (She even poked fun at herself on this point when she was being urged to quit the race in 2008. "It's not over until the lady in the pantsuit sings," she said while clad in, yes, a butter-yellow pantsuit.)

Atlanta mayor Shirley Franklin worked in city government for three black mayors before she was recruited to run herself. Franklin, who was by then in her fifties, sees another reason for the ceilings many female candidates confront. "I did not think that I was worthy to serve," she told me as we sat in her airy city hall office. "Now I'm sixty-three. My generation is different from the one you're going to meet at thirty-five and forty-five and fifty-five."

Franklin remembers old debates about whether successful black women were keeping black men down, but says she hears that less now. Her challenge—which she considers an advantage—is incorporating her blackness, her femaleness, and her municipal expertise into a single package.

"I can see things as a woman, and I can see things as an African American," said Franklin, who decided to support Obama early on. "And I can see things as a mayor. I can put on a lens: How do I feel about this as a mayor? Who has the best policy for urban America? That's seeing it as a mayor. I can look at the historical exclusion of women and say, 'I don't care who he [any opponent] is; it's time for a woman.' Or I can look as an African American and say, 'This is the progression of leadership that Dr. King talked about, and people before him.'"

But this race-gender power conflict has been playing out for decades. The civil rights movement that forced racial change on a nation always seemed somewhat conflicted about the role of women. Rosa Parks may have been hailed as the mother of the movement for refusing to give up her seat on a municipal bus in Montgomery, Alabama, and Fannie Lou Hamer may have forced her Mississippi Freedom Party into the state's all-white delegation to the 1964 Democratic National Convention, but many more of the movement's women essentially stayed in the background, laboring in obscurity as the Kings, Youngs, and Abernathys led the marches.

Dorothy Height, the venerable ninety-six-year-old leader of the National Council of Negro Women, credits women with roles in all facets of the civil rights movement in her 2003 memoir, *Open Wide the Freedom Gates.* But one of the most telling photos contained in the book shows Dr. Height standing with the NAACP's Roy Wilkins, the Congress of Racial Equality's Floyd McKissick, A. Philip Randolph of the Brotherhood of Sleeping Car Porters, Whitney Young of the National Urban League, and Martin Luther King Jr. The caption reads: "The one woman in the crowd." In another photo, capturing the crowd gathered around King at the Lincoln Memorial at the March on Washington in 1963, the only recognizable women are Height, Coretta Scott King, and gospel singer Mahalia Jackson.

There has been documentable improvement. The Department of Education reports that more than two-thirds of all bachelor's degrees earned by African Americans are awarded to women, a number that rises for master's degrees.[36] Still, a study conducted by the Brookings Institution found that eighty-three nations have greater percentages of women in their national legislatures than the United States, and that the number of women in public office had not changed markedly in a decade.

The reason, according to the report, is not sexism; it is an ambition gap. "The fundamental reason for women's under-representation is that they do not run for office," the report concluded. "There is a substantial gender gap in political ambition; men tend to have it, and women don't."[37]

"It's like the train left and we weren't on it," one black female politician told me. "I think we decided we didn't even want to get a ticket. And that's the difference."

The ceiling for women in general, and for black women in particular, really kicks in at the executive level. In 2008, there were eight women governors—including Republican vice presidential nominee Sarah Palin—but none was black. And only two big-city mayors—Baltimore mayor Sheila Dixon and Atlanta mayor Franklin—are black women.

Dixon's rise is a case in point. When she was elected the city's forty-eighth mayor in 2007, she received 88 percent of the vote. But she had a major advantage: She had been elevated from city council president the year before, when the previous mayor, Martin O'Malley, was elected governor.

She too sees gender as a greater challenge than race. After decades of community and church work, Dixon now comfortably occupies the second-floor executive suite. But she clearly remembers the resistance another woman—Kathleen Kennedy Townsend, the daughter of Democratic icon Robert F. Kennedy—encountered when she ran for Maryland governor in 2002. "I was a woman in meetings with individuals who made it very clear, 'I'm not supporting no woman for no governor,'" Dixon recalls of being the only woman in the room. "I mean, here I was sitting at the table!" Townsend lost.

But there are considerably more women in the crowd in Baltimore these days. When she took office in late 2007, Dixon became the lead in an unusual foursome of municipal leadership. She not only was the city's first female chief executive but also made the journey to city hall in the company of three other black women who were elected city council president, comptroller, and state's attorney. This was the first time that had happened in Baltimore's two hundred years.[38]

At her inaugural at the city's historically black Morgan State University, Dixon's pastor, Frank M. Reid III, prayed, "We thank you, God, for the women who opened the door of opportunity and would never turn back." In the address that followed, Dixon quoted abolitionist, former slave, and early feminist Sojourner Truth, who said women together ought to be able to turn the world "right side up again."

"It took a long time for a woman to prevail and earn the right to represent this city and its people," she said. "Too long."[39]

That night, she wore a floor-length one-shoulder gown and pearls to her inauguration ball. For the first time in history, the mayor's fashion choice was news.[40]

Still, some of the hesitation black women face differs little from the choices all women make. Political life, said Dixon, who is divorced, also took a toll on her personal life. "It's a lot of work if you're really committed," she confided while sitting at the conference table in her city hall office. "It's a lot of sacrifices you make with your family. In my case, my second husband had a real tough time dealing with the fact that I had ambitions. And, God knows, don't call him *Mr. Dixon*. His name is Hampton. He had a real problem with that."

San Francisco district attorney Kamala Harris, who is single and has no children, is just as blunt when she describes the challenges facing an ambitious woman who wants to rise in politics. The round-the-clock commitment elected politics often requires, she confessed to me, "is based on a lifestyle that a mother cannot have. But it's not because she's not up at midnight doing the work after the babies have gone to sleep. She may not be at a cocktail reception after work. She might not be at the community meetings at seven o'clock because she's got to get those babies fed and get their homework done and get them in bed."

Karen Carter Peterson, the speaker pro tempore of the Louisiana House, got married last year and is considering a second race for Congress. "Certainly my husband and I are talking about kids," she says. "I'm thirty-eight years old, I'm speaker pro tem of the house, so how does that play into our future goals? Am I going to be a pregnant congresswoman? How does that impact a new marriage? There are a lot of realities that I think that men do not have." More recently, Peterson has been mulling a 2010 run for New Orleans mayor.

Women are not the only ones taking stock of the race-gender divide and looking for ways to close the gap. Florida Democrat Kendrick Meek, one of a group of African American members of Congress who endorsed Hillary Clinton in spite of pressure to hop aboard the Obama bandwagon, said his decision was heavily influenced by the experiences of the woman whose seat he inherited, Carrie Meek, who served in Congress from 1993 to 2003.

"I look at my own mother, who should have been a U.S. senator, in my opinion, or should have been governor of the state of Florida, because that's where her qualifications were—thinking-wise, she carried that wisdom," he said. "But she couldn't do it because of the limitations of people saying, 'You know, Carrie, you have to wait,' or 'We're not quite ready for that kind of thing.'"

But Clinton's near-miss presidential campaign did end up putting the possibility of a female president tantalizingly within reach. Obama's campaign sealed the deal on race. What about black women, though?

"The reality is no one seriously thinks that if you're a white female who has qualifications and can raise money that there is any impediment for you running for governor or senator," Representative Artur Davis told me. "We're still not certain about the presidency, but for governor or senator, there is no one who believes that in any state in the country, if you are a strong enough candidate, there is a barrier if you're a white female.

"We obviously haven't reached that point with race," he added.

CHAPTER FIVE

ARTUR DAVIS

We don't have any illusions about race. We absolutely know for a group of voters that race will be an inaccessible fact. Most of those voters I'm not going to reach. But the whole premise is that there are enough voters left over who are willing to move beyond their racial bias.

—REPRESENTATIVE ARTUR DAVIS (D-ALA.)

ON A SIZZLING DAY IN DOWNTOWN BIRMINGHAM, ARTUR DAVIS IS strolling through the heart of the four-acre Kelly Ingram Park, pointing out the truly fearsome statue of bare-fanged dogs snarling at terrified children. This is not the bronze Confederate general that would normally occupy a place of honor in a southern town square.

The park is peaceful today, occupied only by a few men lounging under shade trees, who rouse themselves to call out a hello to Davis, their forty-year-old congressman. "Keep doing a good job in Washington," one says.

"I will if we get Obama elected," he responds.

Forty-five years before this hazy summer day, there was nothing at all peaceful happening in this park. The snapping dogs in the statue were real, and they were lunging at the child protesters who had gathered there to participate in a civil rights march. High-pressure fire hoses were turned on them too, all under the approving eye of public safety commissioner Bull Connor and the disapproving eye of photographers on hand from national publications. (One of the photos taken that summer, coincidentally, is mounted on the wall facing Mayor Cory Booker's desk in Newark, New Jersey.)

Davis and I returned here to talk about struggle and ambition. Across the street from the park stands the Sixteenth Street Baptist Church, where four young girls were killed when attackers placed a bomb just outside the building four months after the hoses were used in the park. On another corner, the Birmingham Civil Rights Institute preserves much of that history in exhibits that include original drinking fountains labeled "white" and "colored."

"I wasn't even born yet," Davis mused aloud. "But the history means too much to me not to absorb it." Davis, a 1986 graduate of Birmingham's Jefferson Davis High School, now wants to make history again. This time, he has his eye on the governor's office in Montgomery once occupied by George Wallace, who used it to launch his cry of "Segregation forever!" Talk about the audacity of hope.

"Something is happening here in our lifetimes," Davis said to a group of visiting Virginia schoolteachers he encountered at the Birmingham Civil Rights Institute on the day we visited. "It's what happened in Doug Wilder's lifetime. When you see history begin to move and bend in real time, you have to be moved by that."

Artur (pronounced "ar-TOOR," as his mother, a French teacher, intended) Davis was born in Montgomery in 1967, well after the worst racial strife in his native city had played itself out. Bus boycotts and church bombings were by then hallmarks of the nation's ugly past, but the echoes of segregation still lived on, even in Davis' own story. He lived with his divorced mother and grandmother in a house near the railroad tracks; his father had left the family when Artur was two years old.

The two men talk occasionally now, but Davis credits his ambition to the women who raised him. It was his mother who introduced him to the possibility of a government career in 1977, on an Easter-weekend visit to the state archives in Montgomery. By the time he graduated from high school, Davis wanted to expand his horizons and leave Alabama to go to college. He chose Harvard, where he earned undergraduate and law degrees—with honors.

It would not be far off the mark to read his biography after that as a carefully plotted political career map. Davis interned for Alabama senator Howell Heflin, clerked for U.S. District Court judge Myron Thompson, and worked for the Southern Poverty Law Center before moving on to become an assistant U.S. attorney for four years. After a stint in private practice, the young man turned his eyes to elective politics, and he never looked back. Just over twenty years later, after two tries, he was elected to Congress by defeating an entrenched black incumbent.[1]

"It was very much a leap of faith," Davis says now. "Very much a long shot."

Davis was something of a student of political breakthroughs. While he was at Harvard in the 1980s, he watched carefully as Atlanta's Andrew Young, Virginia's Wilder, and New York's David Dinkins all claimed big offices for the first time.

"Eighteen years ago, the common theme appeared to be that strong black candidates were showing an ability to raise money and ability to trump race in their particular contest," he told me. "It seemed reasonable to think that other strong candidates would come along who would demonstrate the same capacity. For whatever reason, that didn't happen."

Some of the breakthrough candidates, such as Illinois senator Carol Moseley Braun, won election and then struggled in office. Others, including North Carolina Senate nominee Harvey Gantt and gubernatorial nominee Ron Kirk in Texas, reached for the brass ring and fell short.

So Davis picked his path, and his target, carefully. Earl Hilliard, then sixty years old, seemed ripe for an ambitious thirty-four-year-old's maiden political assault.[2] When Hilliard was elected to represent the fourteen counties that make up Alabama's Seventh District in 1992, he became the state's first black congressman since Reconstruction. Before that, he served eighteen years in the Alabama state legislature, mastering the ropes and pulleys of power. It didn't take long for Hilliard to settle comfortably into the rhythms of Washington and to establish enduring ties with other members of the Congressional Black Caucus and with Democratic leaders.

When he decided to challenge Hilliard in 2000, Davis ran head-on against all of that entrenched support, raising only $85,000 in a naive and cautious campaign. Even his advisers suggested he prepare to run and lose his first time. Still, with the help of an endorsement from Birmingham's new African American mayor, Bernard Kincaid, the ambitious political neophyte came within five percentage points of victory, exposing a flank of political weakness he would be able to exploit two years later.

"It's clear to me, as I look back over the conversations we had, that he knew exactly what he was doing from the outset," said Natalie Davis (no relation), a political science professor at Birmingham Southern College. "He knew exactly how he could win, and when he found, in the second go-round, the vulnerability that Hilliard had, he was able to put together a winning coalition."

Part of Hilliard's vulnerability arose from redrawn district lines that moved him away from his base of support, adding more white voters to his district. Part of it came from the fact that Davis had a lot more money to spend the second time around, courting just those white voters—he raised and spent nearly a million dollars.[3]

In 2002, neither candidate won enough votes in the June primary to avoid a runoff. That set the stage for a furious three-week campaign funded in large part by nonlocal supporters. The money went to pay for ads, such as one run by Davis that accused Hilliard of accepting $1.3 million in congressional salary over ten years but failing to introduce education, health care, economic development, or civil rights bills. Instead, the ad concluded tartly, Hilliard sponsored legislation regulating endangered rabbits.[4]

Hilliard responded in kind, with ads accusing Davis of selling out to out-of-state contributors who funneled money into his campaign—including Republicans who supported George Bush. This, as it happened, was true. But both candidates benefited from out-of-state support. The *Birmingham News* discovered that Hilliard received 87 percent of his money from outside Alabama, while Davis received 77 percent.

"The first thing you do is isolate a community the incumbent had offended," Davis said.[5] The community Hilliard had offended: Jewish Democrats. Hilliard had angered pro-Israel groups all over the country by traveling to Libya in 1997 and by voting against a resolution that condemned Palestinian suicide bombings.

Davis' pollster, John Anzalone, said the disenchantment with Hilliard "ignited the money that allowed Artur to communicate. He became a congressman by getting the white vote."

Whenever I asked Alabamians—whether they were Davis' friend or foe—about what made the difference in the young congressman's election, the response was the same: "Jewish money." Southern politics can be incredibly blunt. One flyer that surfaced during the 2000 campaign read: "Davis and the Jews: No Good for the Black Belt." Hilliard said he had nothing to do with it.[6]

But Hilliard also decided to find a community sensitive to offense. He chose African Americans suspicious of law enforcement. "The only thing he's ever done for black people is put them in jail," he said of the former federal prosecutor.[7] And just to be safe, Hilliard played the flip side of the law enforcement card as well, asserting in a live television interview that Davis had once been charged with date rape. This, it turned out, was *not* true.[8]

Hilliard did attempt to exploit the advantage of incumbency. Party leaders, including Richard Gephardt and Nancy Pelosi, campaigned for their colleague. Well-known activists, including actor Danny Glover, Martin Luther King III, and Al Sharpton, rallied to his defense.

Sharpton, in particular, traveled to Alabama to suggest that Davis was not to be trusted. "The new challenge is to try and buy leadership, and to have money come in and use people that look like us but that are not for us," he told a breakfast rally at the East Birmingham Church of God. "Everybody that is our color is not our kind." Sharpton went on, "It seems there are those who now want to impose their will and call it new black leadership when it is really old leadership with black faces on it. It is more a facelift of manipulation than an example of democracy."[9]

"He tried to racialize the contest and inject religion in the contest," Davis said. "And there was a backlash against that in the final days."[10]

Years later, Sharpton told me he got involved in the Alabama race only because he had family members in the state who asked him to lend his weight to Hilliard's cause. But some local Alabama politicians watched such developments with no small measure of disquiet.

"Sometimes those of us in leadership positions are so closed-minded that we don't include people," said State Representative John Knight, sixty-two, a civil rights veteran who once ran for the congressional seat Davis now holds. "We don't give them the opportunity. We do to them what was done to us—that in order to get in, we had to kick the doors down."

But Sharpton was not the only one railing at the newcomer. Hilliard's campaign paid for an anti-Davis television ad in which a white man smoking a cigar morphed into a photo of Davis. The voice-over intoned: "A vote for Artur Davis isn't funny, it's an auction." Another voice chimed in: "Sold!"

Davis won 56 percent to 44 percent in 2002, and Hilliard, who was one of only five incumbent congressmen to lose that year, was bitter in defeat. "I see a future with a great deal of conflict between African Americans and Jews in this country," he said. "It's going to get worse before it gets better. I don't think African Americans are going to sit back and let this continue. There will be retribution."[11]

In 2007, after being reelected twice, Davis challenged his state's political power brokers once again. This time he jumped onto the Barack Obama bandwagon early in the race, while the state's African American old-guard Democrats were sticking with Hillary Clinton.

When Obama won the Alabama primary and then the party nomination, statewide polls began to show Davis' early bet paying off.

By picking the right horse, Davis dramatically enhanced his national profile and his own already semideclared intention to make a credible run for governor in 2010.

"I think what is happening is voters are thinking, 'Wait a minute, if a black can be elected president of the United States, then the idea of a black being elected governor of any state is not so implausible,'" he told me.

Davis, a political junkie who admits he spends more time thinking about these things than he does socializing (though he did become engaged late in 2008 and married only a few months later), carries the numbers in his head. He figures if he can get 38 percent of the white vote to complement what he assumes will be a higher, energized black turnout—up to 28 percent of the overall electorate from 23 percent—he can pull it off. He has memorized the examples he hopes to emulate: Former governor L. Douglas Wilder got 39 percent of the white vote when he broke the color line in Virginia; former congressman Harold Ford Jr. got 41 percent of the white vote in the Senate race in Tennessee, even though he lost.

But Davis' task became considerably tougher on the day Barack Obama was elected president. Exit polls showed Obama did drive African American turnout to 29 percent of the vote total in Alabama, but he managed only 10 percent of the white vote in that state, well short of what Davis estimated he needs.[12]

"I have no doubt if I'm the Democratic nominee there will be a massive effort saying, 'If you don't like Obama you certainly won't like Davis,'" he said after Obama's dismal showing in Alabama. "But my sense is in a statewide race you have the opportunity to move around in a two-year period and introduce yourself to voters and tell them who you are and what you're about."[13]

Obama was a big part of Davis' formula all along. The two first met at Harvard Law School when the future Illinois senator, then in his third year, gave an orientation talk to Davis' first-year class. "I firmly believed he was either going to be a Supreme Court justice or a political figure," Davis said years later.[14] The two remained friendly as they pursued separate but similar tracks through private practice, civil rights work, and politics.

In 2002, they encountered each other again at a Washington party thrown during the Congressional Black Caucus' legislative weekend by Harold Ford Jr., then still a member of Congress from Tennessee. Davis and Obama had just waged campaigns against black incumbents—Davis successfully against Hilliard and Obama unsuccessfully against Representative Bobby Rush. They were not the most popular people in the room.

"Barack had run against another CBC member, and we were damaged goods to most of the people in that room," Davis remembers. "We ended up standing in the corner talking about politics. I have a vivid memory of people looking at us, and one person pointing to us. I think they were probably thinking, 'There are the two losers over there.'"

By the time Obama, now a U.S. senator, was poised for his national run, Davis was right there with him as the first lawmaker outside Obama's home state to endorse him. His profile continued to rise when he started appearing as a surrogate on Obama's behalf, taking on the role of the guy who would say things the candidate couldn't.

On one such occasion, he appeared on the ABC Sunday news program *This Week with George Stephanopoulos* with three other elected officials. When another black lawmaker, Representative Sheila Jackson Lee of Texas, said Hillary Clinton was working hard to win over African American voters, Davis had his riposte ready.

"I have enormous respect for Bill Clinton and Hillary Clinton. They've been pioneers of the American South on race," he began in grandiose fashion.

"Sounds like a 'but' is coming," Stephanopoulos interrupted, grinning.

Indeed there was. "They have frankly chipped away and they've eroded their own legacy because this constant talk that says that, well, Senator Obama is not electable," he said. "Let's call a spade a spade."[15]

Stephanopoulos may not have flinched at the use of the term *spade*—at least not visibly. But as I watched the exchange on television, I certainly did. Months later, Davis likened Bill Clinton's behavior during the South Carolina primary to "a verbal pat on the head."[16]

As Davis progressed on the national stage, he made like-minded friends along the way, including Newark mayor Cory Booker, who had also run against an entrenched incumbent. Booker agreed to help raise money for the aspiring Alabama congressman.[17]

Davis was lucky to end up on the winning side of the argument in 2008. Well before Obama's campaign caught fire, Davis predicted to me that the time would be right. "It is my belief what has quietly happened in American political life is that white voters have gotten accustomed to seeing blacks in authority positions—Colin Powell, Condoleezza Rice, and now Barack Obama," he said confidently as he sat behind the immaculate desk in his congressional office in the summer of 2007. "So it is no longer a radical event for a white American to contemplate seeing a black person in a serious role." He is counting on that same enlightenment to kick in by 2010 in Alabama.

On the night Barack Obama trounced Hillary Clinton in the Alabama primary, Davis was ecstatic. "If we can do this, we can do anything we want in the state of Alabama," he crowed at the victory rally. There was reason to be optimistic that primary night. In choosing Obama over Clinton, 56 percent to 42 percent, Alabama Democrats decided to follow Davis' lead, spurning the old guard. "They got it wrong," Davis said of the mainline Democrats who endorsed Clinton. "They misjudged the black community and they misjudged the white community."[18]

The man who misjudged the moment the most was Joe Reed, the executive secretary of the Alabama Education Association and chairman of the Alabama Democratic Conference. Those mild-mannered titles, however, do nothing to capture the power Reed has wielded for decades in Alabama politics. A natty dresser, smooth talker, and consummate master of the inside game, Reed was, for all intents and purposes, the dean of Alabama's black political old guard. This meant most black incumbents owed him their careers, and he was the man to see for any national politicians seeking a foothold in Alabama.

For Davis to gain his heart's desire—to be elected Alabama's governor in 2010—he had to defang Reed, a notion that flew in the face of the way things had been done for decades in Alabama. Reed was the de facto gatekeeper to the black vote for white politicians as well as black ones, and few who challenged him survived to tell the tale.

But Davis did. "You're not going to have a plebiscite on whether the state is ready, willing, and able to elect a black governor or senator," Davis told me. "The election will be about whether you are a stronger candidate or better candidate than John Jones or Pete Smith."

So instead of running the racial gauntlet, Davis—like Obama—decided to mount his appeal on the bet that he could win votes from whites as well as blacks—the only possible way he could win statewide. "It's going to require me going into communities that have not typically had black politicians on the ballot. It's going to require me going into places all around the state and saying, 'Look, I'm not that different from you.'"

That's a tall order in a state such as Alabama, where many voters—white and black—are less than a generation away from a time when segregation was legal and voting restricted. The only African Americans ever elected statewide were a pair of state Supreme Court justices.[19] That may be in part because there are so few black Republicans in what has been a reliably red state.

The 2008 Obama-Clinton primary race turned out to be a rematch and a foreshadowing, with Davis on one side and the black establishment on the other. "The first time that I publicly said anything about running, people's reaction was, 'Well, that would be a nice thing to do one day,'" he told me. "It was always 'someday,' 'one day'—but the code word was definitely 'not now.'"

Few challenge the claim that Reed and his powerful Alabama Democratic Conference helped place black elected officials in every chamber of state government.

"Keep in mind, I was born in 1938, when segregation was legal," Reed told me when we met at a Birmingham restaurant. "Some of us are warriors. Real warriors. Because we had to fight every step of the way to get where we are." Reed is not sure that a generation of politicians born thirty years after he was understands that.

But the handwriting had been on the wall for the seventy-year-old Reed for some time. Former Birmingham mayor Richard Arrington split from Reed's Alabama Democratic Conference to form the New South Coalition, which supported Obama. Davis won without Reed's support twice, and then in the spring of 2008, Alabama State University's board of trustees—on which Reed served—stripped his name off the campus' 7,400-seat basketball arena. The dispute was not about politics—Reed had sued the board over a personnel matter—but the action served as a symbol of Reed's declining influence.

"Joe and I, we're old men," said Montgomery state representative Alvin Holmes, who has known Reed since they were ASU undergraduates. "The new generation? Hell, they only know that Martin Luther King made the 'I have a dream' speech and they get a day off for his birthday. They don't know who Ralph Abernathy was, who Fred Shuttlesworth is, who Thurgood Marshall was, let alone who Joe Reed is."[20]

(By the time the general election rolled around, Holmes had changed his tune. In a preelection radio ad, he exhorted black voters to go to the polls. "For the first time in the history of the United States we have an opportunity to elect a black president," he fairly shouted as Ray Charles' rendition of "America the Beautiful" played in the background. "So on November the fourth, go to the polls by the thousands.")

Holmes seemed aware that the old bulls were losing their grip. In his *Birmingham News* interview, Holmes added: "I think sometimes Joe has a hard time with not being 'the black leader.'"[21]

Reed insists this is not true. Although he takes pride in his role as an old-style wheeler-dealer—he arrived for our summertime interview in a straw fedora and seersucker suit—he claims to be unbothered by the rise of a class of politicians who pay him little mind, if any. Although he supported Hillary Clinton out of loyalty, he said he had no real problem with Obama. "I'm going to do everything I can to help Barack Obama," he told me during the summer. "And if they don't want me to, that's okay too."

His power, he insisted, has not waned. "Nobody in his right mind is going to try to run for governor of Alabama as a Democrat without coming to the Democratic organization," Reed boasted. "They're just not going to do it. No way. If they want to do it, it's at their own risk."

Reed says he would support Davis, but he made clear in our interview that he is open to other offers. "They don't even want to wait in line," he complained of ambitious newcomers such as Davis. "Their whole thing is, 'It's mine, and if it's out there, I've got a chance to go after it. And I want it. And if you're old, you ought to get back and let me have it. And if you don't get back, I'll challenge you for it.'"

But Obama ignored Reed's organization and won 85 percent of the black primary vote. Davis, anxious to make a clean break with the old guard, says he plans to follow suit. "Honestly, if I was seen as being the ADC candidate, I would not be electable," he told me bluntly. "If I was seen as being the candidate of the black political leadership, I wouldn't be electable. We're not going to spend an inordinate amount of time trying to get endorsements from those groups because it would be counterproductive."

But Davis insists he sees promising signs all around him. When Democratic candidates shocked the Republican Party by winning special elections in Louisiana and Mississippi in 2008, Davis was ecstatic. "The Republican hold is eroding in the South," he exulted.[22] But just to make sure, Davis was a more conservative Democrat in Washington than his friend Obama was, with a 60 percent liberal and 40 percent conservative voting record; Obama was rated 84 percent liberal, 11 percent conservative.[23]

In a summertime poll Davis' pollsters happily released to the press, the campaign declared that the "Obama phenomenon has dramatically changed the way Alabamians view the viability of African American candidates at the national and state level," with 25 percent more of those polled saying the state is ready for an African American governor than had thought so only six months before.[24]

Davis represents the swath of cotton states prairie known as the Black Belt—the fertile, mostly rural farmland stretching from Virginia to Texas that is home to 40 percent of the nation's black population.[25] It is an area rich in real and fictional connections to America's long conflicts over race. Davis has called it "hallowed ground."[26] The small town of Monroeville, Alabama, was home to novelist Harper Lee, who wrote the coming-of-age classic *To Kill a Mockingbird*. And Selma and its Edmund Pettus Bridge was the site of one of the civil rights movement's historic standoffs—1965's "Bloody Sunday," when hundreds of protesters were clubbed and gassed by local police determined to deny them the right to vote.

Well aware of recent history as well as the potential for the future, Davis has invested much of his political capital in convincing outsiders that Alabama is winnable for a Democrat. His political future depends on whether he can persuade fellow Alabamians—only 26 percent of whom are black—of that fact as well.

But then, taking on the black political establishment has already become a defining feature of Davis' political career. At the time Davis defeated the five-term incumbent Hilliard, most black lawmakers were elected from districts where lines were carefully drawn to enhance their chances of victory, thanks to a consent decree dictated by the 1965 Voting Rights Act. The Alabama Seventh Congressional District— 62 percent black—was no exception. But Davis created a new blueprint, one that Obama was to mimic on a national scale six years later.

"We were able to reach out to rural whites, rural blacks, suburban blacks, suburban whites, and really put together a biracial coalition," he said shortly after his election. "I have a very strong commitment to expanding opportunities for excluded people, whether they are black or white, whether they live in urban areas or rural areas. Does that make me a new leader?"[27]

It did and it does.

In Washington, Davis set out making a name for himself. In the fall of 2007, he stepped up to the plate at a House Judiciary Committee hearing to grill Justice Department voting rights chief John Tanner. Tanner, a Bush appointee, had been called before the committee to explain to unhappy Democrats how he had come to make a controversial, if not astounding, declaration at a national Latino group's meeting in Los Angeles. Tanner, captured on tape that eventually made its way to YouTube, was trying to explain why he believed voter identification laws would not disenfranchise minority voters in the long term because they would not live long enough to suffer the indignity of being denied the right to vote.

"Our society is such that minorities don't become elderly the way white people do," he told the audience at a panel discussion. "They die first. There are inequities in health care. There are a variety of inequities in this country. And so anything that disproportionately impacts the elderly has the opposite impact on minorities. Just the math."

Davis, reaching back to his roots as a federal prosecutor, decided to take issue with Tanner's math in a brutal cross-examination that left Tanner stammering.

"Is that accurate?" Davis asked, glaring straight at Tanner.

"It was a very clumsy statement," the unfortunate Tanner replied, looking clammy underneath the lights and C-SPAN cameras.[28]

Then Davis really bored in. In Alabama, he pointed out, elderly blacks were more likely to vote than elderly whites. In fact, he continued pointedly, elderly black people—like most older voters—became more engaged, not less, as they aged. The very idea that they would die before they became disenfranchised was flabbergasting.

"Once again you engaged in an analysis without knowing the numbers," Davis lectured Tanner. "You're a policy maker, sir. You are charged with enforcing the voting rights laws in the country. . . . If you are basing your conclusions on stereotypes rather than facts, then it suggests to some of us that someone else can do this job better than you can."

By December, Tanner was gone.

Davis also decided to tie his future to the middle by becoming a featured player in the Democratic Leadership Council, an organization of moderate Democrats that launched Bill Clinton's national career and was now the political home of Tennessee's Harold Ford Jr.

The middle ground seemed to be the safest place for southern Democrats in general, and for black southern Democrats in particular—especially if they harbored statewide ambitions. "Mainstream values that reflect our best conservative and progressive instincts are what voters chose in the last election," he wrote in 2007 for the DLC's now-defunct *Blueprint* magazine. "They sensed that a politics based on a rigid liberal/conservative divide is just not adequate to today's challenges."

"The most profound moments in politics usually happen unexpectedly," he added.[29]

Because he believed this—and as his early support for Obama would demonstrate—Davis left little to chance. In a political soap opera that claimed local and national headlines, Davis also became a featured player in the fight to exonerate former Democratic governor Donald Siegelman.

Siegelman, who was convicted in 2006 of bribery, conspiracy, and obstruction of justice, argued that he was targeted by Republicans—most notably President Bush's political guru, Karl Rove—who directed federal prosecutors to bring him down. Davis became the former governor's point man on Capitol Hill, where the House Judiciary Committee, on which Davis served, convened a series of hearings.

Davis became one of Siegelman's chief defenders—even appearing on *60 Minutes* to support him—but he also worried that a knee-jerk defense of a convicted politician can smell of the old-fashioned partisan politics he claims to eschew. When I asked him why he was such a high-profile Siegelman ally, Davis said that as the sole member of the House Judiciary Committee from Alabama, he had no choice but to support an inquiry.

"Barely know him, barely know him," he said of Siegelman. "He was my governor. He was my nominee. I know him as one politician to another. But remember, he was going as I was coming. We kind of missed each other."

Davis said he expected most Alabamians to ignore the complicated Siegelman controversy, and was counting on it to fade away well before 2010. Siegelman himself was eventually released pending an appeal.

Davis' decision to back Obama fast won him fans in high places, including at the editorial board of the *Birmingham News*. "Davis was on board early," the editors wrote of his support for Obama. "Davis is not just riding a fast-breaking horse, though. He is also riding a trend in which voters are attracted to youth, vitality, and change. He and Obama represent a new generation of politicians, appealing to a new generation of voters."[30]

Still, when people active in Alabama politics are asked whether Davis can be elected governor in 2010, they pause a bit before answering. John Knight, the state representative who has broken with Joe Reed, picked his words carefully when we spoke in his statehouse office.

"I would never say it's pie in the sky, and I don't ever criticize somebody for what their ambitions might be," he said. "I think all of us have to have high ambitions, the desire to want to do things, and I admire him for his ambitions and what he is trying to do." But then he added: "I would say, realistically, that this is Alabama."

In Washington, older black politicians have been skeptical as well.

"I think Artur is too intelligent," District of Columbia representative Eleanor Holmes Norton told me when I broached the idea of Davis running for Alabama governor. "Artur can't make himself into a white old boy. I think it would be much more difficult given the state, not for Artur, but the state. Of all states, that's the worst state I could think of now to run in. A terrible state."

She added: "The country's so polarized; I do not see a southern governor as our next step, frankly."

But Norton said this months before Obama clinched the Democratic nomination, and Davis was counting on the Obama win to be an object lesson for skeptics.

"For all kinds of reasons, Obama is not in the position to win this state," Davis admitted to me months before voters even went to the polls. "But that does not mean that a moderate black Democrat who ran the right campaign could not win in 2010."

By mid-2008, Davis had already stashed another $1 million in his campaign war chest, and he regularly dipped into it to salt the coffers of other Democrats around the country. This is a very reliable way to be popular on Capitol Hill.

By joining the Democratic Leadership Council, Davis also set out to signal that he was not too liberal for Alabama. Yet, unlike Harold Ford Jr., another black southerner who tried to walk that partisan tightrope, Davis also forged ties with Washington liberals. One key example: Ford challenged Nancy Pelosi for the House leadership in 2002 to burnish his credentials as a conservative Democrat. Six years later, Davis chose another tack. He invited Pelosi to Birmingham to speak at the Alabama Democrats' 2008 Jefferson-Jackson Day dinner.

Some of Davis' political courage could be laid to timing. In neighboring Mississippi, Travis Childers, a white Democrat, had just surprised almost everyone by winning a special election for a House seat long held by Republicans. Add to that Obama's overwhelming Alabama primary win, and Democrats were feeling downright optimistic about the

South when, in another year, bringing Pelosi to town would have been akin to inviting a chicken into the wolf's den.

Davis counts carefully. In spite of the general election results, he remembers that Obama received 25 percent of the white primary vote in Alabama. In the short run, Davis' boldness has been rewarded. It is hard to count out a skilled politician who wants the job so badly, and one who has the resources that make it impossible for skeptics to turn away. His friends began leading the chorus.

"I think in a state that saw 80-plus percent of black voters turn out for Obama Tuesday, you'd see 90, 95 percent turnout for Davis and that would do it," said John Rogers, a black state representative from Birmingham.[31]

Davis also knows that his election hinges on how he is seen at home, not necessarily how he is seen in Washington. By championing the concerns of Black Belt farmers in Washington, Davis hoped to raise his spotty statewide profile, especially in areas such as Huntsville and Mobile, where he was not well known.

He did this by concentrating on the things that get members of Congress reelected, such as delivering $3.1 million in federal disaster funds for the state's catfish industry, significantly affected by a drought. (Alabama is the nation's second-largest producer of catfish.)[32] And because the Black Belt is the poorest area of the state, Davis also railed against the lack of education financing in his home state, as well as a regressive tax structure that penalizes the poor.

"We still tax infant formula and baby food, but yet we have a tax break for animal feed," he says. "That's an indefensible posture."

Still, there are always tightropes to be negotiated. Taking his cue once again from Obama, Davis has spent as much time focusing on possibilities as on problems.

"We have stumbled into an array of blessings that for so long a time would have been considered inconceivable," he told a Kiwanis Club meeting in Montgomery. "The question is, 'What do we do now?' The question is not whether we have the resources because we have more resources than ever before. The question is, 'Do we have the commitment, the resolve?'"[33]

But Birmingham Southern's Natalie Davis tried and failed to win her own race for the U.S. Senate in 1996. She is white, and she is not so sure any of this will be enough.

"In the general election, for a Democrat to beat a Republican, a Democrat has to get about 40 percent of the white vote," says Davis. "I do not know how you get there. If you're *white*, I don't even know how you get there. If you're black, it's that much more difficult."

Artur Davis may have taken note of Natalie Davis' electoral difficulties. He decided not to challenge Republican U.S. senator Jeff Sessions in 2008, even after the Obama primary rout. The Senate race, which he estimated would cost $10 million to $14 million, would have been overshadowed by the presidential campaign.[34] Sessions ended up being the state's top vote getter in 2008.

Still, Davis estimated that only 25 percent of the voting public would cast ballots for or against him because of his race.[35] "The only two political coalitions that exist in Alabama are the future versus the past," he told me.

"There has been just an equation, which is, you have to work harder if you are a Democrat down South because there's a price of admission," said the pollster John Anzalone, who has made something of a career of advising unlikely southern Democratic challengers. "You have to hit a credibility level with white voters, whether you're white or black."

In any case, 2010 will not be a vacuum for Davis. In his attempt to win the Democratic nomination for governor, he is likely to face popular former Alabama governor and current lieutenant governor Jim Folsom. Folsom, fifty-nine, is the son of a legendary former governor, "Big Jim" Folsom, and served as governor briefly when, in 1993, he replaced H. Guy Hunt, who had left office in disgrace. The younger Folsom also has run for office in Alabama a dozen times—including for the U.S. Senate and House—so his name recognition is sky-high.

"If Jim Folsom runs, it's going to be a replay of Hillary and Obama," said Natalie Davis. "The ties to Folsom in the black community are quite strong." Another Democrat told me the face-off would be a "battle royal."

But Davis lucked out. Folsom not only decided to skip the race. Another potential challenger, Chief Justice Sue Bell Cobb, passed as well. That left agriculture commissioner Ron Sparks as his major competitor. Former lieutenant governor Jere Beasley, a forty-year state political veteran, agreed to chair the Davis campaign, leaving six Republicans competing for the GOP nomination. Among them: former state Supreme Court justice Roy Moore, a state judge best known for his campaign to place an engraved Ten Commandments tablet at the State Capitol.

But Alabama is still a thoroughly red state, and Davis is prepared to use the Obama campaign and all it represents to throw down the political gauntlet in a state that otherwise might not have him.

"One of the reasons I have to be so overt about my ambitions is I can't run a shadow campaign," he told me after leaving church on a Sunday morning, where he was repeatedly approached about running. "I have to be overt about it because if I didn't make it clear to people that I was interested in running, people wouldn't automatically presume that the black congressman would be interested in running."

Davis also tells anyone who will listen that he's not particularly interested in any other job. Not lieutenant governor. Not attorney general. Not cabinet secretary in an Obama administration. "I think Artur wants to make history," said Natalie Davis.

Whether he runs for governor or eventually accepts a role in the Obama administration, Davis states bluntly that he does not plan to spend the rest of his career as a member of Congress.

"The longer you stay in the Congress, you will accumulate more difficult votes, you will accumulate more difficult positions that may be hard to reconcile with your national base or your local base," he told me, speaking with more political candor than most lawmakers allow themselves. "That will get worse over time. The longer you remain in the Congress, the more you become part of the backdrop, the more you become a long-term congressman. If you're in the Congress fifteen years, people say, 'You've been there for fifteen years; why not stay twenty?'

"Ultimately, I think we can run a campaign that just doesn't get too tied down to the anchor of race. Race is going to be a topic of conversation. But we're not going to get bogged down in these internecine fights among black political leaders."

CHAPTER SIX

LEGACY POLITICS

A political career is just like any other career. Plumbers'
sons become plumbers. Politicians' sons and daughters be-
come politicians. The odds of you going into politics if your
parents are in politics are much greater.

—DAVID BOSITIS

INHERITING POWER IS NOTHING NEW IN AMERICAN POLITICS. THE
nation's second and sixth presidents were father and son, as were its
forty-first and forty-third. In fact, the nation's political history is peppered with the names of grand political families—up to and including
the Adamses, Tafts, Bushes, and Gores.

But African Americans, who did not get the fully protected right to
vote until the mid-1960s, have only recently begun to establish enduring political legacies. Across the country, these bloodline power grids
are beginning to take hold.

★ ★ ★

STEPPING UP: THE JACKSONS

Jesse Jackson Jr. is standing dead center in the rotunda under the ornate dome of the U.S. Capitol. His arm is extended straight above his head, and he is spinning around in a circle.

This is no dance. He is in full congressman mode, down to his tailored suit and polished black shoes. But he has a point to make. Emphatically, as Jacksons tend to do.

"When you walk into the Capitol rotunda by the stairs and look around, from Christopher Columbus all the way around to the Wright brothers is something called the story of America," he says, pointing out the painted frieze that encircles the room fifty-eight feet above the heads of the tourists. The nineteen images start with Christopher Columbus and end with the birth of aviation.

Jackson exclaims to me, "There's not a single African American in the entire story of America to the Wright brothers."

He has told this story many times before, but Jesse Jackson Jr. is still outraged. Rushing over to nearby Statuary Hall, he expounds some more. There are a hundred statues—everyone from Ethan Allen to George Washington to Huey Long. There is not one black face.

The younger Jackson has found his cause. He has helped engineer the decision to bring a statue of civil rights icon Rosa Parks to the hall and, along with conservative white Tennessee Republican representative Zach Wamp, cosponsored legislation to rename a portion of the new Capitol visitors' center "Emancipation Hall."

He has come a long way from his first days in politics, playing factotum for his father, Jesse Jackson Sr., during the elder Jackson's 1988 run for president. He is now a seven-term member of Congress, published author, and father of two. His wife, Sandi, joined the family business in 2007, running and winning a seat as a Chicago city alderwoman.

So Junior, as others call him, has emerged from his father's shadow, right?

Not quite.

Jesse Jackson Jr., one of five children, says he has been giving a lot of thought to what he terms the "continuum" of black politics, something his father speaks about as well. But while the father thinks back to the arc of a movement that started in the 1950s, the son is more focused on saving black folk from the sins of their fathers.

"There's a movement in the black community towards accountable leadership," the younger Jackson told me as we sat in his congressional offices one rainy Washington morning. "The paradigm for the unaccountable leaders has radically shifted. I consider very respectfully—and this is for the record—my father to be a part of the unaccountable leadership, even though I completely believe in and trust his mission and his motives for that which he does.

"But the press conference, television visibility, lack of follow-through, everything-is-a-civil-rights-issue paradigm with leadership is profoundly unaccountable to the masses of people and to history."

Remarkable words, coming from the son of the man who practically invented the everything-is-a-civil-rights-issue campaign.

Don't get him wrong, Junior continues. There is a place for the agitation and protest politics of a Jesse Jackson Sr. and an Al Sharpton. But it is not here. Not now.

The elder Jackson is keenly aware of his son's apostasy. "I encourage in our house vigorous debate, and there is no punishment for a different point of view," he told me. "We have different roles." Jackson senior is the agitator. The younger one is the negotiator.

Even though both father and son endorsed fellow Chicagoan Barack Obama's 2008 campaign for president, they viewed Obama's candidacy through fundamentally different lenses. At one point, during the height of the presidential primary campaign, they took their disagreement to the pages of the *Chicago Sun-Times*.

"The Democratic candidates," the elder Jackson wrote, "have virtually ignored the plight of African Americans in this country."[1]

Jackson junior responded immediately, penning his own op-ed under a headline that read: "Jesse Jr. to Jesse Sr.: You're Wrong on Obama, Dad."[2]

"While causing quite a stir, Jackson's comments unfortunately dimmed—rather than directed—light on the facts," the younger Jackson wrote about his father. Obama, he argued, represents "powerful, consistent and effective advocacy for African Americans."

The father-son split was put on dramatically wider view later in the campaign when, as we've seen, the elder Jackson was caught on camera whispering into an open microphone that he was so angry that Obama was "talking down to black people" that he wanted to "rip his nuts off."

Jackson senior quickly apologized, and Obama shrugged off the criticism and crude language, but not before Jackson junior declared himself "deeply outraged and disappointed" in his father's off-the-cuff remarks, which he also denounced as "ugly rhetoric" and "reckless."

It is a rare thing to see a family political dispute aired so publicly, but the split in the Jackson family was irresistible in that it mirrored a more general split within the community at large. Senator Ted Kennedy and his niece Caroline cast their lot with Barack Obama, while another niece and nephew, Kathleen Kennedy Townsend and Robert F. Kennedy Jr., opted for Clinton. Similarly, congressional sister act Linda and Loretta Sanchez in California split their primary choices, with one (Linda) supporting Obama and the other (Loretta) Clinton.[3]

But within the African American community, such splits cut much more deeply, in part because most had never had reason to disagree before. "If Jesse makes certain moves, if he needs to distinguish his own name and reputation from mine, I understand that," the elder Jackson said, noting his son's insider responsibilities and mixed-race constituency. "I see the gist, the transition, what his options are now. Where he's hugging them in '08, I was putting them out in '72." He laughed. "I find joy in that."

Congressman Jackson's effort to get out of his father's shadow was put most eloquently on display at the 2008 Democratic National Convention. It was in this venue that Jackson senior in 1984 gave perhaps his most memorable national speech, as the delegates in San

Francisco cheered his refrain, "Our time has come." Twenty-four years later, he was not even offered a speaking role. Instead, the son took center stage.

"I grew up in the lessons of another generation, the Selma generation, my father's generation," the younger Jackson told the crowd in Denver. "I know his stories of struggle and sacrifice, of fear and division. I know America is still a place where dreams are too often deferred and opportunities too often denied."

The Selma generation, he did not have to say, represents the past. "I know, for the sake of our children, for the sake of our families and the future we hold in common, he is the leader we need right now," Congressman Jackson said of Obama.[4]

His father supported Obama too. But the elder Jackson sees the history differently. And given the opportunity, he can catalogue every breakthrough along the way because he was often present, for the big victories as well as the small humiliations. He remembers the night in 1967 when he joined Martin Luther King Jr., Ralph Abernathy, and Andrew Young for a trip to Cleveland to celebrate the election of that city's first black mayor. The group gathered in a hotel suite awaiting their summons to join the victor onstage in the ballroom downstairs. The call never came.

"As I've said to my son and others, what does one generation owe the other?" Jackson told me after retelling the story of the forty-year-old election night insult. "Remember. Be grateful. And do well. Remember, because sometimes you have to go back over the same path."

THE HARLEM RENAISSANCE: THE PATERSONS

David Paterson got his first taste of politics on the back of a sound truck wending its way through Harlem. As the truck mounted with speakers moved through the streets of America's most famous black neighborhood, the sixteen-year-old bellowed into the microphone, urging residents to vote for his father. "I tried to make my voice deeper to create the illusion that I was older," he remembers now.

It was 1970, and Basil A. Paterson, then a member of the New York state senate and later secretary of state, was running for lieutenant governor on the doomed Democratic ticket with gubernatorial nominee Arthur Goldberg, a former Supreme Court justice and United Nations ambassador. They were easily beaten by Republican Nelson Rockefeller.

If they had won, Paterson would have become New York State's first black lieutenant governor. His son was watching carefully, and decades later was still able to recount the events of that year in sports play-by-play fashion.

"Interestingly enough, he wins the primary; he gets 71 percent of the vote. He wins every county in the state except the home county of the person he ran against," Paterson said. "Here's an African American winning in these heavily white areas overwhelmingly. So this is shocking. But when the general election comes, his likeness never appears in any ads for governor. They don't use him at all."

The younger Paterson smelled a squandered opportunity, and took careful note of the fact that no one seemed to give his father credit for the strengths he brought to the ticket. Lessons learned in that race informed a critical decision the son made thirty-six years later.

That is when David, by now the minority leader of the New York state senate and a mere two seats away from claiming the powerful majority leader's post, decided instead to join Eliot Spitzer on the Democratic ticket for governor as lieutenant governor. Democrats thought he was crazy. But Paterson was reliving his father's past.

"I wonder if the reason I ran for lieutenant governor was not just because I thought Eliot Spitzer was going to really be a super reformer and I wanted to be on the team, but that part of it was me wanting to avenge the loss," he told me.

On election night in 2006, when it was Paterson's turn at the microphone, he reveled in the notion that he had attained the brass ring his father had deserved but not gotten. "I said to the audience that I've never compared myself to my dad," he told me. "I've never seen myself as a replacement for him. I'm just a closer."

He was more skilled than that. David Paterson learned names, faces, and the ways of electoral politics at the knee of the city's most skilled practitioners—his dad, Congressman Charles Rangel, Manhattan borough president Percy Sutton, and Mayor David Dinkins.

Basil Paterson worked the levers of power in New York State for decades. He served as Ed Koch's deputy mayor and as Governor Hugh Carey's secretary of state. He was an insider's insider in New York City politics.

"I'm a Harlem guy," Basil said when asked to compare his style to his son's. "Born here. Grew up here. I knew a lot of people, some people that I don't admit I knew anymore. So we're different that way. Yet I know if I walk down the street with my son—long before he became governor or lieutenant governor—everybody knew him.

"I always came home and talked about what I was doing," Basil told me. "I couldn't help myself."

Legally blind after a childhood infection robbed him of sight in one eye and severely limited his vision in the other, David Paterson grew up on Long Island and never ran with the political pack. He took up the family business only after exploring careers in the law and journalism. But everything he did learn about politics happened in Harlem. "To be honest, my father never said to me, 'I expect you to take the reins, son,' or that kind of thing," the governor told me. "It was almost like an effect of your identity."

His father remembers it the same way. "I'm not sure this is something that I wanted him to do, as much as he saw it as the thing he wanted to do."

The governor says he was first drawn to the idea of a political career at the age of ten as he watched Robert Kennedy speak at the 1964 Democratic National Convention. Watching another family's legacy play out on a public stage resonated. "He was following in the footsteps of John, Hillary follows in the footsteps of Bill," said David Paterson, who supported his home state senator in the 2008 Democratic primary. "So I always relate to that kind of family member who has to deal with that shadow."[5]

With his father as his guide, Paterson became a keen observer and practitioner of black political leadership. "There is always this discussion of who is the leader," he told me. "Is it Jesse Jackson? Is it Reverend Al Sharpton? The question isn't who's the leader. The question is how badly we need them. If you lived in Scarsdale in New York, who cares who the leader is? Everybody's doing great. What do you need a leader *for*?"

Ultimately, David proved his own leadership skills by building a twenty-three-year power base representing Harlem in the state senate before he moved on to the lieutenant governor's job. And through a quirk of fate and political misfortune, in less than two years the younger Paterson became the state's first African American governor. "No one was more surprised than he was," his father chortled.

Paterson stepped into the job in 2008 after Spitzer was implicated in a seamy scandal in which it was revealed he had paid high-priced prostitutes to service him in a Washington hotel. Paterson's rise may have appeared sudden, but it was not out of the blue. He had spent more than two decades as a blind man learning the political ins and outs of Albany, listening to voices and detecting intentions. He even had to memorize his speeches.

"People think he just got there, but he worked hard for a long time," Basil said tartly. "Black folks, whenever we get there, it's like it was overnight. It didn't matter how long we worked for it."

At the age of fifty-four, David Paterson was only the nation's fourth black governor. Virginia's L. Douglas Wilder and Massachusetts' Deval Patrick had preceded him. A more obscure chief executive, Pinckney Benton Stewart Pinchback, rose from lieutenant governor to Louisiana's top job for five weeks in 1872 and 1873, after the governor he was serving was impeached.

Paterson and Patrick have compared notes about the difficulty of being a governor and a representative of the larger black community. The New York governor is particularly annoyed at what he considers to be coded judgments aimed at him. In an address to the NAACP annual convention in 2008, he complained that he is frequently referred to as the state's "accidental" governor, because he was not elected to the job.

"We counted twenty-seven references to the 'accidental governor' that were reserved just for me," Paterson told me, the trace of irritation still in his voice weeks later. "And my question is, why is that going on?"

Most of the time, though, Paterson took the edge off uncomfortable situations with a joke or an easygoing smile. On the day Paterson was sworn in, he was greeted with applause as he arrived in the capitol's Red Room. "If most of you weren't being paid, I'd be flattered by that," he said, and everyone laughed.[6]

But, weirdly, on the very next day after he took office, Paterson and his wife, Michelle, stepped before the cameras in Albany again, this time to admit that they had been unfaithful to each other—he with multiple partners. The disclosure echoed loudly, a jarring aftershock to the Spitzer scandal.

But those initial scandals faded as Paterson set about negotiating the thicket of state governance. At about the time he was settling in at the governor's office in Albany, the state's economy hit the skids as the global financial crisis that froze the national economy hit the Empire State's budget hard. Taxes derived from Wall Street businesses typically provided one-fifth of the state's revenue.

Paterson shaved the state budget by $1.5 billion his first summer in office, and by October was faced with begging the state legislature for help in closing a $1.5 billion deficit. None of this could be learned at Daddy's knee.

So little could. While Obama enjoyed an extended honeymoon in Washington, Paterson's stock in New York dropped like a rock. The fiscal crisis mushroomed into a political one. A fifty-fifty deadlock in Albany left the governor on the sidelines for a month, unable to break the tie.

His effort to appoint a lieutenant governor to fill the job he'd vacated was challenged in court. In the midst of all this, more than 60 percent of the state's voters told Quinnipiac University pollsters he was doing a bad job as governor and should not be elected to a full term.

"In my short time—and I know I am just sipping at what Barack Obama has to go through gallons of every day," Paterson told me, "the energy that takes away from your effort is immense."

THE TENNESSEE WALTZ: THE FORDS

Harold Ford Jr. is a son of Tennessee, but like former vice president Al Gore, he really grew up in the rarefied confines of Washington, D.C., as the privileged son of a member of Congress. He went to private schools and spent his off time working on Capitol Hill as a congressional page and an intern.

As he approached his final year at the University of Michigan Law School, Ford junior began thinking about taking a year off to work in Bill Clinton's White House. So he sat down with his father, who held the congressional seat representing Memphis, and had a little talk. Dad, it turns out, had a plan to make sure young Harold got that law degree.

If Harold junior finished at Michigan, his father would retire from Congress. His son could replace him. And true to the terms of their deal, when graduation approached, the younger Ford phoned his father. "He called me up and said, 'Look, are you going to step down?'" Ford senior told me. "And I said, 'I'll keep my promise. Are you ready to run?'"

The promise counted for a lot. Harold junior was in school out of state and was only technically a Memphis resident. But the Ford name would help erase any carpetbagger accusations. With the help of campaign signs that simply read JR. and a campaign strategy that got the twenty-six-year-old invited to as many hometown elementary school graduations as he could wangle, he won.[7]

"You never know when an opportunity will present itself," Ford said years later in a speech to the University of Arkansas' Clinton School of Public Service in Little Rock. "In the strangest, weirdest of circumstances. Out of defeat, out of turmoil, out of just difficulty you never know when an opportunity may lurk.

"My dad was one of fifteen," Ford told the students. "I cannot imagine not having running water. I can't imagine some of the things my dad did not have. They worked hard to make things better for me."

Together, the two Fords held the Memphis seat for thirty-two years. The elder Ford had broken through thanks to education, collecting degrees from Tennessee State University and Howard University. With his newly acquired expertise in mortuary science, he worked at building a family funeral home business that allowed the Fords to establish deep roots and loyalties within Memphis' black community. He was elected to the Tennessee House of Representatives in 1971.

Harold junior, taking advantage of those roots and the seat his father essentially handed off to him, headed to Washington for five terms as a member of the House. By 2006, he was ready for a change, and launched what became an $11 million run for the Senate.

But Ford discovered that the family ties that had gotten him elected to Congress could be a real disadvantage in a statewide race. The Ford family's by now formidable reputation in Tennessee ranged from heartfelt support in mostly black Memphis to hardwired suspicion in mostly white east Tennessee. Republican nominee Bob Corker, although a well-connected former Chattanooga mayor himself, was able to brand young Harold as part of "the Ford family machine."[8]

There were indeed a lot of Fords involved in politics. When Harold senior defeated an incumbent Republican to win a congressional seat in the post-Watergate election year of 1974, he did so by only 574 votes. On that same night one brother, John, won a state senate seat, and another, Emmitt, clinched a state house election.

But there was a stain. Over the years, several Fords had also endured tangles with the law. Four Ford brothers were each indicted at one point or another on various fraud and bribery charges. Two were convicted and two acquitted: Edmund Ford Sr. in May 2008, and Harold Ford Sr. in 1993, after being accused and tried twice. Furious members of the Congressional Black Caucus said Harold Ford was unfairly targeted, calling it "a classic example of the continued harassment of black elected officials."[9]

Still, the cloud continued to hover. Just before Harold junior announced his Senate candidacy, his uncle John was indicted on wire fraud charges, for which he was later convicted and sentenced to fourteen years in prison. Those were to be served consecutively after he completed another five-and-a-half-year sentence on a bribery conviction.[10]

Sometimes the problem wasn't alleged criminality but embarrassment. In 2008, father and son were forced to establish arm's-length distance once again—this time from Harold junior's two brothers, Jake and Isaac, who chose the fortieth anniversary of Martin Luther King Jr.'s Memphis assassination to make racially charged remarks about Representative Steve Cohen, the white man who had succeeded the Fords in the majority-black Ninth Congressional District.[11]

I asked the younger Harold about family baggage when he was running in 2006. It was a question he had become accustomed to. "I am who I am," he replied. "And I think voters know my opponent has made clear to everybody that I'm black, that my family is big and political and sometimes finds itself in a newspaper for things for which they didn't do, but I can't do anything about that but be me."[12]

For his part, the elder Ford does not think the family issues cost his son the U.S. Senate election. Instead, he believes Republicans beat his son at the money game, sending millions of dollars into the state to help Corker pay for weeks of withering television ads. One that became instantly notorious claimed Harold junior frequented Playboy clubs, and featured a buxom blonde who whispered at the end: "Harold, call me." Corker denounced the ad, which was paid for by an outside independent group, but he still profited from it. With one stroke, the ads managed to remind voters that Ford was black (read: not like you and me) and at the time unmarried (read: not like you and me) and to hint that he was engaged in miscegenation (read: not like you and me). "They ran the race card on him," the elder Ford said. "And he just couldn't overcome it in the last couple of days."

By Election Day, everyone in Tennessee was convinced Ford would lose, but by much more than he did.[13] Ford won 95 percent of the black vote and 41 percent of the white vote. But if voters lied about their preferences, it helped him. He got 48 percent of the vote overall, a closer margin than the twelve-point loss preelection polls had predicted.

Still, a loss is a loss. Harold junior disagrees with his father on what brought this to pass. He says his party affiliation hurt him more than his race.[14] But there is some evidence that in this case father knows best. In that same election year, Phil Bredesen, a white Democrat, rolled up overwhelming majorities in his race for governor, sweeping every county. A third of those Bredesen supporters, however, declined to vote for Ford.[15]

"It hurt," Harold junior later admitted. "It was the first time I ever lost anything."[16]

Still, Ford had done something brand-new for a black candidate running in the South. He appealed to white voters by shedding the liberal label, denouncing same-sex marriage, labeling himself "pro-life," and even filming one campaign ad in a church.

In conservative east Tennessee, I saw him run into traffic to shake white voters' hands. He engaged one young man in a sidewalk conversation so penetrating and intense that the voter came away leaning toward voting for Ford. The man told me later he'd never voted for a Democrat in his life.

"Democrats have to be willing to meet people where people are, and meet their lives where their lives are, and don't be ashamed to talk about the things that we care about," Ford said some time later. "We need to cross the hurdle on national security and fiscal restraint. And we need to demonstrate that our values are consistent with other people's values, that they are mainstream not only in Arkansas and Mississippi and Tennessee but around the country."[17]

Two years later, in an open letter published in *Newsweek,* Ford urged Obama to run as he had. "People know that the candidates running for president don't live just the way they live," Ford wrote. "But they want to know that they're understood, and that their daily struggles are respected."[18]

Ford remains adamant that straddles like these are essential for the new breed of African American politician. "I bring a little bit of a different orientation to it," he told interviewer Charlie Rose early in the 2008 primary process. "I'm a member of the National Rifle Association, although that's not something that my party fully embraces yet."[19]

Not even his father fully embraces that, but neither man seems particularly concerned about their occasional differences. "You can have disagreements with father-son," Harold senior said, noting the public split within the Jesse Jackson family. "Harold junior and I, we're extremely close, but that's not to say we agree on everything. I respect his positions, and he respects mine and we talk about it a lot."

But the two are still more alike than different. "If you notice my record in the Congress, I was really a middle-of-the-road-type guy," said the elder Ford, who now works as a lobbyist. Other, more liberal members of the Congressional Black Caucus, he said, viewed him with suspicion.

The younger Ford too became suspect in some liberal circles when he agreed to become chairman of the middle-of-the-road Democratic Leadership Council. The DLC has made it their mission to separate the word *liberal* from the word *Democrat.* Jesse Jackson Sr. often dismissively derided the group as the "Democratic Leisure Class."

Ford, however, decided the DLC represented the Democrats' future. "We can achieve the progressive ideals of the party," Ford said in 2003. "But only if we campaign and govern like the innovators of our party's proud past."

As head of the DLC, Harold Ford Jr. now travels the country defending Democrats and Republicans alike. "The reason Harold Ford likes me so much," perpetually endangered Connecticut Republican

Christopher Shays once said, "is because when I realized that I wasn't going to be president, I went up to him and told him that he was one of the three legislators that I thought would someday."[20] Shays, however, won't be in Congress to help. He was defeated in 2008.

The DLC has devolved into something of a spent political force in the years since the election of one of its own—Bill Clinton—to the White House in 1992. Since then, it has become a refuge of sorts for the party's most conservative members—and certainly for its southerners. Its annual meeting, which used to host top candidates every year, failed in both 2007 and 2008 to attract either Hillary Clinton or Barack Obama. The snub was particularly apparent in 2008, when the group met in Chicago. The Illinois senator, by then the party's putative nominee, was actually in his hometown that day, but didn't bother to drop by.

Speculation continues to swirl that Ford, married and spending the bulk of his time in New York as a vice chairman for Merrill Lynch and a television commentator, might return to politics. He has continued to keep a hand in, teaching at the LBJ School at the University of Texas in Austin and at Vanderbilt University in Nashville. His name still surfaces regularly in Tennessee commentary as a potential candidate for the 2010 gubernatorial race, but his prospects remain unclear. As a columnist for the Nashville *City Paper* warned: "Another loss would mean the end to a very promising career."[21]

In fact, Ford is keeping his Tennessee connections intact. He told the Little Rock audience that when he is in Memphis, he stays at his condominium and regularly gets up in the morning to run a route that takes him past the National Civil Rights Museum, on the site of the Lorraine Motel, where Martin Luther King Jr. was shot.

"I do think that we've made enormous progress and I think we can all appreciate that," he said. "And then, I look up at the balcony and think we've got a long way to go.

"And then," he added, "I look back up and think I have not done nearly enough to try to make the kind of difference that I know that all of us are capable of making."[22]

His father's advice? "I hope he stays on Wall Street and makes a little money."

THE LOYAL SON: THE CLAYS

William Lacy Clay Jr. freely admits that he won his first political office because his father's name was William Lacy Clay Sr. This was not his plan. In part because he grew up in a household where his father always seemed to be off somewhere else—picketing, getting arrested, agitating—politics was not his goal.

"To be honest with you, when I was growing up, I hated politics," Clay, now a member of Congress from Missouri, said. "I hated what it did to people."

But after he struggled through high school and college to finally land at Howard University School of Law, he was presented with a slam-dunk chance to win election to the Missouri state legislature. His father, by then something of a kingmaker in St. Louis politics, was on the hunt for someone to fill a vacant state house seat. His son, who at the time was still living in Maryland, where he had essentially grown up, volunteered for the job. His main qualification? He had the right name. A mere six weeks later, he was on his way to Jefferson City.

By the time Bill Clay Sr. gave up his congressional seat seventeen years later, the younger Clay—known as Lacy to differentiate himself from his dad—had established a reputation and a name of his own. When he arrived in Washington to take over his father's seat in 2000, Nancy Pelosi swore him in. Standing nearby, his father teared up.

Bill Clay Sr. was a member of the first wave of decades-long members of the Congressional Black Caucus. He got elected the old-fashioned way, climbing up through St. Louis ward politics and defeating seven white and four black competitors along the way. One of the white candidates owned a Howard Johnson's restaurant where Clay was once arrested while trying to get served.

His breakthrough came in 1968, the same year New York's Shirley Chisholm and Ohio's Louis Stokes were sent to Congress. He would remain in Congress for thirty-two years.

"The three of us—Stokes, Chisholm, and I—came to Washington determined to seize the moment, to fight for justice, to raise issues too long ignored and too little debated," Clay wrote in his 1992 book on blacks in Congress. "We were described by the media as militant, aggressive new leaders determined to make changes in the way black members of Congress had been viewed in the past."[23]

Clay and the others promptly created the Congressional Black Caucus, and set about rattling the status quo on Capitol Hill and, ultimately, in the Nixon White House. They went to war with Nixon over everything from the creation of a Martin Luther King Jr. Day holiday to programs for low-income housing and other Great Society antipoverty programs.

Father and son bear a striking physical resemblance to each other, and their liberal politics are nearly indistinguishable, but Lacy Clay is the first to admit he lacks some of his father's considerable street political skills. He remembers faces but not always names. "In St. Louis people sometimes refer to me as the milder version of my father," Lacy Clay says.

But he was not *that* mild. He once kicked a group of labor leaders (who backed another candidate) out of his office after they showed up with a list of demands even though they hadn't supported his candidacy. His father, always closely linked to organized labor, never would have done that.

He also resists the kingmaker label his father enjoyed for so many years. "I had an eighty-year-old guy tell me, 'You're a congressman. You can do anything,'" he remembers, chuckling at the thought. "I said, 'Look, pal, I only know one person that ever walked on water, okay?'"

But when the 2008 presidential campaign was threatening to devolve into a political death match between Barack Obama and Hillary Clinton, Clay did not hesitate to throw down the gauntlet and cast his lot with the growing chorus of Obama supporters who tried to force Clinton out of the race.

"If you have any, any kind of loyalty to the Democratic Party," he told Clinton, "perhaps you need to rethink your strategy and bow out gracefully in order to save this party from a disastrous end in November."[24]

The son was told repeatedly that he would have trouble filling his father's big shoes. His response was to tell his critics they were absolutely right.

"I said I'm never going to be him, because he was the first African American legislator from Missouri," Lacy Clay said. "He was the first this and that. I won't be the trailblazer that he was, because he's done it all. He's laid a path for me."

Lacy Clay is now a fully entrenched member of the Congressional Black Caucus, an inheritor of a safe seat in a majority-black district, and an admirer of the lions of the civil rights movement who preceded him. He listens carefully to the critique of younger activists and politicians who declare it time for a new approach to black politics. And to some extent, he counts himself among their number.

"I think we have deference to that, to the previous generation," he told me as we sat in his congressional office, surrounded by the photographs and framed newspaper articles linking him to his father. "We have a profound respect for them. And we know most of us know and realize how we got here. It was on the shoulders of them. They paved the way for us to make it to these new heights.

"Look what they did, the Lou Stokeses, Bill Clays, John Conyerses, and the Charlie Rangels and the Adam Clayton Powells," he said. "I don't know if any of us would have had the will or the strength to do all of that."

But the battles are different now. Black lawmakers couldn't even get a haircut on Capitol Hill when they first came to Congress. Their sons and daughters are struggling instead to alter the agendas they have inherited. Lacy Clay remembers having a tough conversation with his father when he tried to explain why he supported charter schools to supplement public education. The two had to agree to disagree.

As simple as the politics of inheritance may seem, Clay was only the second African American member of Congress to step into a parent's shoes. Harold Ford Jr. preceded him; Kendrick Meek followed.

MIAMI NICE: THE MEEKS

Kendrick Meek was a young Florida state senator when he made his first significant mark on electoral politics in January 2000. The issue was affirmative action, and the target was Republican governor Jeb Bush.

Meek and fellow Democratic state lawmaker Tony Hill wanted to kill Bush's plan to replace the state's higher education system's racial preferences with a plan to guarantee admission to high school seniors who graduated in the top 20 percent of their classes. Bush called it "One Florida."[25]

Meek and Hill opted for a 1960s protest tactic neither was old enough to have actually witnessed: They would stage a sit-in at the governor's Tallahassee office. It lasted twenty-five hours.

As it happens, what ensued was a clash between two men who benefited from the politics of inheritance. Jeb Bush, the brother of the man who would become president later that year after a fractious electoral recount in Florida, was the scion of one of the nation's most dominant political dynasties. His father, George H. W. Bush, was a one-term president from 1989 to 1993, and his brother George W. Bush would go on to serve two terms of his own from 2001 to 2009.

Meek's own political heritage was nowhere near as illustrious, but it may have played a more critical role in shaping his ambitions. His mother, Carrie Meek, was a member of Congress from Miami from 1993 to 2003.

Indeed, the former Florida A&M linebacker and highway patrolman's introduction to politics came through working to elect his mother in 1979. The party elders in Miami had discouraged her from running for the state legislature to replace another legendary black woman, Gwen Cherry, who had been killed in a tragic car accident. They had a man in mind for the job. "What they forgot was that I had been a college professor for many years, and I had taught all the people of voting age during my tenure at the college," Carrie Meek told me.

Her son joined in the effort, directing traffic, recruiting volunteers, and doing whatever else needed to be done. He was thirteen years old at the time. "We ran, and we did little campaign signs and we even drew them up," he recalled of the bare-bones campaign. "She worked at the community college and, I mean, with no money whatsoever, she ended up winning that race. She was able to pull it together, but it was not like she was recruited to pull it together."

Meek, too, learned politics literally at his mother's knee—or perched on her hip. She remembers lugging him along to community meetings while she fought to desegregate the community's schools and colleges. The politics of it all just sort of seeped in. "He had a knack for it," she told me. "He really did."

The younger Meek promptly followed his mother's path in 1994, winning a seat in the Florida state legislature at the age of twenty-seven. When Carrie Meek decided to retire from Congress in 2002, Kendrick was there once again—making use of the family name and Tallahassee connections to step onto the path she'd cleared for him. "I know there will be other candidates," the seventy-six-year-old congresswoman said at the time. "But there's just one Meek."[26] There were no other candidates. Meek made a beeline for Washington.

"He became a member of Congress without standing for election," said David Bositis, who studies black politics at the Joint Center for Political and Economic Studies. "Not only did he not have a primary opponent, he didn't have a general election opponent. His mother usually didn't have a general election opponent. He actually became a member of Congress without having to run."

But before he could get to Washington, Meek had to make his mark in Tallahassee. On that Tuesday night in 2000, Meek and Hill were joined at their sit-in by dozens of students and lawmakers, who crowded the halls at the state capitol. When reporters arrived to cover the protest, Governor Bush was widely quoted as telling an aide to "kick their asses out," an ill-advised retort he subsequently apologized for.[27]

"I'm a sitting member of the state senate," Meek recalled. "This is not what you do. But at the same time, I wouldn't have been able to sleep well knowing that Governor Jeb Bush was doing away with affirmative action through executive order."

Watching Meek on Capitol Hill today, it is hard to believe he was once such an upstart. Buttoned into handsome suits and looking every inch the Washington insider, he is a well-liked junior lawmaker whose best friend in the House is an equally handsome white Democrat, Paul Ryan from Wisconsin. He has been known to share a fine cigar with Republican congressman Mario Diaz-Balart, another Florida statehouse alumnus. He makes a point of attending every weekly meeting of the Congressional Black Caucus and fiercely embraces the responsibility of representing the needs of a district that is 57 percent black. He is also cochairman of House Speaker Nancy Pelosi's "30-Something" working group and—because so many of the residents of his south Florida district were born in Haiti—he concentrates on trade issues affecting the Caribbean nation.

But unlike many members of his generational cohort, Meek resisted appeals to endorse Barack Obama for president, instead becoming a useful and vocal defender of Hillary Clinton, appearing frequently on television on her behalf. And when Bill Clinton got in trouble for making what were widely interpreted as racially dismissive criticisms of Obama, Meek rose to his defense as well. Throughout the primary process, Meek resisted the Illinois senator's entreaties.

"Barack's conversation with me was something like, 'You know, if you come on board, we want to make you a significant player in the campaign. If I do well, you do well in the future. I'm going to cut the path for you,'" Meek said, recalling the conversation. But he had a different response. "I think Carrie Meek cut the path for me."

On this decision, mother and son parted ways. Carrie Meek desperately wanted to support Obama, if only because she was excited at the possibility of electing a black president. But she initially kept silent out of deference to her son's political decision.

"I asked him, 'What are you going to do? Because I really like Obama.' I could feel the beating of the drums, and all that crazy stuff," she told me, laughing. "And he said, 'Mama, I'm going to support Hillary.' We both had some affinity for Hillary, because we knew how strongly her husband had supported us. But all along—I have to share this with you—I was an Obama fan."

Once again, the 2008 presidential campaign showcased the generational divide between parents and children who agree about almost everything else. Carrie Meek admits she was drawn to Obama because she felt his success would demonstrate "black power"—a phrase it would never occur to her son to use. "I don't think they look so much as deeply as we did toward color," she said.

Her son agreed. "Just because Senator Obama is black doesn't necessarily mean that every black person elected or nonelected must be, because of the 'race thing,' on the bandwagon with him," he said.

In the end, Kendrick Meek was the odd man out on the national political stage in 2008, but he kept busy building a base on Capitol Hill as a member of the powerful House Ways and Means Committee. He still carries his mother's congressional identification card in his wallet, and he is casting an eye on the possibility of running for statewide office back home in Florida. Even though he did not endorse Obama in the primary, he studied his historic run carefully.

"Everyone has a balance beam to walk," Meek said. "But when you're black, you're in uniform, you're not undercover." Laughing, he gestured at the gold pin on his lapel that identifies him as a member of Congress. "When I take this pin off and I walk down Pennsylvania Avenue, I'm just another black man."

THE FAMILY BUSINESS: THE MALLORYS

When Mark Mallory was twelve years old, he used to accompany his father to work at the statehouse. Representative William L. Mallory spent twenty-eight years in Columbus, Ohio, and when he took his youngest son to committee meetings, he would grill him later about who said what.

That was Mallory's first taste of politics. His father also had been introduced to politics at the age of twelve, when his mother's physician brought him along to political club meetings and let him listen in. William Mallory says he never meant to create a family dynasty. It just worked out that way.

When the time approached for the elder Mallory to step aside, his five sons had a meeting. Two were judges, one was the vice mayor of a Cincinnati suburb, and the youngest, Mark, was a midlevel manager at the public library. A daughter, Denise, who works for the Ohio Lottery, is the only one uninterested in elective politics.

Someone, the sons decided, was going to have to plan to succeed their father when he gave up his seat in the Ohio state legislature, where he was currently the well-respected Democratic floor leader.

"I said, 'Well, I think you're right. Which one of you is going to do it?'" Mark Mallory said when his brother Dale took him aside. Unbeknownst to baby brother Mark, the die had already been cast.

At his siblings' insistence he went to his father to tell him he had reluctantly been recruited to take over the family business. To his surprise, his father did not immediately embrace the idea. "He looked at me and he said, 'Well, why do you want to do that?'" Mallory recalled. "And that caught me off guard, because I was expecting him to be excited—you know, 'My son's going to follow in my footsteps, and this is a great thing.'"

The elder Mallory remembers it differently. Mark, he said, wanted him to step aside before the election so the son could be appointed to replace the father without first standing for election. "I said, 'No, we can't do that, because if I do that people will always say you could never have won this seat on your own,'" William Mallory lectured his son. "'They will always say I gave it to you.'"

So young Mark got the third degree. Was he doing this because he wanted to do something for himself, or because he wanted to do something for the people he would represent? "He wanted to know that my intentions were correct," Mark says now, recalling the conversation with his father.

It took another three years before the senior Mallory was ready to step aside, and there was nothing ceremonial or torch-passing about it. Mark read about his father's decision to resign his seat in the newspaper.

"I prevailed, and he was elected on his own," William Mallory, now seventy-seven years old, told me. "And even though he was elected on his own, people still said I gave him the seat."

Mark Mallory, now forty-six, spent two terms in the Ohio house and another term in the state senate. While there, he sponsored a resolution for the Buckeye State to—belatedly—ratify the Fourteenth Amendment to the Constitution, granting full citizenship to former slaves. He left the legislative post to run and win election as Cincinnati mayor in 2005, becoming the city's sixty-eighth chief executive, and the first African American elected directly by the voters.

"During that campaign I kept hearing the same thing over and over again," the mayor said, ticking off the objections to the campaign he ran against city councilman David Pepper. "'Mallory, you're not qualified. You haven't been on city council. You don't know city government. You've been away at the state[house], so you don't know the issues that are important in Cincinnati. You will not be able to raise the kind of money that it takes in order to win the mayor's office. You have 50 percent name recognition. People don't know you. They don't know who you are. This is an uphill battle for you. Why don't you just, you know, step aside and wait for a time later?'"

Well, he wasn't stepping aside. In this, he says now, he was like Obama was in 2008. "There were people in this city who took a chance and said, 'I'm going to go with the message of hope. I'm going to go with the intangible, with this Mallory guy.'" Mallory beat Pepper 52 percent to 48 percent.

"My father never said to any of us, 'I want you in politics,'" the mayor told me of his unusually political family. "The things that we got from my dad and my mother were 'You have to do something.'"

Mark Mallory also says he is keenly aware that African American politicians have a different row to hoe now than they did when his father first went to Columbus. "Back in the old days when you had a dispute with someone, you didn't do character assassination like you do these days," William Mallory told me, chuckling. "You just punched them out." But to this day, the younger Mallory will not set foot in the Columbus Athletic Club because it once did not allow his father to dine there.

The elder Mallory cut his teeth in politics knocking on doors and registering voters in Cincinnati's largely black Eighteenth Ward. The younger Mallory, who did not have to work nearly so hard, sees his role as dramatically different. Instead of advocating for, say, voting rights as a way of helping a largely African American constituency, Mayor Mallory is convinced he can do as much or more for his African American constituents by advocating for health care, housing, and education. "By the time I got to office, there were an additional set of issues that people expected you to work on as an African American," he said.

Mark Mallory's was a sought-after endorsement for Barack Obama. Unlike other breakthrough elected officials around the country, he did not embrace the black candidate right away. Instead, he conducted a high-profile political dalliance with both Obama and Hillary Clinton. Ultimately, he said, he decided to support Obama because he saw echoes of his own experience running for mayor. He endorsed Obama before thirteen thousand supporters at a late-February megarally in Cincinnati.[28]

Now, after three years in office, Mayor Mallory is happily fielding rumors that he might become state treasurer or state attorney general or follow Obama to Washington. His only plan, he says, is to run for reelection. But he is happy to let the rumors live a life of their own. "I figure, as a politician, you know, you really shouldn't, you know, promote them or kill them unnecessarily."

IT IS NOT ENTIRELY shocking that sons and daughters follow their fathers and mothers into the family business. "Nobody questions the Ford children when they want to go into the car business," said Essex County (New Jersey) freeholder Donald Payne Jr., whose father is a member of Congress. "The examples you have growing up are naturally going to cause you to lean that way, and when it comes to my father, why wouldn't I want to be like him?"[29]

In 2006, Payne was one of two sons of Newark's black political establishment elected to the city council. Ron Rice Jr., who followed in his father's footsteps onto the city council, split with his father politically when the son decided to align himself with another young leader, Newark mayor Cory Booker. This was particularly significant because the elder Rice was Booker's opponent.

"I ran for city council against my own father's judgment and without his support," the younger Rice told me candidly. "I ran with Cory Booker against his support—against him, to be frank. But it wasn't because I loved Cory Booker more than my dad. It was because my dad's generation told him constantly to wait your turn, wait your turn."

But legacy politics does not always take. John James, the son of former Newark mayor Sharpe James, ran for city council the same year and lost. And although Representative Carolyn Cheeks Kilpatrick, a Michigan Democrat, was able to pass on her political genes to her son, Detroit mayor Kwame Kilpatrick, he became ensnared in troubling behavior that ultimately tarnished the family name.

At the height of the 2008 presidential campaign, the younger Kilpatrick was so enmeshed in a lurid sex scandal that even he admitted his endorsement would not help Obama. "He's running a very smart campaign," Kilpatrick conceded. "And his campaign is not to be walking, holding hands, singing 'Kumbaya' with Kwame Kilpatrick."[30]

True enough. When Kilpatrick was eventually forced to relinquish the mayor's job and sent to prison for obstruction of justice, Obama was far away. And Carolyn Cheeks Kilpatrick's political legacy was extinguished.

Sandpaper scratches. Almost all parents can enumerate ways their offspring can disappoint. But in politics, the family name is the coin of the realm. It opens doors like a charm, but it falls to the legatee not to abuse the advantage—or get sunk by the baggage.

CHAPTER SEVEN

CORY BOOKER

The real test of leadership has never been who can get people to follow them. We've got charismatic leaders who get followed a lot. The real test of leadership is to motivate people to be leaders themselves and to carry the burden.

—CORY BOOKER

IT'S ONE THING TO WIN AN ELECTION. IT IS ANOTHER THING TO GOVERN.
No one knows that more keenly than Cory Booker, the young and energetic mayor of Newark, New Jersey, who is the living embodiment of a warning parents have long issued to their children: Be careful what you ask for.

Booker, with his six-foot-three football player's build, big eyes, shiny pate, and strikingly youthful demeanor, had managed only thirteen months in office before the truth of those words came back to haunt him.

Four students were hanging out listening to music on a playground in the city's Ivy Hill neighborhood on a Saturday night before they headed off to Delaware State University in the fall. One by one, three were shot and killed execution-style. The fourth was gravely wounded.

The violent and apparently unprovoked attacks on Terrance Aeriel, eighteen; Dashon Harvey, twenty; Iofemi Hightower, twenty—who were all killed—and Terrance's sister Natasha, nineteen, who was shot but survived, shocked the city, the state, and the nation. Mere months later, it became fodder for an episode of television's *Law and Order* franchise.[1]

The mayor's BlackBerry started going off after midnight.[2] By the time the sun rose, it had become clear he had a full-fledged municipal crisis on his hands.

Within days, five people had been arrested for the murders. One of them surrendered personally to Booker.

Less than a month before, the new mayor had ordered the city's flags lowered to commemorate the fortieth anniversary of the six-day riot that virtually burned the city to the ground in 1967.[3] Now a shocked city saw that not enough had changed.

Recidivism was rampant. Eleven-, twelve-, and thirteen-year-olds were being released from the Essex County juvenile detention center with nowhere to go but right back to jail. "That's absurdity," the mayor fumed to me. "That's absurdity. We pay a whole lot of money to warehouse them, but we're not going to invest to keep them from going back again?"

The schools were crippled. And the schoolyard killings brought the year's total of homicides in the city of 280,000 to sixty. Soon enough, Newark would surpass the previous year's miserable murder rate.

Into this mess walked Cory Booker, thirty-seven years old, incredibly bright, and almost unbearably optimistic. That is, until Terrance, Dashon, and Iofemi were killed. At the funeral of one, a group called Morticians That Care displayed signs reading HOW MANY BODY BAGS WILL IT TAKE?[4]

For Booker, the killings and the outpouring of grief that followed were transformative. He took to his adopted city's pulpits in what sounded like a primal scream of frustration.

"Get this evil out of my city," he cried at one funeral at New Hope Baptist Church. "How dare I or any other Newarker crumble to the ground? How dare we give in to this fear? How dare people turn on their brothers and attack them, blame them?"

For the time being, the new Newark he had been promising was obscured by old demons. The new downtown development, the new leadership in city hall—none of it seemed to matter. People walked up to Booker on the street, screaming at him that he had blood on his hands.

"This really hurts," he told a *New York Times* reporter at the time. "I still believe we're going to move the city forward, but this is a powerful blow. This was going to be a summer we were going to brag about. This overshadows everything."[5]

In perhaps the most shocking way possible, Booker was being forced to cope with the realities of urban leadership. "I think the murders in the city were the cold reality for him," one adviser told me. "That he had to stop being superficial and roll up his sleeves and really get down to the work."

Another political ally found herself on the defensive when Newarkers blamed the mayor for the periodic spikes in violence. "I said he's not Batman, Superman, Spider-Man," city council president Mildred Crump told me. "He cannot see through steel girders and concrete to see that crime is taking place, and fly through the air and prevent it. He can't be everywhere, so it is not fair to blame him."

And violent crime was just one part of the challenge. By the end of that already awful month, Booker would be forced to deal with another big-city mayor's dilemma, less shocking but no less unappetizing—laying off two hundred city workers as part of a plan to save $12.5 million. The city was struggling under the weight of a $180 million budget shortfall, and his critics—who, it seems, had been lying in wait all along—were calling for his head.

When Booker assumed his chief executive role at Newark's city hall in 2006, he was surrounded by a halo of approval not only from the streets of this tired East Coast city but also from pundits and politicians around the country. He'd fought hard for the job, and he knew when he won that he was inheriting, among other things, a city with more than its share of entrenched difficulties—including the fact that one in three of its residents subsist below the poverty line.[6] The reality of it all dealt a severe blow to the urban-savior story line that had sprung up around Booker, who was surely the only mayor ever to be featured in an Oscar-nominated documentary

The first time Booker tried for the mayor's office, he lost. Actually, in the political sense, he was mugged. That was the story of the 2002 documentary *Street Fight*. Booker was the outsider, the kid with a Yale Law degree, an all-American tight end's confidence, and a big mouth. He'd been president of the senior class in both high school and at Stanford University. In between Stanford and Yale Law, he'd gone off to Oxford as a Rhodes scholar. Mayor Sharpe James—who had held the city's reins for twenty years in a thirty-six-year municipal career—was not about to willingly hand over his Broad Street office to an outsider, a snot-nosed kid. James' backers trafficked extensively in rumor-mongering about the new upstart. He was really white. He was Jewish. He was gay. Worse, he didn't really live in Newark. None of this was true, but whisper campaigns don't necessarily have to be.

Sharpe James, who in 2008 would be convicted for shady real estate dealings and sentenced to twenty-seven months in prison, had had bigger names than Cory Booker for lunch. Booker, the child of a gilded, virtually all-white suburb, was an easy target. He possessed a distinguished and distinctly nonghetto pedigree, including the Stanford-Yale-Oxford triple threat. Newark hardly seemed the place someone with Booker's options might choose to land.

Steve DeMicco, a New Jersey political strategist who worked for James in that first campaign, figured Booker was a fairly easy mark. He decided to brand the young outsider as a carpetbagger. "It didn't take a lot of doing to figure out which of the voters were susceptible to that message and to get across to them that Cory was someone who was not to be trusted, that he was not of the city," DeMicco told me. The strategy worked.

Slapped down by James in 2002, Booker retreated to the city council and prepared for a comeback four years later. He won in 2006 in no small part because James, who had decided to step aside, was no longer his opponent. And this time around, DeMicco's firm was working for Booker, not against him. Booker's old foe decided to use what he'd learned in defeating Booker in 2002 to Booker's advantage in 2006. "We basically said to Cory, 'You can't make this campaign about you,'" he said. "He was already going down that path. Cory was already constructing a campaign around himself, which is his tendency. He sort of gravitates to that naturally. We felt that if he was going to make a real connection to the voters in the city and overcome some of that suspicion which was still hounding him a little bit from 2002, he had to really speak to voters and make the campaign about *them* and not about *him*." It was very, very clear that 2006 was going to be different from 2002, that the hunger for change was greater.

The city's voters finally seemed to be tiring of the old ways. James' handpicked successor, Ronald Rice Sr., ran hard. (During the campaign, the *New York Times* posted a photo on its Web site of a flyer taped to a table in Rice's campaign office that read: WARNING DO NOT VOTE BOOKER: THIS NAZI NEGRO REPUBLICAN MUST GO.)

Other political possibilities were dangled in front of Booker. "I had everybody from the governor down to the local councilpeople working against me, threatening people who even wanted to try to write me a check," he told law school students at Harvard's Class Day.[7]

But Booker clocked Rice, clobbering him with 72 percent of the vote. Two years later—five years after James defeated Booker—the former mayor returned for the ceremonial opening of the new downtown arena. Booker was the only one to acknowledge the now-disgraced former mayor's presence. The two former rivals hugged.[8]

At his inauguration, Booker declared that Newark would "lead our nation in an urban transformation."[9] But it took him a while to fully grasp the depth of the city's inferiority complex. "Newarkers have this sense that their city was abandoned and that the only people who benefited lived outside the city," he said during a talk in his suburban hometown of Harrington Park. "They have this belief that these people are going to come back from over the hills and take over."[10]

Even a year later, when the first signs of that transformation were realized with the opening of the city's new $375 million, 18,500-seat arena, an ESPN hockey analyst who had never been there told a national audience to stay away from downtown Newark, "especially if you got a wallet or anything, because the area around the building is awful."[11]

Transforming attitudes, Booker was to discover, is even tougher than transforming downtowns. One unlikely ally is the son of the man he defeated, city councilman Ron Rice Jr. The younger Rice was as interested as Booker in knocking down a few political walls in Newark. But he knew his friend's task was more daunting than his own.

"Cory wasn't born in Newark," said Rice, whose family has lived in Newark for three generations. "He wasn't raised in Newark. And Newark, like many other cities, is very xenophobic. And I even kowtowed to that a little bit myself. Look at my résumé. I always say I'm a third-generation Newarker. It gives me street cred in a way that Cory didn't necessarily have, and struggles, I think, on some levels to still have, in Newark."

Booker says his move to Newark was as much a calling as a choice.[12] He grew up in that part of New Jersey where homes are widely spaced and most of the people in them are white. In order to move into Harrington Park, his parents, a pair of IBM executives, hired a white couple to pose as them.[13] And they dragged their sons to civil rights rallies.[14] Dinner-table conversation in the Booker household was as likely to be about sit-ins and protests as about what the two Booker boys had done at school that day.

No one was more shocked than Cary and Carolyn Booker when their son Cory chose to use his suburban upbringing and elite education to save Newark, of all places. His father, born in the mountains of North Carolina, expected him to go make money on Wall Street. His mother, whose schoolteacher father was paid in crops before they left Louisiana for Detroit, hoped (and still hopes) that he will find a good woman and settle down. Maybe that way he wouldn't spend *every* night roaming the streets with his security detail, looking to roust drug dealers.

But the Bookers have thrown themselves into what they now see as their son's mission. Along the way, they say they have discovered how deep the city's problems go and how entrenched its politics are. "The sense of abandonment of poor black people in this city was stronger than I think I had ever seen anywhere," Carolyn says.

Now Booker's parents travel from their Georgia home at least once a month to work the streets of Newark on their son's behalf. "We think there's so much promise here," Carolyn says. On the day we met, they breezed into the mayor's office fresh from visiting a nursing home, where Cary Booker had cheekily advised senior citizens on the wisdom of using condoms. When they're not in Newark, they spend their days worrying about the son who jumps out of bed in the middle of the night to rush to crime scenes, or invites ex-offenders to live under his roof to offer them a second chance. He spent the early hours of one Christmas Eve touring police stations, dressed in a gray hooded sweatshirt.[15]

"It's their fault," he says with a shrug. "That's how they raised me."

Carolyn Booker raised two boys, Cory and his elder brother, Cary junior. From the start, Cary—now an educator in Memphis—was the easier of the two.

"If you said, 'Cary, sit in that chair and don't move and I'll be back in a few minutes, I've got to do a few things,' he would sit there," Carolyn told me, sitting with her husband one winter day while her son worked nearby in his city hall office. "If you said to Cory, 'Sit in that chair, I'll be back in a few minutes, I've got to go do something,' you know Cory would just look at you and laugh, as if to say, 'You know I'm not going to sit in this chair.'"

"He would say, 'Why?'" her husband piped up.

"Cory was the child who saw the world as a big question mark," she continued. "As something to explore and to examine, and to engage you in a conversation about why things had to be this way."

"My parents used to tell me as a young kid that we were a country that was formed in perfect ideals but a savagely imperfect reality,"

Cory Booker said. "You had people that were enslaved and in chains seeing the most horrible and heinous realities, but yet, somehow, they saw freedom and they saw liberty."[16]

Booker talks like this all the time—in perfect and eloquent loops that leave you nodding in amazement. That's what happened the first time I met him, in 2006 at the Community Tabernacle of Deliverance Church in Stamford, Connecticut. He had only been mayor for a matter of months, but had been persuaded to come north to campaign for Senator Joseph Lieberman, the embattled Connecticut Democrat who was at the time fighting a losing battle for his party's renomination.

Lieberman had gone from being his party's history-making vice presidential nominee in 2000 to persona non grata in his own party six years later. He supported the Iraq war and would not back off. Later, he famously endorsed John McCain over his own party's nominee, Barack Obama.

Booker had no business in the middle of the Connecticut mess in 2006, but Lieberman was among the string of national party luminaries who'd made their way to New Jersey to help Booker. The new mayor, with his steadily rising national profile, was willing to repay the favor.

"When I've called on Senator Lieberman to help me, when I've asked him to stand up before, he has stood strong," Booker told a summer Sunday crowd. "When it came to issues that affected me and my city—getting guns off streets, helping putting more police on, countless times in health care, countless times with the people I serve—he has stood with me."

Booker could not have known that just up the interstate that Sunday in Hartford, veteran black Democrat Maxine Waters, a California congresswoman, was leading Lieberman's challenger, Ned Lamont, on a vigorous Sunday morning black church tour of her own. Waters, you see, had never forgiven Lieberman for seeming to waffle on affirmative action. And it was not the last time Booker and Waters would be on opposite sides. He supported Obama in 2008—even giving his chief of staff a leave of absence to work for Obama in the general election.[17]

Waters supported Clinton in the primaries—a foreshadowing of the establishment-versus-upstart dynamic that linked Booker to other new-generation politicians.

"I think it's generational as much as anything else," said DeMicco, the political strategist. "I think that actually this has been a great advantage for him because I think a lot of the people who are supporting him support Barack—whether they're the same people, the same type, the same demographic that supported Cory or the younger people who were looking for a change in the system, not just a change in character."

But on that day in Connecticut, Booker was getting his feet wet in national politics for the first time. He may have picked the wrong battle. Lieberman was defeated in the primary and reelected to the Senate only by quitting the party that had spurned him and running in the general election as an independent. Perhaps campaigning for the increasingly renegade Lieberman was not the smartest risk for anyone with national political aspirations. Booker insisted he did not hold such ambitions, of course. But his presence at Lieberman's side, far from Newark's crumbling city hall, suggested otherwise.

Something else happened that day too. When Booker climbed into the Connecticut pulpit and began to tell his story, heads snapped up. Suddenly everyone—including a clutch of national political reporters in town to cover Lieberman—was paying attention. And when he climbed back into pulpits and onto stages two years later to campaign for another young and ambitious black man with multiracial aspirations, he had a little more wind under his wings.

Of all the young black politicians breaking through, Booker may have taken the most unusual route to elective office. Setting aside his Ivy League education and comfortable suburban upbringing, Booker chose to get to know his adopted hometown of Newark by moving into a drug-plagued inner-city public housing project.

"Cory jumped in and kicked the door down," Ron Rice Jr. told me. "And we'd be dumb if we didn't follow him, because he is our generation, and he does have the right vision for our city, and he had the resources."

Booker was still in law school in 1996 when he went knocking on doors trying to organize tenants on behalf of New York's Urban Justice Center. There, he met Virginia Jones, a seventy-four-year-old resident of Brick Towers whose son had been gunned down in the lobby of her apartment building in 1980. Sixteen years later, a thriving open-air drug market still flourished there.

Booker had bright ideas about how to save the building, but all Jones wanted to know was whether he was committed. The road to hell, she reminded him, was paved with good intentions.

"Boy, what do you think you are here for, to be a lawyer or to help the people?" he remembered her saying. "If you want to help, run for office! If you want to be a lawyer, well, run along then and be a lawyer."[18]

So, with Booker working with Jones and other tenants to face down the landlord and make demands on city government, change began to take root. Police protection appeared. Slumlords were held to account. And Booker's political career was born.

Booker moved into a $600-a-month two-bedroom apartment in Virginia Jones' public housing project on Martin Luther King Jr. Boulevard. He was elected to the city council at the age of twenty-eight by defeating a fourteen-year incumbent.

"Boy," Jones told him, "you need to understand that what you see outside of you is a reflection of what you see inside of you, and if you're one of those people who sees only problems, darkness, and despair, that's all there is ever going to be. But if you are one of those people who sees hope, opportunity, and love, then you can be somebody who makes a difference."[19]

Brick Towers' two 16-story, 300-unit buildings, where Booker lived for eight years, were razed not long after Booker moved out to take over the top floor of a multifamily home in the city's South Ward. There was a marching band there on the day the towers began to fall, and Booker got out of his sickbed to watch. A new mixed-income residential and retail development is to rise in its place.[20] "This is finally our community finding redemption after all these years," the mayor said.[21]

Sometimes Booker thinks he was born in the wrong generation. A conversation with him is likely to be littered with references to Martin Luther King Jr., Mahatma Gandhi, and Langston Hughes—but also to Chris Rock and Cornel West. On the desk in his office, there is a stack of five books: the Quran, the Bhagavad Gita (the core beliefs of Hinduism), a Hebrew Bible, and two Christian Bibles (he is Baptist). He takes part in the civil rights marches led by liberals, but also supports school choice, favored by conservatives—which he supports as a way of "giving grassroots people power back."

"I think we all share this reverence for where we come from, but we also realize that in many ways we have just as severe challenges but they're even more complicated than they were in our parents' generation," he says. "We have black-on-black violence now. Blacks are being killed at rates untold of in terms of comparison to whites killing blacks."

Newark's city hall is as good a metaphor as any for the city itself. Outside, a handsome façade and golden dome signal the seat of government within. Inside the hundred-year-old building, the paint is peeling and cracked plaster is falling seventy feet to the floor of the tall rotunda. The plaques honoring police valor have not been updated since 1970.

But the mayor's office, where men wearing suits and speaking with Jersey accents come and go at a brisk pace to do business with the city, is a busy place. Outside the mayor's office on the day I visited, the steps leading up to the building's ceremonial front doors were crowded with hundreds of people—many of them students still in school uniforms—ending a march the mayor himself had led.

This day, Americans across the nation—but especially in Jena, Louisiana—were rallying to protest the imprisonment of six black teenagers in a remote southern town. The plight of the Jena 6, as they had come to be known, sparked an old-fashioned civil rights outcry. Fueled by the Internet and black radio, the protest had a distinctly new-fashioned feel that reached even to Newark. The front page of New Jersey's largest newspaper, the *Star-Ledger,* carried a story about Jena. The headline read, "A Civil Rights Phenomenon."[22]

Echoes of the civil rights movement surround the erudite young mayor, and Booker embraces them. Even though his presence in the corner office signifies how far the nation has come, the wall opposite Booker's desk features a framed vintage photograph of a child being blasted with a fire hose in a 1963 Birmingham, Alabama, voting rights protest. In many ways, Booker worries, the wrong lessons have been learned, both within and outside the black community.

"The reality is we're still in a place and a time where everybody knows who JonBenet Ramsey is, or who Natalee Holloway is," he says, referring to two famous cases of white females who disappeared under mysterious circumstances. "But so many people, even within my own community, cannot name a black child that died within our communities in an unsolved murder. So you still see a world in which there is a different value sometimes placed, or different degrees of horror or response, or where there are consistent and persistent and insidious divisions between black and white."

At practically every step in his career, Booker has been forced to delve into the thorny world of racial politics. When the Reverend Jesse Jackson came to Newark in 2002 to campaign for James, he declared Booker a "wolf in sheep's clothing."[23] Al Sharpton also campaigned against Booker the first time. He says Booker's mistake during that first campaign was to think he could work around the old-line leaders.

"I think the thing that a lot of guys mistake, my age, younger and older, is that they're going to take a shot at civil rights leadership and we ain't gonna shoot back," Sharpton told me.

But by 2006, Booker had bigger challenges to deal with than an outsider's criticism. Once he moved into city hall, the problems piled up: struggling schools, violent crime, an unmanageable city workforce. "We came in and we had 4,000-plus employees and 3,500 outstanding workmen's compensation claims," he said.

After a hundred days in office, he was able to publish a shiny report touting his successes, including a Safe Summer Initiative that created sixteen "safety zones" targeted for increased police protection and community outreach activities. The result? Murders dropped by 50 percent in the targeted neighborhoods.[24] In 2007, the FBI reported a 20 percent overall drop in crime—including rapes, robberies, assaults, burglaries, and car thefts.[25] By 2008, murders had dropped another 40 percent from the year before. Shootings were down nearly 20 percent.[26] On top of that, population jumped 3 percent, making Newark the fastest-growing city in the Northeast.[27]

And there was other good news. The U.S. Census Bureau reported at the end of the summer in 2007 that average household income in Newark had actually climbed 28 percent since 2000. Neither the state nor the nation outpaced that growth rate.[28] But Booker knew one bad weekend could easily obscure the good news he worked to emphasize.

Even some of his supporters worry that he is racing so fast toward the lofty goal of turning Newark around that he is failing to listen to good advice from people who see the pitfalls at his feet while his eyes are on the horizon.

"I remind him every now and then that it didn't get this way overnight," said Mildred Crump, who once ran her own losing race against Sharpe James. "And he can't expect to snap his fingers like in a movie and it's resolved overnight. You have to be in it for the long haul."

Booker occasionally does acknowledge how tough the job he has undertaken is. Speaking at the Harvard Law School event, he offered the rare admission of a weak moment.

"I tell you, there are days as mayor that I go home, crawl up on my couch at eleven-thirty, and turn on Stephen Colbert and pray that he'll make me laugh," he said. "I've realized that the biggest, most important challenge is to not change myself, but to be myself. To have the courage to live my truth. This is integrity. This is the challenge of every single day and living in accordance to your highest values, to your highest ideals. No matter how insane that might seem or where that might take you."[29]

There is an element of insanity in Booker's ambitions for his city. The city's struggling schools and depressing crime rate are enough to rob even the most determined optimist of his sense of humor.

"You certainly can't blame Cory Booker," said former New Jersey governor Brendan T. Byrne. "I told him early on that he shouldn't make commitments with respect to homicide, because you can't."[30]

As elemental and nonracial as these challenges seem, Booker does not pretend they are unrelated to inequities rooted in race. Even though Newark is a majority-black city, nearly a quarter of the urban population is white, and nearly 20 percent is Latino, Asian, or other.[31] Anyone on the hunt for a black politician who believes that his success suggests racial transcendence will have to look elsewhere.

"If you ignore race, you do it at your own peril," Booker says. "I mean, how can you ignore [that] racial realities exist in the United States of America? How could you ignore that I live in a state with 14 percent African Americans, but the prison population is over 60 percent black? How can you say that's not—that race has nothing to do with it? Let's not talk of it?"

In fact, one of Booker's pet projects is a subject that comes up repeatedly in conversations with African American leaders around the country—what to do once these underserved and undereducated prisoners are released back to their communities. In Newark, twenty-three hundred felons return to the streets each year. Sixty-five percent are headed back to jail within five years.

Booker recruited fifty local companies to help ex-offenders return to the workforce, but he had some trouble getting the initiative off the ground. The first two people he hired to run the program quit. "We're making progress, but it's like running on the beach," the mayor said.[32]

The day we talk, Booker has spent the morning at yet another funeral, this one for a twenty-two-year-old black man who, he believes, could have been a gift to his generation. Instead, he was shot in a gang-related assault.

"Racism is not a black problem," he adds. "It's not a white problem. It's our problem. I think that's the kind of dialogue we're looking for on race."

Booker embraced Barack Obama's presidential candidacy. The two were introduced in 2005 by magazine editor and Oprah Winfrey confidante Gayle King, and their trajectories—Ivy League education, multiracial political support base—seem similar.[33] Each was embraced more readily by white supporters than by black ones. And each has been working to expand the definition of what it means to be a black politician. Standing beside each other at campaign rallies, they look like a pair of brothers, big and little.

"We're in the foothills of transforming our nation," Booker said as he campaigned on the streets of his city. "But it's a big hill to climb."[34] Indeed it is. Booker worked hard for Obama—traveling the country to campaign for him, and predicting brashly but incorrectly that the Illinois senator would stage an upset win in the Garden State primary. At home in Newark, the results pointed up Booker's own political weaknesses. Obama won in Newark's black neighborhoods, but Clinton dominated in the white and mixed-ethnicity North and East Wards, which Booker had previously won.[35] (The loss, Booker told me one week later, was "sobering.")

A few months later, Booker suffered another political setback when his slate of local candidates was roundly defeated in a largely African American section of the city—in the mayor's own neighborhood. It was a week of contrasts. On one day, he was addressing Harvard Law School's graduating class. On another, he was getting spanked at home in Newark, as city leaders who had once run with Booker explicitly turned their backs. Mildred Crump said she had begged the mayor not to take on the district leader fights because she knew from her longtime insider connections that he would lose. But he ignored her. "And so he got embarrassed," she said.

His political opponents could not have been more pleased at the outcome.

"The people have spoken," said councilman-at-large Donald Payne Jr. "They say: 'We support Booker to a certain level, but this is who we support at home.'"[36]

Steve Adubato Sr., a white veteran Newark ward leader, is seventy-six years old. Although he is proud of the fact that he was one of the first white power brokers to support Newark's first black mayor, Kenneth Gibson, in 1970, he has often been at odds with this mayor.[37] He called Booker's performance in the district races "pathetic."

"We beat the shit out of him," he told me. "He got killed in the South Ward, East Ward, Central Ward, every place he runs, he gets killed, all the time. I'm not exaggerating. It sounds crazy, but that's a fact."

Adubato, who says he was once a Booker fan, is now one of the mayor's most outspoken critics. He has little respect, he explains, for someone who seems to have done so poorly at the nitty-gritty of urban politics. For all of the appeal Booker exudes on the national stage, says Adubato, he is missing the boat locally.

As it happens, Adubato's son Steve junior has been watching the evolving politics from the sidelines as a talk show host and commentator on New Jersey television. Having himself served one term in the New Jersey legislature, he comprehends the crosswinds at work.

"Here's the catch," the younger Adubato told me. "I don't believe that Cory has ever really mastered, or understands that there's a need to master, showing the proper respect. Touching the right bases. Frankly, kissing the right asses to put himself in a position where he could, if not ameliorate, just minimize some of that negativity."

Perhaps it is only to be expected that any breakthrough leader would attract some level of censure from the people he blew past. Comparisons to Barack Obama abound.

"I like to distinguish Obama from Cory," said Princeton's Eddie Glaude Jr., who chats regularly with Booker and with Cornel West, another Princeton professor who sometimes acts as Booker's political muse. "Cory is the mayor of a black-power town, of a black-power city. So he's had to make some very interesting moves in that space in order to govern."

One of those interesting moves came when Booker was drawn into a confrontation with the city council over the suspension of police chief Anthony Campos. Campos was a Booker-picked lieutenant who had run afoul of local politics. He also happened to be white. So when

Booker stuck by him in the face of displeasure from the majority-black city council, his tenuous ties to the elected officials who won with him in 2006 were strained. Even council president Mildred Crump, a Booker supporter, said, "There is no respect for the council."[38]

Booker had already angered some of his supporters by promoting Campos to the permanent position in the first place. Campos was a twenty-one-year veteran of the force who had served as acting chief for a year. But in selecting white men for both of the city's top law enforcement jobs (police director Garry McCarthy was the other), and passing over a black candidate to do it, Booker had broken an unwritten rule. "I felt betrayed," Crump told the local newspaper at the time.[39]

"Newark is a very unique community and we lean on relationships," Crump told me a year later. "And Mr. McCarthy came in with none."

The mayor's opponents were not above theatrics either. At one city council meeting just before the Ivy Hill murders, a clutch of them showed up wearing T-shirts that read RECALL and WE SUPPORTED BOOKER AND ALL WE GOT WAS THIS LOUSY T-SHIRT.[40] "For a lack of a better term I don't think he gets it," said the Reverend Jethro James, a Booker critic.[41]

And shortly before the schoolyard killings, he was forced to apologize for a story he had told at a Democratic fund-raiser about a recently deceased Newark activist whom he described as not only fat but profane and corrupt. He also described dodging bullets in Newark like the character Neo from the movie *The Matrix*. When video of the event surfaced on YouTube, it became clear the mayor had thought his description of the activist was affectionate and funny; the crowd laughed. But what those who hadn't been in the room saw was the black mayor making fun of a revered black figure, perpetuating negative stereotypes, and, worst of all, making white people laugh at black folks' expense.

"It is racist," declared Newark council member Dana Rone. "Why deliver this story in a room full of white people? Tell a positive story."[42]

That rap had followed Booker before. He liked, for instance, to tell stories in front of elite white audiences about a young man he said he met when he came to Newark, named T-Bone.

"I said hello to this guy, and I'll never forget he leaped off the steps where he was standing and looked at me and threatened my life," Booker said during a February 2007 speech at Manhattan's New School. "He said: 'I don't know where you come from, but if you ever so much as eyeball me again, I'm going to bust a cap in your . . .' let's say posterior region." The audience laughed.[43] But it was the kind of laughter that sounds entirely different coming from white people when the target of the joke is black.

These undercurrents at home were part of a provincial uneasiness about the bright young mayor that never entirely went away. Plus, Booker has never been above the occasional publicity grab, such as pitching a tent in a terrible neighborhood in 1999 to protest open-air drug dealing. In *Street Fight* he allowed cameras to follow him day and night. He looked like nothing less than a hero, and he knows that some of his tactics—hunger strikes and tent pitching—come across as stunts.

"Absolutely!" he says, reaching back, as he often does, to the civil rights movement he was too young to experience. "But was it a stunt for my heroes to get on a bus and drive down to the South knowing that you're going to get all of the press following that bus, and knowing you're going to get chain-whipped? And the bus is going to get blown up? Absolutely. Start bringing attention to the problem."

But the comparison falters when one considers that people lost their lives during Mississippi Freedom Summer, and all Booker stood to lose was his political standing. After he had been mayor for a year, some residents began to question why he hadn't bought a house and demonstrated his willingness to assume some of the city's tax pain himself.[44]

The mayor's mother, who raised her son to befriend everyone, bemoans the racial minefields she sees everywhere in a city such as Newark. "Everything is measured through the lens of black and white," Carolyn Booker says, remembering how someone complained to her after her son delivered his annual state-of-the-city address that there weren't enough black people in the audience. "I mean, in front of us were black people, behind us were black people." She says she thought, "What section were you sitting in?"

The mayor has assembled a supernova of celebrity support as his national profile has risen, attracting people such as former New York Giants running back Tiki Barber, Miami Heat basketball player Shaquille O'Neal, former Dallas Cowboys running back Emmitt Smith, and actor Keenen Ivory Wayans to the city to explore development opportunities.[45]

Booker dismisses critics who grumble when he airs the black community's dirty laundry in public. "A whole bunch of nitpicking going on," he complained to me.

Some of the nitpicking thrives because Booker, like all neophytes, may have set the bar for change impossibly high.

"He is extremely passionate, but he oversells things," said Byron Price, who resigned from the city's prisoner reentry program after only three months, complaining about a lack of resources. "You can go out and give big speeches, but you have to deliver."[46]

All the same, Booker seemed to recognize he had supplied his own distractions, simply by overpromising what a bright and brash newcomer could accomplish in a city beset by rampant political and social insecurities. By the time he climbed into the pulpit at Terrance Aeriel's funeral in the summer of 2007, he was regretful. "I want to repent to this church," he said. "In the days leading into Saturday, I was saying things that hurt this city. But I broke down. I was broken down, but in the pit of my despair, I heard the Lord speak."

More often, he takes his critics on, especially if they are outsiders. Booker was infuriated by an *Esquire* magazine article that catalogued the city's many ills and, among other things, portrayed Newark as a place "racked by decades of ruin, a town known only for murder, blight and feckless negritude."[47] He sent off a blistering reply.

"ENOUGH!" he wrote in a letter on city letterhead. "There has not been an article written since I have been mayor that has made me and my fellow Newarkers more angry than this one. It is altogether a tired song that has been sung by people who don't know our city. This music has played for decades, and the people of Newark have endured enough disrespect, disregard, and contempt. Enough!"[48]

Internally, Booker takes note of his critics more calmly, and occasionally even strives for the greater dose of humility that might help mute their complaints. "I've come to a point of greater knowledge, greater respect and greater awareness of my own weaknesses," Booker told his hometown newspaper. "But in that weakness, I discovered a greater strength . . . connecting with other individuals in the community and drawing on their strength."[49]

Some of those individuals were still calling for Booker's head, and the mayor gives them credit for drawing attention greater than their numbers warranted, and for standing down once the schoolyard killings forced political disputes to take a backseat to sad reality.

"Most people at that point who were of good conscience put down their swords and pulled, and joined arms," he said. "I wish and hope as a leader that I could help sustain more of that unity. Because ultimately, as the African proverb says, 'Spiderwebs united could tie up a lion.' You know we need to find more of that unity."

But Booker's critics are not going away, and his mother, as one might expect, is baffled by it. "As much as this kid works 24/7, it's amazing to me that they still don't think he's visible enough and that he's with the people enough," Carolyn Booker says.

Like all wise and ambitious politicians, Booker says he is focused on the task at hand—saving the city of Newark. For now. He leaves it to the legion of others who have bigger plans for him. "My job here, I really feel like I'm on the front lines of the fight to make this country real."

At the end of 2007 the *Star-Ledger* published a New Year's prediction for Booker that seemed only partly tongue in cheek. By the end of 2008, the newspaper guessed, Booker would (a) emerge as a star after showing solid progress on crime, ethics, and education; (b) announce that he was leaving city hall to seek higher office; or (c) be crippled by corruption charges against a close ally and endless confrontations with the city council.[50] None of those three things happened.

ALONG THE WAY, BOOKER became a surrogate big brother to three teenage boys, adapted to the routine of sixteen-hour days, and developed a skin that toughens with every new crisis. Still, it becomes clear in any conversation with the mayor that he has tied Newark's survival to his own. This effort to save a city is an intensely personal quest for the man who was told by his parents that he could do anything.

"I mean, hell, this is the hardest thing I've ever done in my life," says the still-young mayor. "And there are days I definitely feel like just going home and curling into a ball. But what keeps me coming back into the game, strapping on my chin strap, is I look around me and I'm reminded of who I am."

As for who Cory Booker is, he's a walking, talking, philosophy-spouting generational conflict. In his attempt to woo those who would spurn a city such as Newark and mollify those who are defensive about its past, success for Booker lies in forging a way forward. The trouble is, the path forward is littered with the debris brought on by the act of breaking through.

Mildred Crump says Booker's problem is that he surrounds himself with people who tell him he can do it all, all at once, that he is the one who can fix it all. "And I say, 'Sweetheart, no, you're not,'" she told me ruefully. "'You're a baby in this business.'"

CHAPTER EIGHT

THE POLITICS
OF IDENTITY

I'm still not exactly sure what that means, Is he black
enough? *Of course, you would never hear that about a
non–African American, or somebody who is white*—Oh,
he's not white enough. *What does that mean?*

—Philadelphia mayor Michael Nutter

ON THE NIGHT BARACK OBAMA WON THE SOUTH CAROLINA PRIMARY,
his supporters could barely contain themselves. Bouncing back from a
surprise defeat two weeks before in New Hampshire, the double-digit
victory thrilled the multiracial crowd gathered that night in the heart
of the South. When their candidate appeared, they took up a chant.

"Race doesn't matter! Race doesn't matter!" they shouted in a chant
that built and spread throughout the room. Standing at the foot of the
stage in a ballroom just blocks from the state capitol, Obama's pollster,
Cornell Belcher, watched in astonishment.

"Here you are in South Carolina, three blocks from where the
Confederate flag is still flying in front of the state capitol and all the
history that has held in that state," Belcher, who is black, told me later.

"And you have a group of young white people shouting, 'Race doesn't matter.' Now, do they think there is no racism? No. But were they screaming and shouting the world they wanted to exist? Yeah. That is powerful and profound and very different."

This may have been the only night during the course of the campaign where anyone believed that race indeed did not matter. Certainly the candidate at the center of all the euphoria did not believe it.

Obama, like every other elected official in the United States, was keenly aware of how much the nation's mood swings on race could determine the outcome of a competitive election. Sometimes race helped, and sometimes it hurt, but it always mattered.

The first question—usually directed to African Americans by African Americans—was frequently an upside-down identity test: "Are you black enough?" Governors, mayors, and lawmakers of all stripes I spoke with have been confronted with the question—especially early in their careers, and especially if they were new to the game. Even Walter White, the founder of the NAACP, who campaigned against lynching and in favor of equality in education, was deemed inauthentic in some quarters because of his fair skin.[1]

So it should come as little surprise that this same attitude infected politics. "I was not immune to that by any means," former Massachusetts senator Edward Brooke told me. Brooke, a fair-skinned man with wavy hair and patrician features, remembers that the charge was hurled at him when in 1964, as Massachusetts attorney general, he refused to support a group of black parents who wanted to boycott the public schools to protest segregation.[2] "I had to call them as I saw them," he said. "You couldn't keep a child home from school for political protest purposes, and I said so. Now, you can imagine how the black community came down on me on that issue."

Four decades later, the race test seemed peculiar to many of Obama's white supporters, who wanted to believe they did not see race when they looked at their candidate. Barack was bigger than that, they would tell anyone who asked. They were color-blind, they boasted. So they were more than a little surprised and frustrated that the race test never seemed to go away.

Obama dealt with it when he challenged (and lost to) Congressman Bobby Rush in 1999. Rush, a former Black Panther, derided Obama's Harvard credentials, and another competitor, State Senator Donne Trotter, deemed the young interloper "the white man in blackface in our community."[3]

"It was a race in which everything that could go wrong, did go wrong, in which my own mistakes were compounded by tragedy and farce," Obama wrote years later.[4] "His performance reminded me of a comedian dying on stage," the *Chicago Tribune* reporter covering him wrote.[5] Obama ended the race $60,000 in debt.

In 2004, Obama won election to the U.S. Senate, but once he started to run for president, the question popped right back up again. In August 2007, Leonard Pitts Jr., a columnist for the *Miami Herald,* decided to count up the "black enough" references. He discovered 464 instances where Obama's name was linked with the phrase—the first dating to 2003.[6]

Obama, without question, did not fit the corrosive stereotype of what a black man was supposed to be. His speech was precise and grammatical, his clothes tailored and conservative, his demeanor calm and nonthreatening. In much of the black community, however, this meant that white people liked Obama, which in itself seemed to render him an object of suspicion.

"I'm not making an argument that the resistance is simply racial," Obama himself said late in the campaign. "It's more just that I'm different in all kinds of ways. I'm different even for black people. . . . If I were watching Fox News, I wouldn't vote for me, right? Because the way I'm portrayed 24/7 is as a freak! I am the latte-sipping, *New York Times*–reading, Volvo-driving, no-gun-owning, effete, politically correct, arrogant liberal. Who wants somebody like that?"[7]

The Illinois senator's advisers had another theory about why Obama's racial identity remained a subject of comment and conflict, especially early on. Well into his race for president, Obama, they said, was still a mystery man. "The truth of the matter is, four years ago, the average African American didn't know who Barack Obama was," Belcher said.

Roland Martin, the outspoken CNN contributor, took the matter on in two front-page articles in the *Chicago Defender,* a black newspaper he edited. "It's inconceivable that a black man could be married to a black woman and have two black daughters and not be concerned about black folks," he told me.

And, by the way, Obama played basketball, including the morning of every primary and right through the day of the general election in 2008. "Here is a place," he told Bryant Gumbel on HBO, "where black was not a disadvantage."[8]

"He's been black for most of his life as he understands it," said Michael Eric Dyson, the Georgetown University professor and author. "So why all of a sudden would that black card, so to speak—with apologies to American Express—get lifted or taken away by merely suggesting that his melanin or his pigment is not the predicate of his politics? It's not how black his skin is. It's how black his politics are, if that's possible. What are you doing and saying most about the issues that are important to the people of color?"

Writer and poet Bomani Armah called the question "asinine." "What do you expect the first black president to be? A dashiki-wearing, Afro-with-a-pick, fist-waving, ex–Black Panther?"[9]

With black reporters, who asked Obama about his so-called blackness more persistently than white reporters did, the senator occasionally tried laughing the whole thing off, one African American to another. "I want to apologize for being a little bit late," he told the National Association of Black Journalists when he strolled onstage at their convention an uncharacteristic ten minutes behind schedule. "But you guys keep asking whether I'm black enough." Three thousand black people, all familiar with the stereotype associated with black tardiness (known as "C.P. time," or "colored people's time," behind closed doors), exploded in surprised laughter. The white people in the room, unaware of the code, shifted uneasily. Were they permitted to laugh at that, even if they got the joke?

As the campaign evolved and gathered the credibility that comes with momentum, Obama became convinced that cynical political motivations were behind the question. On a bright and sunny campaign day in Laconia, New Hampshire, that summer, I asked him why the question kept coming up.

"There was a political systematic agenda to push that story line into the press," he replied. "And people asked me if it bothered me. I said, 'You know, I went through that stuff when I was twenty. I'm an old man now. I'm forty-five. I know who I am.

"Now, it may indicate the degree with which we as a nation are still confused about race," he continued. "Or there is still confusion within the African American community about who's black and who's not. But I'm sure not confused about it. And the truth is, I don't think most folks are. Most of the folks in my barbershop are not confused about it."

Perhaps not in his barbershop, but the debate was aired repeatedly in other barbershops, beauty salons, and places where black people gathered. Michelle Obama, the well-educated chocolate-skinned daughter of Chicago's predominantly black South Side, told one audience to "stop that nonsense" because "we are messing with the heads of our children."[10] But she also remembered other children telling her as she was growing up that she talked "like a white girl."[11] Matter of fact, I remember that too.

"There isn't one black person who doesn't understand that dynamic," she said. "That debate is about the pain that we still struggle with in this country, and Barack knows that more than anyone."

It is true few people have pondered the question of racial identity more publicly than Barack Obama. In his best-selling memoir *Dreams from My Father,* he wrote almost meditatively about his search for racial identity as a young man born to a white mother and black father.

And in college, he embraced the writings of Malcolm X, the light-skinned, red-haired activist whose autobiography radicalized a generation of young black people.

"[Malcolm] spoke of a wish he'd once had, the wish that the white blood that ran through him, there by an act of violence, might somehow be expunged," Obama wrote. "I knew that, for Malcolm, that wish would never be incidental. I knew as well that traveling down the road to self-respect, my own white blood would never recede into mere abstraction."[12]

Obama was twenty years old when he realized that, and he wrote later in his well-received autobiography *The Audacity of Hope*, he identified himself as African American with little trouble. This puzzled some of his idealistic white supporters. Why, more than one person asked me, did he seem to be rejecting half of himself? When it came to racial identity, Obama couldn't win for losing.

"Nobody asked if I was black enough when I was in the U.S. Senate, right?" he said, thinking aloud to a group of African American columnists. "Everybody was happy to claim me. Everybody thought, 'Man, that's our guy.' Everybody was proud as punch. Suddenly I'm running for president and all these questions start coming up. Well, why is that? What happened? Did I change? Was my background any different? Did I start talking in a different way? Have I run away from any issues that are important to the African American community? No. No, what happened was that I showed up and suddenly people look around and say, 'Where did this guy come from and why is he kind of breaking up the party?'"

In retrospect, it did not take long for the question of Barack Obama's "blackness" to appear moot, almost quaint. Once he won in Iowa, Obama began regularly collecting 80 and 90 percent of the black vote. His competitors blamed automatic race loyalty, but it was clearly more complicated than that. "Iowa became very important to us," chief strategist David Axelrod told me after the campaign was over. "I think that was a galvanic event vis-à-vis the black community, because here was a state that was 98 percent white embracing the candidacy."

In other words, black voters decided Obama could win once white people did. Only then did his candidacy catch fire. Philadelphia NAACP president Jerry Mondesire later called it an "emotional tsunami."[13]

Obama's bigger and more enduring challenge would prove to be the same one that has dogged African American politicians all along: white reluctance, or outright racism—much of it encoded in a way that made it impossible to expose. For instance, when a New Jersey town wanted to block the construction of a public park, some complained that "church groups from Trenton" might start showing up. Whatever might that mean?[14]

Others simply invented reasons not to vote for the black man. "I don't think it's because he's black," one Kentucky county official offered as a way to explain why Obama would not win there. "What everybody says is he is a Muslim."[15] Which, of course, is not true.

Father Andrew Greeley, the liberal white Catholic author and priest, boiled the arguments down to their most pessimistic interpretation in a column for the *Chicago Sun-Times*. "The point is that racism permeates American society and hides itself under many different disguises," he wrote. "The nomination of an African-American candidate was a near-miracle. Only the innocent and the naive think that the November election will not be about race."[16]

Ultimately, Greeley's pessimism was overstated, but double standards still abounded. When Colin Powell crossed party lines to endorse Obama, radio talk show host Rush Limbaugh declared it solely an act of race loyalty. "If I had only had that in mind, I could have done this six, eight, ten months ago," Powell said on *Meet the Press*.

No such assumptions were made when Democratic senator Joe Lieberman endorsed John McCain. And although it made no factual sense, Obama continued to be linked both to the rants of his former pastor—a Christian—and to the unfounded rumors about his Muslim background.

Obama's campaign finally confronted some of the more scurrilous race-based rumors by launching a Web site, FightTheSmears.com, that debunked them all. This was a reversal for Obama, who generally preferred to sidestep overt references to race, although on occasion he challenged white audiences to get past the visuals. "They're going to try to make you afraid of me," he told an audience in Florida after he clinched the party's nomination. "'He's young and inexperienced, and he's got a funny name. And did I mention he's black?'"[17]

Obama was repeatedly forced to confront the matter of his race because every public survey showed it mattered to a significant segment of the electorate.

"Race is intertwined with a broader notion that he is not one of us," said Pew Research Center pollster Andrew Kohut, speaking of how Americans view themselves in general. "They react negatively to people who are seen as different."[18]

The dilemma of identity politics has plagued famous black people ever since they were permitted fame. The glamorous Lena Horne was rightly embraced for her groundbreaking work in films such as *Stormy Weather* by the same black audiences who wondered if her strikingly fair skin wasn't the real reason for her success. Diahann Carroll, the singer and actress who staged her own breakthrough when she became the first African American woman to star in her own television series, told me she struggled for her first film and stage roles against the perception that, even at nineteen, she was exotic and therefore sexually available—a stereotype she confronted routinely. "I thought, 'You have never seen a black person?'" she said. "'Find a way to relate to me.'

"I would do that very often working with writers and producers. 'Look at me! I am what I am. I'm not pretending. I don't know what you thought, but this is who I am. Let's work with it.'"[19]

The comedian-turned-civil-rights-activist Dick Gregory brought the house down at Tavis Smiley's State of the Black Union conference in 2008 by reminding African Americans of their own race identity conflict. Bill Clinton, he pointed out, had been embraced by many as the "first black president," while Barack Obama was questioned for not being black enough. What the heck, Gregory wanted to know, was *that* about?

Obama occasionally tried to turn the notion of racial identity on its head. A recurring part in his stump speech mocked genealogical research that proved he was distantly related not only to Vice President Dick Cheney but also to movie star Brad Pitt. But the danger inherent in arguments about racial identity is that oversimplification is easy and sometimes dangerous. Candidate Ralph Nader stepped purposely into it when he accused Obama of trying to "talk white" to win over non–African American voters and later declared Obama an "Uncle Tom" for not championing enough progressive causes.[20]

Michael Steele, the former Maryland lieutenant governor who lost a 2006 bid to join Obama in the U.S. Senate, looks at the question through a practical lens as well as a political one. "You've got to be able to speak about these things more broadly, because you don't want white folks to think you are a single-issue or single-race individual, which most people aren't," he said. "But the black community also has to hear some authenticity with respect to their issues in your voice."

But biracial breakthroughs have come to occupy an entirely different plane of identity. Obama and other breakthrough politicians such as Maryland lieutenant governor Anthony Brown and Washington, D.C., mayor Adrian Fenty are biracial but identify as black. Still, many white voters are clearly more comfortable thinking of them as half white.

Do you choose to believe a thoughtful man such as actor Don Cheadle, who told Harvard historian Henry Louis Gates Jr. in the PBS documentary *African American Lives*, "You are what you have to defend"? (As James McBride, a biracial writer, put it: "If cops see me, they see a black man sitting in a car.")[21] Or should we listen instead to a thoughtful man such as Harvard law professor Randall Kennedy, who argues that black identity is a choice, especially for biracial achievers such as Tiger Woods?

I put the question to Georgia congressman John Lewis. "This is not a new question," he pointed out. "It's an age-old question. We heard it in the sixties when we were moving into the period of black consciousness and black power. There were people saying that individuals were not black enough. How black do you have to be [to be] black enough? You know, the majority of the population said that if we held just one, a tiny drop, we were black. What does it take? Do you have to preach blackness? Or do you have to be a champion of blackness to be black enough?"

Representative William Lacy Clay Jr. says intraracial identity politics is something any public figure has to learn to expect. "You really have to take it for what it's worth," he told me. "You have to look at who's making the charge. There are still haters out there. We have turned it into an art form."

Aspiring black leaders are often commanded to transcend race, even though no one ever asked, say, Hillary Clinton to transcend gender. This is a precarious race straddle that most members of the breakthrough generation seem to reject. Even the most well-meaning white Obama supporters seemed to take deep satisfaction in this idea. Obama, they insisted, could be raceless, a reassuringly optimistic view of America's deepest burden that ignored countless pieces of evidence to the contrary.

Obama's role as a standard-bearer for a new, postracial politics rankled a stubborn community of left-leaning academics, many of whom wondered aloud in blogs and Internet chat rooms what exactly "postracial" was supposed to mean.

"I don't like that term," Princeton professor Cornel West once said when asked about postracial politics. "You work through race, you don't deny race. It's the difference between being color-blind and lovestruck. You see, if I love you, I don't need to eliminate your whiteness. If you love me, you don't need to eliminate my blackness. You embrace humanity."[22]

But blackness is becoming an increasingly complicated notion. Take the dilemma facing the voters in the Ninth Congressional District of Tennessee. For years, Memphis voters were represented by African American congressmen: Harold Ford Sr. and Harold Ford Jr. But in 2006, the same year Harold junior ran for U.S. Senate and lost, fifteen people ran for his empty House seat, and the man who won, Steve Cohen, is white. As a member of Congress, Cohen backed legislation apologizing for slavery and recognizing the contributions of Memphis soul music.[23] He tried to join the Congressional Black Caucus as a representative of a majority-black district but was denied. Within months, one of the people he beat, African American airline executive Nikki Tinker, began to mount a rematch. Coming in the midst of the racially charged presidential campaign, Cohen's reelection campaign split members of the caucus. Representatives Gregory Meeks and Stephanie Tubbs Jones backed Tinker. Representatives John Conyers and Charlie Rangel backed Cohen.

Meanwhile, back in Memphis, Jake Ford (who also had lost to Cohen in 2006) declared Cohen unfit to represent the district because of his whiteness. "Jake Ford is a black candidate, it's a black district, and we need black representation," said Isaac Ford, Jake's brother. Jake and Isaac are sons of Harold Ford Sr. and brothers of Harold junior. The two Harolds promptly denounced those members of their own family. "I want to make clear my brothers' comments are not mine," Harold junior said in a statement. "I reject them. I don't believe any candidate's fitness for office should be measured or determined by race or gender."[24] The voters rejected it too, and Cohen was reelected.

It is one thing to reject the measure. It is another to dismiss it as unimportant. Of the scores of black achievers interviewed for this book, none was willing to say race had not in some way enhanced or hampered the voters' perception of his or her political fitness. It is striking how many told the same stories. Buffalo, New York, mayor Byron Brown used the word *fascinating* rather than *frustrating* to describe the manner in which his racial identity was questioned.

"I've tried to do what our parents have said to do—get a good education, be the best you can be, present a good image, be articulate, work to improve your community, be active in your community, be a good husband and father, stay away from criminal activity because that can destroy your life and have a negative toll on your family and your community," he said in a rush when I asked him about it. "And even when you do all of those things, for some that makes you not black enough."

Much of the complication when it comes to identity politics is rooted in conflict that African Americans seldom talk about across racial lines, one that is tied in with the nation's painful history. The fact is, many African Americans are direct descendants of the white land-owners who enslaved their forebears.

Cory Booker's parents, Cary and Carolyn Booker, have caramel-colored skin, and their son is considerably fairer. When they travel from their home in Atlanta to visit their son, they regularly discover that black voters are surprised to learn they are both black. But the mayor's father told me of walking Newark's streets and being approached by people who complain about his son: "He isn't black enough and he don't belong here."

"There's always been this division between light-skinned blacks and dark-skinned blacks, you know, that we grew up with . . . as inane as that is," Carolyn said. Because Booker and his brother, Cary junior, grew up as two of the few black children in a white suburb, they came late to some forms of race consciousness. Young Cory, his mother remembers, had trouble grasping the meaning of the refrain in a popular James Brown song, "Say It Loud (I'm Black and I'm Proud)."

"The kids were having a hard time latching on to that," Carolyn says, laughing. Her literal-minded sons would insist they were brown, not black. "And so we'd say, 'Well, you can be brown and proud.'" The pride was the thing. Cory Booker says the pride is still the thing: "I mean, I can go through the different black leaders of the past generation who were always questioned on their authenticity, but always were willing to break the mold."

The proof is not in the name-calling, Cory Booker now says, but in the results. "Some of the gay brothers in the movement back in the day were always questioned about were they really black. In fact, it was a vicious bigotry as well," he recalls.

"It definitely hurts when people throw it at you," Booker says of the "not black enough" criticism. "But when you are centered in what you're doing and how you're moving, and then also say to people, '*Please*, please, nobody was doing anything for minority businesses in this city' . . . and you have evidence to throw in their faces, that gives you even more certainty."

Deval Patrick was born and raised on Chicago's legendary black South Side. But it took only a few years spent at an overwhelmingly white prep school and an Ivy League college to plunge him back into the muck of proving his identity. "You can't be black enough if you speak the king's English," he told me, describing the array of false choices offered to African American achievers. "Or you can't like opera and hip-hop. You've got to pick one—that, in the political context— you can only win a political race if you can lay claim to a black base." But in states such as Massachusetts, where blacks make up roughly 7 percent of the population, that formula is obviously not a workable one. So what's an aspiring politician to do?

Patrick's problem was rooted in his present, not his past. His grass-roots activism was well behind him by the time he ran for governor, and he and his wife, Diane, had evolved into something far more inaccessible. "His worldly set of experiences and his very high-end set of corporate experiences and his personal wealth were a problem for the black leadership and the voting black public," said one Patrick friend, who is black. "They voted for him, but you did hear, 'Who is he? Is he black enough?'"

Elected officials such as Patrick have little choice but to shrug off some of these criticisms. Would black people like him better if he fit some demeaning stereotype of a black man? If he ate chicken wings and watermelon in public? If he were more "authentically black," whatever that means?

It's hard to know. But the demand for that authenticity is without question the most predictably explosive theme in black politics. Sometimes the question is posed in code, as when the *Philadelphia Inquirer* asked Philadelphia mayor Michael Nutter to respond to charges that he—the son of a plumber who grew up in West Philadelphia—was "elitist." Nutter was well educated and well spoken and did not run with the city's traditional black political leadership.

"I don't know what *elitist* means, to be honest with you," he responded. "I mean, I could have come in today with my jeans on—maybe halfway down my behind—and my hat on backwards."[25]

Interestingly enough, Obama also had the elitism charge tossed his way during the primary campaign. The son of a single mother who on occasion relied on food stamps to support her children, Obama ran into a land mine during the Pennsylvania primary when he suggested—at an "elite" fund-raiser in San Francisco, no less—that he was having trouble connecting with small-town voters who were "bitter" over their stations in life and tended to "cling" to guns and religion. This was bad enough coming from the man who had appeared on fashion magazine covers. But it also played into another troubling story arc for a black candidate whose very ambition seemed outsized. Within four days after the comment surfaced, *Time* magazine reported that a Google search of the term *Snobama* resulted in nearly four thousand hits.[26]

But the charge of insufficient blackness, let's call it, touches all sorts of additional, often painful chords when both attacker and attacked are black. Congressman Kendrick Meek thinks he's figured out the reason the question never goes away. Black folk, he says, want to know that the people they elect—with their Ivy League degrees and new power—have not forgotten their roots.

"I keep thinking that we've broken through that, but at the same time, it's a very difficult balance," he told me in a conversation just off the House floor. "It's strange—you have some folks, when you start looking at those broader issues, they say, 'Are you leading the civil rights struggle? Are you leading the struggle for equality? Are you now kicking the ladder down that helped you get up? Can you still talk about Miss Johnson with meaning? Can you still bring the mustard to the debate on her behalf, or are you flying at a higher altitude and not able to see what's on the ground?'"

Sometimes the charge is hard to shake off. Three years after Alabama congressman Artur Davis' race loyalty was called into question by the black man he ousted, Mary Moore, another black state lawmaker, used similar language to downplay Davis' chance of getting elected governor in 2010. "I don't think we're ready yet to elect a black man governor," she told her hometown newspaper. "I think if Davis gets into the general election, he'll find out how black he is."[27]

Other veteran African American politicians pooh-poohed the entire debate. "What is blackness?" scoffed Douglas Wilder. "Is it the way you talk? Do you got to say, 'Dey this, dey dat.' Or the way you dress? Or is it the forgiving of certain things? What is black enough? Is Jackson black enough? Is Sharpton black enough?"[28]

Vernon Jordan has no patience for people who called his decision to support old friend Hillary Clinton an act of treason. "Let me tell you what the movement was about," he told me over lunch. "The movement was about the freedom for you to determine who you want to be and what you want to be in real life. So you can go into the media, and I can go to Wall Street, and Kenneth [Chenault] can go to American Express. That's what it was about. It's not about the right for somebody to have a meeting and tell you what to do with your life."

THE ONLY THING MORE politically debilitating than the "black enough" question is the "too black" question. The latter is seldom asked out loud, and it is never asked by black people. It is, however, the question that can cost mainstream black candidates an election.

At one town hall meeting in Pennsylvania, a white Obama supporter asked his candidate whether Hillary Clinton was speaking in code when she suggested the Illinois senator was out of touch and elitist. "As a white person, this term, the way it's being used against you, it isn't far from 'uppity,'" the man said. "I think the Clintons are getting away with something that they must be called on." Obama dismissed the Clinton critique as mere "politics."[29] Bill Clinton, in the meantime, cried foul, asserting in a radio interview that the Obama campaign "played the race card on me" after he linked Obama to Jesse Jackson.[30]

"I just fundamentally refuse to believe that this wasn't a part of their strategy to try to turn him into the African American candidate," said campaign manager David Plouffe when I asked him about Clinton's remarks. "I will never believe otherwise, because there's too much evidence to suggest that it's true. And I think it's highly unfortunate, but it is what it is."

Far more damaging to Obama's effort to get past the racial identity issue was a videotape showing Barack Obama's Chicago pastor raging in the pulpit against injustice perpetrated by a nation he referred to at one point as the "U.S. of K.K.K. A." Few saw the full sermons. Instead they saw an endless YouTube video loop of an angry black man appearing to blame America for 9/11 and calling on God to visit damnation on the land of the free and the home of the brave. Obama had known Wright—who officiated at his marriage, baptized his children, and blessed his house—for twenty years. This was a problem, and for a time it swamped his campaign.

Obama launched into a series of stuttering explanations. He had never been in church when the Reverend Jeremiah Wright said such things. Well, maybe he had. Wright was like everyone's old uncle, who would say things you did not necessarily agree with. Well, Wright wasn't actually his spiritual adviser. The shifting explanations were made necessary by the subtext that polls showed was troubling white voters in particular: If Obama didn't mind belonging to a church whose slogan was "unashamedly black, unapologetically Christian," was Barack Obama perhaps too black? This was dangerous terrain for a political candidate engaged in a tooth-and-nail struggle for every available vote. Answering that question either incompletely or too completely was bound to alienate somebody, somewhere.

Obama campaign manager Plouffe and others had detected the difficulty inherent in the Wright connection early on. Obama, in fact, had blocked Wright from delivering a public invocation at his presidential campaign announcement. "The overhang is, well, you know, this may be too much for people," Plouffe told me when the first burst of Wright publicity hit the airwaves. "Maybe this will prove that people really aren't ready for an African American named Barack Obama at this moment in time."

This theory demanded a test, and it occurred at the National Constitution Center in Philadelphia, where Obama walked onto a stage crowded with U.S. flags and delivered a speech on race that received roadblock cable television coverage.

"At various stages in the campaign, some commentators have deemed me either 'too black' or 'not black enough,'" he said. Wright, he argued, was a man bound by his past, someone who considered the nation's racial dilemmas to be "static," essentially unfixable. By characterizing Wright in this way, Obama distanced himself from the pastor without alienating black churchgoers. And he used the address to cast himself as the biracial bridge spanning the nation's "racial stalemate."

"I have brothers, sisters, nieces, nephews, uncles, and cousins, of every race and every hue, scattered across three continents," he told a multiracial audience in Philadelphia. "And for as long as I live, I will never forget that, in no other country on Earth is my story even possible. It's a story that hasn't made me the most conventional candidate. But it is a story that has seared into my genetic makeup the idea that this nation is more than the sum of its parts—that out of many, we are truly one."

Obama had not wanted to give a race speech. "But I think in our case we really didn't have an option," Plouffe said. "Our candidacy could have been consumed by this." So when the time came, Obama told many Americans what they wanted to hear: that, contrary to Wright's negative worldview, racial difference need not mean racial division.

"Contrary to the claims of some of my critics, black and white, I have never been so naive as to believe that we can get beyond our racial divisions in a single election cycle," he said. "Or with a single candidacy—particularly a candidacy as imperfect as my own."

At first, the speech appeared a masterstroke—what the *New York Times* called his "profile in courage."[31] "He talked to us as though we were adults," the comedian Jon Stewart said with mock astonishment on his nightly news parody, *The Daily Show.*[32]

"Maybe we'll get a little bit further in the dialogue on race," Esther Johns, a college administrator in Washington State, told the *New York Times.* "The guilt factor may be lowered a little bit because Obama made it right to be white and still love your black relatives, and to be black and still love your white relatives."[33]

Still, the Obama campaign had lingering worries—correctly so, as it turned out. "We're kind of in the penalty box about this with voters," Plouffe said. "I think some voters, some white voters in particular, who were thinking about shutting the door on us opened it back up after the speech. They haven't managed to walk on through yet."

Indeed, Wright did not go away. He was back in a matter of weeks, in a trio of public appearances on PBS, in Detroit, and in Washington, D.C., that stirred up all the old doubts all over again among voters who wondered whether Obama secretly embraced Wright's radicalism. In the end, Obama was forced first to denounce Wright and then to quit his Afrocentric church entirely.

Unnoticed while the cable networks and many nervous voters obsessed over Wright was a less inflammatory but still remarkable statement made by Secretary of State Condoleezza Rice—next to Aretha Franklin, perhaps the world's most famous black woman. No one considered Rice a radical, and because of her close association with President George W. Bush and hawkish Republicans, questions about her racial authenticity had run far deeper than Obama's, for far longer.

"Africans and Europeans came here and founded this country together—Europeans by choice and Africans in chains," she told editors and reporters at the conservative *Washington Times* newspaper. "That's not a very pretty reality of our founding, and I think that particular birth defect makes it hard for us to confront it, hard for us to talk about it, and hard for us to realize that it has continuing relevance for who we are today."[34]

This was not the first time Rice had been moved to address the racial identity question. In a speech she delivered to the class of 1999 as she ended her tenure as provost at Stanford, she declared that "identity and history are double-edged swords."[35] Her eight years working for President Bush would expose her to both sides of that blade, but she seldom spoke about the conflict as openly as she did after Obama plotted out the map.

She could have taken her cue from her immediate predecessor in the chief diplomat's job. Former secretary of state Colin Powell practically dared observers to declare him race-neutral. Although he too moved in many white Republican circles, he just wasn't having it. "I have never let anybody believe that I'm not black and I'm not proud of what those who went before me did," the retired general told me. "I never distanced myself from the Buffalo Soldiers, from any of those guys, 'cause I'm here because of them and I'm not going to let youngsters forget, or white people forget, what we went through. So when they say, 'Well, how can you still support affirmative action?' I say, ''Cause I saw the affirmative action the other folks had for about two hundred years.'" Every black achiever has invariably stumbled into the identity minefield, whether he or she made the choice to engage in combat or not. Because race always makes for a fraught conversation, it should come as no surprise that some version of racialized conflict would become the hallmark of a historic campaign such as Obama's.

The outstanding questions remained unanswered. Will the nation's "birth defect" ever make it impossible for racial politics to be set aside completely? Representative Emanuel Cleaver II, a black Missouri Democrat who supported Hillary Clinton during the primary, worried that Obama's candidacy was letting white people off the racial hook. "They are looking at Barack Obama and saying, 'This is our chance to demonstrate that we have been able to get this boogeyman called race behind us,'" he said. "And so they are going to vote for him."[36] Certainly 95 percent of black voters and 67 percent of Latino voters did go for Obama in the end, outperforming John Kerry's 2004 support with both groups.

Still, a persistent strain of pessimism never went away. Even when Obama was leading McCain by double digits in the polls leading up to election day, debates about race—some of them murmured, some of them conducted at a high decibel level—cropped up repeatedly. In early October at the New Yorker Festival, political activist Donna Brazile sliced through the musings of the four white men onstage who had been debating whether race would ultimately hold Obama back.

"This is a more tolerant, a more open, a more progressive society," she said with force. "And yet we are having these conversations because he is biracial. He spent nine months in the womb of a white woman. He was raised for the first nineteen to twenty-one years by his white grandparents. And yet he got out of school and went to Harvard, and all of a sudden he's uppity and something is wrong with him.

"I tell my friends, 'You may vote against him, but don't ever put me back in the back of the bus,'" she continued. "I'm not going to the back of the bus. I'm not going to be afraid anymore. My black skin does not make me inferior."

The men onstage fell silent. The audience burst into applause.

Once the Congressional Black Caucus got past its divisive primary split, early wounds began to heal there as well. In 2007, many attendees and lawmakers at the caucus foundation's annual gathering spent blocks of time debating whether Obama was black enough. By the time the same conference rolled around in 2008, the title of one major panel was "Does It Matter if You Are Black?" Indeed, an extensive study conducted in part by Columbia University's Center on African American Politics and Society found that 60 percent of blacks say class trumps race when it comes to identity. But 44 percent of the African Americans surveyed said they do not expect racial equality to occur in their lifetimes.[37]

This does not sound like a society that truly believes we are prepared to entirely set race aside. The candidate may be judged not black enough or too black, but one way or another, race counts.

CHAPTER NINE

DEVAL PATRICK

*Don't tell Deval he can't do something—particularly be-
cause he's black, or because it's not his turn. That to him
is a real challenge.*

—DIANE PATRICK

TO UNDERSTAND HOW BIG A DEAL IT IS THAT DEVAL LAURDINE PATRICK
is occupying the blue-carpeted third-floor corner office under the
dome at the Massachusetts statehouse, you have to go back a couple of
decades, and a couple of centuries.

The walls of the more than two-hundred-year-old Beacon Hill
landmark are lined with ornate portraits and marble and bronze busts
of dead white men: Hancock, Adams, Winthrop, Lodge, Endicott.
Their names grace town squares and government buildings throughout a state where the future arrived on the *Mayflower*—not on the
slave ships that docked some distance south.

The governors have all been white. The mayors have all been white,
and the overwhelming majority of the state legislature has always been
white. Deval Patrick, the black son of Chicago's South Side, is well
aware of this as he walks past the paintings and the busts, along the
cracked Italian mosaic flooring, to Nurses' Hall on the second floor,

where a ceremony awaits: A clutch of white male lawmakers have gathered to congratulate the victorious Walpole Little League baseball team—all the members of which, it happens, are also white.

But quickly the new order becomes clear as the Red Sox mascot steps aside and the men on the stage acknowledge the arrival of the most important man in the room. The crowd stands from their folding chairs to applaud respectfully.

"Save it for them," Patrick says, gesturing toward the Little League players. In the remarks delivered from a folded piece of paper he removes from his jacket pocket, he congratulates the boys for their effort, their grit, and—he says this with a little fist pump—their attitude.

It seems that this mild-looking black man knows a thing or two about attitude himself. How else could he have become the first African American governor of Massachusetts, and only the second African American ever elected to run a state since Reconstruction?

When Patrick surprised insiders in and out of the state by winning the top job in 2006, he had just turned fifty-one. No Democrat had held the Bay State's executive job in sixteen years—not since Michael S. Dukakis, who gave up the job in 1991 after having run a dismal and losing 1988 presidential campaign. Patrick didn't just win. He pounded his Republican opponent, Kerry Healey, in a landslide, garnering 56 percent of the vote in a state where African Americans make up just under 7 percent of the population.

Moreover, he defeated Healey after her own attempts to paint him as a weak-kneed sellout lawyer backfired. Central to her campaign were ads that focused on Patrick's 2002 defense of a jailed Puerto Rican felon named Benjamin LaGuer, who was convicted of raping a fifty-nine-year-old white woman in her Leominster apartment. Patrick contributed $5,000 to a defense fund that paid for DNA tests intended to exonerate LaGuer. Instead, they linked him to the crime.

"What kind of person continually defends a brutal rapist?" one ad asked. Another featured a frightened-looking white woman walking alone to her car in a shadowy garage as a woman's voice intoned, "Deval Patrick. He should be ashamed. Not governor."[1] Healey's campaign even sent protesters dressed in the orange jumpsuits prisoners wear to picket Patrick's suburban home. There were no overt references to race in the advertising, but there did not have to be.[2]

Healey's tactics proved controversial and her party unpopular, and her campaign never gained traction even as Patrick's campaign was taking off, Obama-like. So forty years after Edward W. Brooke was elected to the U.S. Senate, Patrick became only the second African American ever to win statewide office in Massachusetts. Brooke, a loyal Republican who no longer lives in Massachusetts, supported Healey. Democrats, he said, "need an opposition."

But party loyalty took a backseat once Patrick won. Retired now and living in Florida, Brooke, eighty-eight, is still keenly interested in politics, pleased that there is a black man in the Massachusetts governor's office, and dismayed—until Obama was elected president—that there was only one in the Senate.

"I take great pride in the fact that Patrick was elected," he told me. "I didn't know him. I had never met him. I met him after he was elected. But he ran a good campaign. And he realized that the only way to win is to put together a coalition."

On first meeting, Patrick looks like the kind of man who got beat up on so many school playgrounds that he took refuge in books. And that is not so far from true.

"Instead of being drafted into gangs, he ran from them," his sister Rhonda said.[3]

His childhood was the kind of hardship tale most politicians have to embellish in order to seem more authentic. When his father, who played saxophone with jazz greats Thelonious Monk and Sun Ra, left the family when Deval was four, he and his sister were raised by their mother in a basement apartment on Chicago's tough South Side. At Mary C. Terrell Elementary School, he entered a school essay contest titled "Why My Father Should Be Father of the Year." Because his dad was long gone, he retitled his essay "Why My Grandmother Should Be Father of the Year." He won.[4]

When Patrick did make good his escape from the South Side, he ran all the way to Milton Academy, a prep school in Massachusetts that, through a program called A Better Chance, was wooing smart black kids with the promise of scholarships and escape. It was a completely alien environment, and he told writer Wil Haygood he was "scared to death."[5] He showed up with a blue windbreaker in his luggage, because he was told he should bring a blue jacket to the prep school. He didn't know they meant for him to bring a blue *blazer*.[6]

One night, on a run for burgers with his housemaster, he was angry, terrified, and rendered helpless when a group of kids in the parking lot began banging on the car windows, chanting, "Nigger! Nigger! Get out of here!" He was fifteen years old. He got out of there.[7]

But young Deval took to Milton, and it took to him. After his first three months there, he returned home for a school break and was greeted in the hallway of the apartment where his family now lived with his grandparents. "You talk like a white boy," his sister Rhonda said.[8]

"I was *devastated*," Patrick recalled to me more than thirty years later. But his grandmother removed the sting. "He speaks like an *educated* boy," she said without missing a beat. Indeed, the Milton education served him well. He applied to five colleges—Harvard, Yale, Princeton, Georgetown, and Trinity—and was accepted at every one. He chose Harvard, a place his approving grandmother had never even heard of. But two Harvard degrees, a civil rights career, and a presidential appointment later, his grandmother was vindicated.

Patrick now shrugs off the sting of his sister's words, but not the lesson they taught him. "It was the beginning of realizing that I either had to choose a world to live in or learn to live comfortably in both," he said. "I had these parents and family members, each of whom wanted me to choose 100 percent of one world or another. And I think that and other experiences like it have left me with a very strong sense of how many choices there are out there and how many of them are false."

By contrast, he mused recently, his daughter Katherine has traveled on three continents and shaken the president's hand. "One generation it took for my family to completely transform our circumstances," he told Brown University students after he became governor. "What will define the character of this generation?"[9]

He told the story of what he called the "one-generation transformation" at his 2008 state-of-the-commonwealth address on Beacon Hill, reminding an audience of lawmakers and residents listening in across the Bay State how far he had come to be there. "I can't think of a time when I didn't enjoy reading," he said, "but I don't ever remember actually owning a book. I got my own bed for the first time in my life when I came east on a scholarship to a boarding school in 1970. In that and so many other ways, coming to Massachusetts was like landing on a different planet."

After he graduated from Harvard Law School in 1982, Patrick went to work for the NAACP Legal Defense Fund, a proving ground for generations of young black attorneys. "He struck me as somebody who was ambitious," said Julius L. Chambers, who ran the Legal Defense Fund when Patrick was there. "I really didn't view him as politically ambitious, but I viewed him as someone who could probably get into just about anything he wanted."

One of the lawyers he worked with was Lani Guinier, who had known Patrick's wife, Diane, since high school. She recalls collaborating with Patrick on an Alabama voting rights case in 1985 where he and another attorney, Dayna Cunningham, went door-to-door in rural Perry County attempting to convince local residents to vouch for the activists who had been working on their behalf. Patrick, Guinier said, would approach a woman sweeping her porch, ignore her attempts to ignore him, and eventually end up cajoling her into talking to him. "Ah, now, why are you being so mean to me?" Patrick would say with a smile. "I ain't that mean, am I?" By the time he was done, everyone was sitting in rocking chairs on the porch, enjoying the host's lemonade.[10]

Patrick and Guinier were also co-counsel when they sued then–Arkansas governor Bill Clinton over the state's voter registration laws. She remembers that even though they were on opposite sides, Clinton, a consummate politician, admired Patrick's people skills. "He has a future as a politician," the future president told Guinier at a Renaissance Weekend retreat in the 1980s.[11]

"I never doubted then that he would assume a leadership role and a public role," she says now. "But I can't say I thought of him as a politician." That would happen years later.

Elaine Jones, who succeeded Chambers at the Legal Defense Fund, did see the politician in him. She told me she was only surprised that Chicago native Patrick chose his adopted state of Massachusetts in which to make his political stand. Patrick, like Obama and other breakthrough leaders, did not seem to buy the notion that politics was the preserve only of those who had spent decades climbing the insiders' rungs. "One thing these guys have in common—and they need it—is some boldness," she said. "They have to be willing to step out there and think differently and believe that they can meet any challenge."

The future governor joined Hill and Barlow, a well-known Boston firm, in 1986, and became one of exactly two black lawyers there. The other was Reginald Lindsay. The two outsiders—the younger one from Chicago, the older one from Birmingham, Alabama—bonded instantly.

Being an outsider meant coping with casual insults, something both men got. Lindsay, now a federal judge in Boston, remembers arriving at Harvard Law School from historically black Morehouse College and being asked by a white student if he thought he "belonged" there. By the time Patrick arrived ten years later, no one was asking those questions anymore.

"I think there's been acceleration in the country about race relations, and about ambition, the ambition of African Americans," Lindsay told me. "There are things I wouldn't have thought of, that people like Deval and Barack think of. The things that I wouldn't have thought possible, they think are not only possible, but *likely*."

Patrick's first brush with national politics came when President Bill Clinton nominated him to be assistant attorney general in 1994 and take charge of the 250-attorney civil rights division. Patrick would be Clinton's second choice. His first choice, awkwardly, had been Patrick's old friend and Legal Defense Fund colleague Guinier, now a University of Pennsylvania professor, whose nomination had just collapsed under the weight of a bitter uproar over some of her writings.

The nomination was rife with meaning, and Deval called Guinier before he accepted Clinton's offer to make sure she would not mind. "It's not that he asked permission, but he said, 'Lani, I won't do this if you object,'" she said.

Patrick took the oath of office in April 1994. "To be a civil rights lawyer, you must understand what the law means," he said after he took the oath of office. "But to understand civil rights, you must understand how it feels . . . to be trapped in someone else's stereotype."[12]

While he was working for Clinton, it fell to Patrick to implement the president's plan to "mend, not end affirmative action," and to police discrimination in mortgage lending. He also won a $45 million racial discrimination judgment against the Denny's restaurant chain.[13] Conservative critics said he was a liberal ideologue, but he had the support of the one who mattered—the president.

When he left Washington in 1996, Patrick headed back to Boston, where his wife and two daughters had remained, and back into private practice at one of New England's largest law firms, Day, Berry, and Howard. One year later, when he was forty years old, Texaco recruited Patrick to become general counsel after the company settled a $176 million racial discrimination suit when executives were caught on tape making demeaning remarks about minority employees. His job: to lead a task force overseeing the settlement.[14]

Another general counsel stint followed, this time at the Coca-Cola Company, where he was, once again, the company's highest-ranking black executive. By the time he landed a $360,000-a-year board position at the parent company of Ameriquest Mortgage, Patrick was comfortably wealthy.[15]

Those who knew Patrick during this time recognized the ambition in the man, but not the political fire in the belly he would display only a few years later in the tough Massachusetts race. "I sure was surprised," Reginald Lindsay told me. "I wondered after Deval had finished hobnobbing with Texaco and with Coca-Cola what would be of interest next. And so governor seemed right. After you've been out to *Par-ee*, you're not going back to the farm."

Diane Patrick, who married the future governor in 1984 and is now a partner at the Boston law firm of Ropes and Gray, always knew her husband was drawn to public service, but found it "stunning" when he decided to run for Massachusetts governor. "That was, in anybody's estimation, a real shocker, an uphill ride in Massachusetts given our demographics, given our history, given that we have an entrenched political establishment," she told me. "And he'd never held office in the state, so it was a real, real, real long shot."

Patrick made his rounds, telling others about his ambition. One of the first people he consulted was another politically ambitious Harvard Law graduate who, in an earlier meeting at a downtown Chicago coffee shop, had asked for Patrick's support as he ran for U.S. Senate.[16] Now it was time to return the favor. "He says, 'I want to run for governor,'" Barack Obama recalled. "I said, 'Let's go.'"[17]

Christopher Edley Jr., the dean of the University of California at Berkeley's law school, has crossed paths with breakthrough politicians his entire career, which included working for the Carter and Clinton administrations, involvement in the 1988 Dukakis campaign, and teaching law at Harvard.

It was at Harvard that he met both Patrick and Obama, ten years apart. Asked to compare the two, he declined. "There's no winning that," he said. Both showed promise early on, said Edley, who famously supported Obama even though his wife, fellow Clinton administration alum Maria Echaveste, was a fierce supporter of Hillary Clinton.

"Deval was amazing. He and Barack both, in that sense, they had a certain kind of presence. This sounds corny, but they glowed."

In Massachusetts, Patrick's decision to return and seek the top job—without as much as a dogcatcher's election under his belt—arrived like a bolt out of the blue. "I've been around here a long time," said Wayne Budd, a black Republican lawyer who served as U.S. attorney and associate attorney general in the first Bush administration. "I was as surprised as anybody."

"I wasn't surprised that he ran, or wanted to run," his friend Reginald Lindsay said. "What surprised me about it was the notion he could win. He came, as far as the political scene was concerned, from nowhere."

Patrick's appearance on the Massachusetts political scene—a tight-knit and hierarchical system that does not welcome outsiders—was not, to put it mildly, universally embraced. Democrat Thomas Reilly, the attorney general, had been anointed as next in line. "People said, 'I think you're a fabulous person and you'd be a great candidate, probably better than the other candidate, but it's not your turn,'" Patrick says now, secure in the knowledge that he proved them all wrong. "I heard that a lot."

He shrugged off their warnings, and the notion of waiting his turn, without a backward thought. "I just don't think it counts for much in a democracy," he said,

Reilly, a well-connected Irish Catholic politician from western Massachusetts, happened to be Springfield native Wayne Budd's best friend. Budd was that most practical of black Republicans. He joined the party because he, Reilly, and a third friend were attempting to create a nonpartisan law firm. Ideology was secondary in a state that had, after all, managed to send a black Republican to the U.S. Senate. Aware of the history-making potential of a black candidacy, but loyal to his childhood friend, Budd was one of those who told Patrick to wait, and perhaps try for lieutenant governor instead.

"He had been out of the state a long time, and growing up here, you always think homegrown people are the only people that really have a shot at running for office," he said. "I just didn't think he had a chance."

Budd was, obviously, very wrong. Patrick rolled over Reilly by 50 percent to 23 percent in the September primary. Just six months before, polls had shown Reilly leading Patrick by double digits, including among African American voters.[18] Reilly was widely seen as a good but awkward campaigner, while Patrick glad-handed voters with the true zeal of a natural-born politician. "On an emotional level, Deval was ten times more attractive than Tom," Budd admitted later.

Patrick then set his sights on Republican nominee Kerry Healey, the lieutenant governor, who theoretically should have held at least a name recognition advantage over the newcomer. But Healey's miserably run campaign allowed Patrick to roll up impressive majorities throughout the state—even in neighborhoods such as South Boston, where mere decades before, residents had rioted at the very notion that black children might be bused into their schools.

Months later, Healey reflected that time had simply run out for Republicans in Massachusetts, and Patrick benefited from that. "People considered this an unusual race and a positive race, in that whoever was elected, there would be a glass ceiling broken, whether it had to do with gender or race."

The perception that Healey had run a racist campaign may also have helped Patrick in the black community, where he was largely unknown. There is nothing like a perceived attack from an outsider to make otherwise warring insiders band together.

"I think that as criticisms leveled against women are often interpreted through the lens of gender, any criticisms leveled at a candidate of color may be seen through that lens as well," Healey told me. "It's very hard to discern that when you're in the middle of the fray."

Add to that fray one more complication. More than a few black leaders were suspicious of this new guy on the block and did not readily welcome him into their club. Especially suspect, among black clergy in particular, was his support of gay marriage and abortion rights.

(Patrick was halfway through his first term before some of the reason for his energetic support of gay rights became clear. His adult daughter Katherine, in an interview with a Boston gay newspaper, announced she was a lesbian. The governor and his wife joined her to march in Boston's annual gay pride parade later that week.)[19]

Patrick decided he could not change the ministers' minds on such a fundamental difference of opinion. He could only plead with them to agree to disagree. "In politics, we need to get past the point where the view is, unless we agree on everything, we can't work together on anything," Patrick told a black church congregation in Springfield.[20] Maneuvering his way through intraracial minefields, he recruited early support from old friends such as Dianne Wilkerson, until recently the lone black female in the Massachusetts state senate. It did not hurt that, as a well-known firebrand lawmaker from a majority-black Boston district, Wilkerson was able to lend Patrick the race credibility he somehow lacked on his own.

"I found myself during the gubernatorial campaign doing a lot of what I call whispering, winking and nodding, hand holding," she says. "Just asking our folk, 'Just bear with us.' My line was that it's not so important that the brother be wearing a dashiki, as it should be that you know he knows what a dashiki is."

Credibility, it should be noted, can cut both ways. In spite of Patrick's support, Wilkerson was defeated in her 2008 reelection primary race. Worse, shortly before the general election, for which she attempted a write-in comeback, she was arrested and later indicted on eight counts of extortion for allegedly accepting $23,500 in bribes.[21] She resigned her seat just before Thanksgiving.

Wayne Budd, for one, believes it actually helped that Patrick was a black man—but not the sort of black man who might scare anyone. "Maybe it's a part of the old Ed Brooke genre," Budd said. "He was very fresh, very alive, very articulate, very charismatic, and people saw him not as a black candidate. They clearly did not." As countless new black leaders have discovered, the key to breaking through often lies in just such a crossover—putting whites at ease without alienating blacks.

Patrick stoked that racially transcendent notion throughout his campaign. "I do need to be not just the first black governor," he would say, "but the best governor you've ever had."

On election night 2006, six thousand jubilant Patrick supporters flocked to Hynes Veterans Memorial Convention Center to celebrate. More Democrats voted in the 2006 primary—915,209—than in any other since 1990, with Patrick's grassroots organizing effort boosting turnout by nearly 20 percent. "You are every black man, woman and child in Massachusetts and America, and every other striver of every other race and kind who is reminded tonight that the American dream is for you too," he exulted.[22]

If history is any guide, there is every reason to believe Patrick was not going to succeed in this America. His childhood fit the stereotype of countless young black men whose futures are derailed. But his mother and grandparents had plans for young Deval. When he was six or seven, his mother took him to hear Martin Luther King Jr. speak in a park on Chicago's South Side.

"I never met Dr. King. I don't remember a single word he said" that day, Patrick says. "I remember what it *felt* like. I remember the sense of common cause with people in that park—people like me. Nothing but hope."

Years later, even Kerry Healey gave Patrick credit for pulling off what had seemed politically impossible. "He was able to overcome the good-old-boy system, the very traditional, almost Tammany Hall–style politics that has dominated the state for a number of years," she said. "Deval was able to build a successful grassroots candidacy and overcome all of those structural disadvantages in ways that were quite extraordinary for the Democratic Party."

On the day he was sworn in as governor, he took his oath on the Mendi Bible, an artifact freed slaves presented to former president John Quincy Adams. On his office wall, he hung a portrait of former governor John Albion Andrew, who urged Abraham Lincoln to create the first black Civil War regiment.[23]

Like many change agents, Patrick brought a full head of steam into his first months in office, but not a lot of knowledge about how best to make that change actually happen. Shortly after the election, Patrick presented Doug Rubin, the campaign strategist who later became chief of staff, with his wish list of state projects. Rubin recalls, "I went back to him like an hour later and I said, 'This is a great list for your first four years.' He said, 'No, this is my first-six-month list!'"

Then, during his first one hundred days in office, the new governor hit a wall. His supporters charitably called them "rookie mistakes." His critics called them the bone-headed missteps of an arrogant neophyte. His supporters say they were shocked to arrive at the statehouse and find that the Republicans had not left anything behind to work with—not even furnishings for the governor's office.

"We were ready to roll, which meant that everyone, the sixty-five people we had hired for the governor's team, was in place, in their offices, ready to go to work," said Joan Wallace-Benjamin, Patrick's first chief of staff. "Very few people walk into a company, even when a company has been bought, and there is nothing there from the old owner, and you just kind of start brand-new making new paper from the first day. And that to me was very surprising, even scary."

Right away, Patrick started making unforced errors. He decided to replace the chief executive's old Ford Crown Victoria with a new Cadillac DeVille DTS—which cost over $20,000 more than a new Ford would have.[24] He couldn't have sent a worse, more racially loaded signal if he'd started break-dancing at his inaugural ball.

Talk radio hosts, tabloids, and bloggers jumped all over him. He was dubbed "Coupe DeVal." He was accused of "pimpin' his ride."[25] Even his political opponents were taken aback at the racially tinged vitriol. Diane Patrick said it was "frankly racist" that Boston media could denounce her husband's "tricked-out car" when it was identical to the model other governors used. "It didn't have boom boxes, speakers on the outside, but they called it tricked-out," she told me, the astonishment still in her voice.

Another double standard? No doubt. But Patrick could have learned a thing or two from the flamboyant former San Francisco mayor Willie Brown, who wore custom-made suits and drove a Porsche Turbo while he was Speaker of the California House. He settled for a Lincoln Town Car from the city fleet when he became mayor, though, because if he got the Caddy he wanted, he wrote later, he knew he would give "my enemies an opening to attack me as a princeling."[26]

Then Patrick shelled out nearly $30,000 of taxpayers' money to outfit his new office—$12,000 of it just for pricey, custom-designed damask drapes for the historic twenty-foot-tall windows overlooking Boston Common.[27] Never mind that the previous governor, the millionaire Mitt Romney, had bought all his own furniture—and took it with him when he left, including the drapery. "You can't go to Linens 'n Things and buy curtains for these windows; they have to be cut to fit," Wallace-Benjamin said. "It was so ridiculous, it would have been funny if it had not been us living it."

Yet while they were racing along at breakneck speed, Patrick and his new staff failed to grasp one of the fundamentals of politics: appearance often trumps reality. In what was to become a familiar Patrick feint, the new governor at first defended the expense, then derided the critics who wouldn't let it go. Then, belatedly, he apologized, offering to swallow the nearly $30,000 it had cost to refurbish his office, as well as a portion of the cost of the Cadillac's lease. "He's learning how important symbolism is," the state minority leader said.[28]

The governor's political naiveté came back to haunt him within a month, when he decided to call an old pal to vouch for a controversial mortgage lender now seeking backing from a top bank. The pal was Robert Rubin, who had been Bill Clinton's treasury secretary when Patrick was at the Department of Justice. Now Rubin was a top official at Citigroup. Patrick had only recently served on the board of Ameriquest, the home lending firm, which was now struggling under the weight of accusations that the company was involved in predatory lending. The company needed cash, and Citigroup had it. Less than a week later, Ameriquest and Citigroup struck a deal, and Patrick's call began to look mighty suspicious—especially since the big New York bank did business in—and was regulated by—the state of Massachusetts.

Once again, Patrick insisted he'd done nothing wrong since he no longer served on the Ameriquest board. But he was the governor now, and the insider's intercession stank to high heaven. No wrongdoing was found, but Patrick learned the hard way—as he often seemed to—that good intentions can be trumped by bad appearances. This was a politically costly lesson for someone who had won office in part because he seemed so squeaky clean. He called them "stupid mistakes."[29] Few of his critics were even that charitable, and the whole affair left an unnecessary early stain on his new administration.

Wallace-Benjamin herself, who headed the Urban League of Eastern Massachusetts for eleven years, was one of the problems. New to government and its insider ways, she had earned her stripes as an executive in the nonprofit world, also running a well-regarded children's charity called the Home for Little Wanderers. None of that could have prepared her for the upheaval of hardball politics. She was among the first to go.

"There was a steep learning curve," the Wellesley graduate said after she left government. "But I've had learning curves before in my life. I can learn anything I want to learn. It wasn't that I couldn't learn; it was, did I want to learn it?"

Part of the problem was staff, but a lot of it was the self-confident governor himself. "He genuinely has a tin ear," said Stephen Crosby, dean of the McCormack Graduate School of Policy Studies at the University of Massachusetts, Boston. "Patrick's first year was uniquely of his own making. He didn't have a network. No one had ever heard of him. The political class in Massachusetts had never heard of him."

Doug Rubin, the next chief of staff, says the early problems were magnified by confounded insiders who had spent decades climbing the rungs of Massachusetts politics. "You can never paint him as one of the guys. He wasn't part of the establishment," Rubin says. "He was new, he was different, but he wasn't, I guess, what the stereotypical African American candidates were. I think early on people didn't have a box to put him in."

Patrick was trying to construct an entirely new box, one in which transcendence was a concept that went beyond race. "I believe the challenges before us transcend party partisan politics," he said when he endorsed Obama in October 2007. "We don't just need a Democrat— we need a leader."

"People want to find ways to each other," he said later, sitting with me in his massive office one fall afternoon after the Little Leaguers left. "They don't want to be told that there aren't differences, that the paradigm is color blindness. People, they understand their differences, and some of them are sharp."

When Patrick talks like this, he sounds as if he has been studying from a shared Obama playbook. When Patrick ran for governor, he adopted the slogan "Together we can," a variation on the resonant union chant "Yes we can" ("Sí se puede"). The political language they used was so similar, in fact, that it briefly caused a stir in the presidential campaign: Was Obama stealing Patrick's lines or vice versa? Hillary Clinton even accused Obama, who campaigned on a platform of "change you can believe in," of plagiarism—"change you can Xerox," she said in one debate. The Texas audience booed.

The truth was, neither had to steal from the other, because their thinking was so much alike. They even shared political consultants. While campaigning in Iowa for Obama, Patrick told reporters he and Obama shared a signal characteristic: Each serves as a bridge between different worlds.[30]

It would not be the only strategy shared by the two friends. Patrick, Obama joked, "stole a whole bunch of lines from me."[31] Payback came in the form of Patrick's 45,000-strong list of political supporters, each of whom was peppered with pro-Obama e-mails.[32]

"The political commentators and self-appointed experts start telling us that we can't have what we want," Patrick wrote in a *Boston Globe* opinion piece during the final days of the presidential primary campaign in neighboring New Hampshire. "I heard that throughout my own campaign. I don't care if it's not his turn, because I know in my head and in my heart that it is his time."[33]

Obama lost the primary in Massachusetts, but when he won the nomination, he appointed Patrick one of fourteen national cochairs of the campaign's fifty-state voter registration drive. All this—coupled with Patrick's energetic weekend campaigning on Obama's behalf throughout the 2008 campaign—naturally led to speculation that Patrick would follow Obama to Washington. "Goodness no," Patrick responded. "This is the greatest job going."[34]

But Obama's Bay State primary defeat exposed some problems for Patrick back home. Among Democrats, Patrick was no political match for the pro-Clinton party veterans arrayed against him—Boston mayor Thomas Menino and House Speaker Sal DiMasi. DiMasi, in particular, took pains to compare Obama with Patrick, and not in a flattering way: "I really don't want my president to be there in a learning process for the first six months to a year."[35]

National conservatives gearing up to run against Obama liked that line of reasoning and seized the opportunity to recast the story line about the two breakthrough politicians into one about the perils of naiveté and inexperience. "If Deval Patrick is indeed a preview of Barack Obama," the conservative magazine *Weekly Standard* wrote, "the lesson is buyer beware."[36]

Breaking through has its costs. John Lewis was hit in the head with a brick at Selma. Vernon Jordan was shot. And families pay a price as well: Martin Luther King Jr.'s wife and children were threatened, and shortly after Patrick moved into the corner office on Beacon Hill, his wife, Diane, dropped out of public sight to receive treatment for depression. "I fell out splat in front of the public," she told a Chamber of Commerce luncheon more than a year later.[37]

She described the first few months of her husband's term as a "roller coaster" and herself as a "deeply private person," which hardly fit her new highly public role as the commonwealth's First Lady. After receiving the treatment—the nature of which she never disclosed—Diane Patrick returned to the public eye, where she says her husband is happiest. But she maintained a low profile.

When we sat down to talk in her high-rise law office with its sweeping view of Boston Harbor, she admitted that the adjustment was a difficult one. "I have to tell you, it took me a long time and a lot of pain to get to where I am now," she said. "I didn't like the scrutiny. I didn't like the criticism. I didn't like the lack of privacy. I didn't like that everything he did, said, where he went was fodder for all the talk radios, all the newspapers, all the magazines, all the columnists, and I felt like they don't know him, how can they say these things about him?"

The governor too chafed at the claustrophobic nature of the job. Once, he told reporters, he canceled what was to be a leisurely bike ride when he discovered his security detail was blocking traffic near his vacation home in western Massachusetts. "I put the bike in the truck and said this is not working out," he said.[38]

That was personal. The public miscues were, in many ways, more troubling. And along the way, Patrick sometimes allowed his impatience with the new rules of the road to show. "If I walked on water," he complained, "critics would say, 'You know, he can't swim. What's wrong with him?'"

None of this stopped Patrick from plunging headfirst into breathtakingly ambitious multibillion-dollar plans. He drew up a sweeping proposal to provide free education for every Massachusetts resident from the age of three through community college. He pushed plans to spend $1 billion on biotechnology, put a thousand more police officers on the street, reduce property taxes, and dramatically overhaul the state's transportation agencies.

Much of this optimistic agenda shrank before the governor's eyes when the economy collapsed in 2008, taking the Bay State's tax revenues with it. In mid-October, he announced he would be forced to cut a thousand state jobs and order $1 billion in spending rollbacks.[39]

Earlier in the year, however, prospects had been considerably brighter. During his annual state-of-the-commonwealth address, Patrick was able to boast of the creation of twenty-six thousand new jobs.[40] "Three hundred thousand adults and children who were uninsured a year ago are insured today and have access to affordable, reliable primary care," he told his statehouse audience. "The state of our Commonwealth is strong, and the evidence of that strength is tangible. My goodness, even the Red Sox, the Celtics, and the Patriots are on fire!"[41] The Patriots, in fact, were undefeated that year, right up until they fell to the underdog New York Giants in a shocking Super Bowl.

But the nation's slowing economy was already placing pressure on the new governor to come up with new sources of revenue. Just before the anniversary of his first year in office, he decided to launch a plan to allow three resort-style casinos to operate in the state. This measure, Patrick hoped, would allow Massachusetts to hang on to between $900 million and $1.1 billion in gambling cash otherwise headed over the border to the Indian casinos in Connecticut.

The timing, he reasoned, was ideal. As he told a joint legislative committee in December 2007, the state during his time in office had moved from forty-ninth in job creation to fifteenth. "My late mother used to ask me to take her to Foxwoods," Patrick told the lawmakers, referring to a casino in neighboring Connecticut. "And if she were alive today, my mother would be like the many adults I meet from all across the state who tell me . . . that they have been making their own decisions about what's best for them for a very long while. And they do not need the state to tell them how they should and shouldn't spend their entertainment dollars."[42] Patrick's argument that the plan would create twenty thousand jobs and $2 billion in related profits, as well as raise $400 million in taxes to pay for roads and bridges, was supported by the Greater Boston Chamber of Commerce.[43] And as late as the previous September, six months before the vote, a poll showed that 53 percent of voters supported the casino idea.[44]

But the Patrick plan went down to embarrassing legislative defeat, rejected 108 to 46, and the governor lost a high-profile battle with the wily and well-connected DiMasi, who should have been a critical ally. The Speaker did not immediately reject the casino proposal, but he eventually became its worst enemy, telling the Boston Chamber of Commerce on the day before the House killed the proposal that casinos would "absolutely cause human damage on a grand scale."[45] It ultimately turned out to be a political master's class in how to defeat a neophyte. "The fix was in pretty early," Patrick ruefully told reporters after the vote.[46]

The blueprint for defeat seemed pretty apparent in retrospect. Patrick disappointed some of his earliest and most liberal backers over the casino proposal. "He promised a new kind of politics," said State Senator Susan Tucker. "But casinos represent politics as usual at its worst."[47] One *Boston Globe* columnist derided the plan—which would raise money, in part, for education—as "the old slots for tots hustle."[48] And one constituent, in a tartly worded letter to the editor of the *Globe,* suggested Patrick abandon the search for "phantom income" from the casinos, and stump for Obama while he was at it: "Perhaps Patrick's time on the campaign trail could be better spent meeting with Massachusetts legislators to convince them his proposals deserve their support."[49]

Patrick later patched things up with DiMasi, meeting him on his turf—a restaurant in Boston's Italian North End. Patrick called it a "come to Jesus" encounter. DiMasi said, "We got together and bared our souls." For both men, it was a necessary healing.[50]

Another recurring theme that never went away was the appearance that Patrick was simply too ambitious. When he flew to New York and signed a $1.3 million book deal with Broadway Books on the same day his allies were back at the statehouse defending his doomed casino plan, even his supporters worried that he was spending more time burnishing his own national reputation than tending to the fires back home. Blue Mass Group, a usually supportive political blog, published a critique titled "D'oh Deval!" that called the book trip a "political embarrassment."[51] The less-friendly *Boston Herald* called Patrick an "author-tunist."[52] Immediately after the casino collapse and the brouhaha over the book, a Rasmussen poll showed a whopping 66 percent of Massachusetts voters ranked the governor's performance as "fair" or "poor."[53]

Once again, the conservative magazine the *Weekly Standard*—by now Patrick's most assiduous national media critic—weighed in. "It is becoming increasingly evident that Deval Patrick is far more than your garden variety maladroit pol. He is instead proving himself a political bungler for the ages."[54] And another conservative news organ, the opinion page of the *Wall Street Journal*, also piled on, declaring Patrick "a pedestrian liberal governor who is remarkably quick to retreat in the face of pressure from the status quo."[55]

But Patrick pushed back. John F. Kennedy, he said, had been ambitious, and no one seemed to have a problem with that. Patrick insisted his ambitions, unlike those of governors who preceded him—three or four of whom sought higher office while in office or immediately after their terms—ended at the state line.

"In Massachusetts we've had a series of governors who have lost interest in Massachusetts and started to look south," he says.

Although Patrick insisted he would not use the commonwealth as a launching pad, potential challengers watched his ups and downs closely. Health insurance executive Charlie Baker, once an aide to Republican governors William Weld and Paul Cellucci, took note of the state's bleak economy in mid-2009 and decided to challenge Patrick. "It's a pretty dark picture," he said at his announcement. "And I don't think we're doing the things we need to do to make that picture better."

Baker's leap into the race revived the flagging Massachusetts GOP. He may not have been as well-known as Patrick, but Patrick was also an unknown factor politically when he got into the 2006 race.

It's not like Patrick could not see some of the setbacks coming. State lawmakers, he admitted in a candid moment, urged him early on to slow down, to let *them* show *him* how to do the job. Democrats had had free run of the state legislature for sixteen years, exercising their balance of power in the best way they knew how: putting the brakes on a succession of governors from the other party. They'd forgotten how to work with someone who was on their side—whatever that means in politics. Then along came Patrick, who was still an outsider.

"I'm new, I'm brash, I had a big political victory in terms of the numbers against a lot of odds and most expectations," he said. "And nothing wears worse than the appearance of being arrogant. And that's not what I mean to project, but I do know I have to be sensitive to that because I don't want to be counterproductive. I just want us to *move*."

But the Democrats in the state legislature put Patrick firmly in his place. He had, after all, leapfrogged over everyone else on Beacon Hill. ("I certainly know that I cut the line by running for governor," he said.)

IN MANY WAYS, MASSACHUSETTS is the perfect place for black history to be made. Crispus Attucks, the first casualty of the American Revolution, was shot and killed on the night of March 5, 1770, during the Boston Massacre. He was black.

But two centuries later, the state—especially its capital—became the site of black history of a negative sort. In the 1970s, anti-busing riots consumed its schools. In 1988, then-governor Michael Dukakis saw his presidential aspirations go up in smoke after a Republican campaign ad linked him to a scary-looking black convict named Willie Horton, who raped a woman while on a weekend furlough granted by Dukakis.

With that kind of history, race is never far from the center of the conversation for the state's chief executive, and there are sharp differences of opinion about whether his race hurts or helps. Wayne Budd, the black Republican, is one of those who believes Patrick's race helped him, even in a state still wrestling with its conflicted racial history. "For him to be successful as our governor, he has to take on not shades of black, but he's got to be the governor of everybody," said Budd. "So he has to get beyond the race question. He has to be sensitive to it and he has to be responsive to it, but his overall image has to be that of our governor. And if I'm Irish, if I'm Italian, if I'm Jewish, if I'm whatever, he's still my governor and I can identify with him."

Easier said than done. The minority community in Massachusetts may not be very large, but it is vocal—especially in Boston. "The black legislative caucus was impossible," one Patrick supporter told me. "They were so difficult, so demanding. They now had their guy. They wanted access. But I just found some of their approach with him unreasonable. It just kind of boils my blood."

Still, as governor, Patrick had the job of picking up dropped balls. Former governor Mitt Romney's administration never followed up on a pledge to explain why minority drivers were pulled over on state roads in disproportionate numbers. Activists wanted to know what the black governor would do about it. "We have an African American governor in the corner office; I would like to think our law enforcement personnel would recognize that times have changed," said one.[56]

Some of the challenges laid at Patrick's feet would normally fall to municipal officials. But when race was a factor, Patrick was a factor. In late 2007, when thirteen-year-old Steven Odom, a black boy, was shot to death on his way home from playing basketball, all eyes turned toward Patrick. Why hadn't he stopped the violence? Why hadn't he paid prompt respects to the boy's mother? No one had asked this of previous governors. The difference was that Patrick was being held to a new standard, one dictated by his race.

Some of those critics, however, worried about Patrick for reasons that had little to do with race. When Patrick supported a Massachusetts law that legalized same-sex marriages, some socially conservative black pastors ended up siding with some of the governor's fiercest critics, the state's dwindling collection of conservative Republicans. "I had to explain to my grandson the other day why it's not okay for boys to marry boys," groused David Tuerck, who runs the Beacon Hill Institute, a conservative think tank. "I don't want to have that conversation with my grandson. And I don't want to have a national health care system, and a Canadian health care system. I don't want to surrender to al-Qaeda. Compared to that, race is a nonissue."

Patrick agrees with Tuerck on little else other than the idea that race should be a nonissue. "The challenge, in my view, is not about the right versus the left," he told students at Brown University. "It's not about race or gender or ethnicity or religion. It's a challenge of citizenship, and the need fearlessly to reclaim American ideals."[57]

Like so many other breakthrough black politicians, Patrick does not fit society's stereotype of how a "typical" black man looks and behaves. A Harry Potter fan who snapped up three copies of the final installment in J. K. Rowling's series of books, he is happy to note that he and Harry share the same birthday. But he appears untroubled by the balance beam he treads daily—proving his blackness to his own minority community while not allowing that same race consciousness to alienate the majority.

"In so much of the work I've done, I've found that you had to put people at ease on the question of race before you could even start to talk about what you were doing. I don't fit a certain expectation that some people have about black men. And I don't mean that as anything other than an observation about my life."

That said, it can be fun to be governor. The Red Sox mascot—a huge kelly-green fuzzball in a red-and-white jersey, nicknamed Wally the Green Monster—comes to your events. The state trooper patrolling the halls has a "Hail to the Chief" ring tone on his cell phone. And the potential for history-making plays out on the mild yellow walls of the anteroom leading to the governor's office. There, giant oil paintings of living former governors stare down at visitors. Jane Swift, the only woman, is wearing a shapeless black suit. An odd, sepia-toned abstract of Michael Dukakis, who ran for president and lost in 1988, is portrayed in an equally shapeless brown suit. Bill Weld, the patrician Republican, is in blue jeans.

But will ambition and reality collide? One year after Patrick took office, the *Boston Globe* gave him only a middling grade for his ambitions. "'Mission Accomplished' it is not," *Globe* columnist Steve Bailey lamented.[58]

"I'm learning fast," the governor assured the state's leading newspaper. "Good," the editorial assessment responded. "Because graduate school is over."[59]

On a side table in Doug Rubin's office rests a silver-framed campaign-night photo inscribed with the words "Together we did," an updated version of Patrick's "Together we can" campaign slogan. Rubin is one of the true believers who are convinced that Patrick's success depends on the governor's willingness to push back when he has to. "There were a long list of pundits in the state who said, 'You can't win. Who is this guy? He can't raise the money. He's never going to be successful. He can't organize,'" Rubin recalled. "But he'd kind of blown away all of their kind of political wisdom. I think there were a lot of people looking for him to fail."

Stephen Crosby, who did his own stint in state government as secretary of administration and finance under Governors Paul Cellucci and Jane Swift, believes Patrick missed his chance to truly govern as an outsider. "Those branding mistakes—the curtain, the car, followed by the book deal, and his inability to ever take responsibility for it," Crosby said, ticking off the early missteps. "He believes the problem is the press, that the press does not let him ever focus on the issues that matter. I think he's one serious mistake away from an indelible brand."

It remains an open question whether Patrick will be strong enough to seek a second term without drawing a significant challenge. "People are making a mistake if they are presuming there is a trajectory here that is clear and defined," Charlie Baker told me. "I think it could go in either direction."

For now, the governor is content to look east, as far as the Boston neighborhood of Dorchester, where he was struck one day by the expressions on the faces of the children at a school he was visiting.

"I looked up, and outside the window are a dozen or more of these little black faces. They're about this big," he says, gesturing. "Backpacks on, they're all beaming and pointing and waving and everything." The governor's eyes are gleaming. "When I look at the excitement in their eyes, it's not for the history we made, it's for the history they might make. That's what they're excited about. They see a possibility they might not have seen because I'm in this job."

CHAPTER TEN

THE NEXT WAVE

*We look different, we sound different, and what's so strik-
ing about the way in which the old guard responds to us
is that they don't quite know what to do with us. And we
don't quite know what to do with ourselves either.*

—EDDIE GLAUDE JR.

A GROUP OF YOUNG, GIFTED, BLACK, AND INCREASINGLY IMPATIENT
politicians, artists, and academics were standing backstage at talk show
host Tavis Smiley's sprawling State of the Black Union conference in
2006. Lined up in the order in which they would eventually be introduced as "emerging leaders," they fidgeted and chatted among themselves, killing time as they waited their turn. Waiting their turn was
something most of them had been doing their entire lives.

Thirty-five speakers with varying levels of notoriety were scheduled
to take part in hours of panel discussions. At the moment the stage
was occupied by the civil rights lions, including Louis Farrakhan, Al
Sharpton, Cornel West, and Harry Belafonte.

As the oldsters waxed on, the younger folk backstage began to murmur among themselves. It occurred to more than one of them that the big-name civil rights veterans preening in front of the C-SPAN cameras were perhaps lingering onstage a bit too long.

A writer for a blog called One People's Project later captured the mood. The younger leaders, the blogger wrote, "were unfortunately given short shrift since long-winded speeches and CPT [colored people's time] delays meant little time was left when they finally got their chance."[1]

This was a minor thing at its root, but as good an example as any of a recurring and familiar conflict in the black community, in which rising stars are forced to temper their ambitions and egos out of deference and respect to the leaders who broke through first. The NAACP's Ben Jealous remembers a similar scenario playing out during the 1993 March on Washington for Jobs, Justice, and Peace.

There were two stages—the historically powerful Lincoln Memorial podium, and what Jealous and others called the "kiddie stage," on the grounds of the Washington Monument. "Everybody was talking about 'time to pass the torch, time to pass the torch,'" said Jealous, who was a twenty-year-old AFL-CIO organizer at the time. "It didn't sit well with me."

Instead, Jealous listened to the words of one of the older speakers, civil rights activist Julian Bond, who had gotten wind of the discontent and was speaking on the main stage. "If you perceive that I have a torch that represents power and you want it," Jealous heard Bond tell the crowd at the march, "you shouldn't be asking for it. You should snatch it."

As power shifts begin to take root in local, state, and national politics, a fraught and delicate relationship has sprung up between the past and the future in the black community. Armed with their college degrees, their private-sector backgrounds, and their own ideas of how to gain and hold on to power, these young leaders are often finding that the biggest hurdles to leadership exist at home.

Barack Obama's rise has affected many of these budding careers, rendering many of their ambitions more plausible. But they are not solely an Obama generation. Some are older than he is, and many have been laboring in the political vineyards for decades. "Some of these people had the courage to step out there, even before Obama said he was going to become a candidate for president," said Cleveland Sellers Jr., the veteran civil rights activist whose son is a member of the South Carolina state legislature.

Still, the network of political relationships Obama cultivated within the African American political class during his presidential campaign provides a useful guide to the next wave of black political leaders. It becomes instantly clear that this new breed is not defined by birth date as much as by their ability to stake claim to another tier of political power. There have been black mayors, legislators, and elected law enforcement officials before, but the ones I profile in this chapter represent the broad swath of African American political talent that has quietly taken root in city halls, statehouses, and Congress just within the last decade. And if the past is any guide, their success is likely to spawn yet another new generation of black political leadership as well.

SAN FRANCISCO DISTRICT ATTORNEY KAMALA HARRIS

When Kamala Harris, forty-four, decided to run for San Francisco district attorney, she came armed with a policy theory and a political plan. She would redefine the traditional idea of a law-and-order candidate by pointing out that the people who suffered at the hands of criminals often looked just like her—black and female. "I come from a background where law enforcement was not necessarily our friend," she says. "And the heroes for me growing up were the architects of the civil rights movement."

To do this, she had to win over an overwhelmingly liberal constituency more likely to be suspicious of law enforcement than supportive of it. She would even have to win over her own mother. "My mother said to me when I was running, 'You be careful, because when people close their eyes and think of who can keep them safe, and who holds these types of positions, it's not you.'"

Indeed, with her lustrous shoulder-length hair, chic suits, and heels, Harris, who became the first female and first African American to hold the job when she was elected in 2004, is more glamorous than gritty. But she likes to point out that, as the city's chief law enforcement officer, she now carries "a big old badge in my purse."

Harris' late mother was not trying to impose limitations on her daughter when she gave her this advice. She was just warning her daughter that change is hard. Shyamala Harris, a native of India, was a scientist at Lawrence Berkeley National Laboratory. Kamala's Jamaican-born father, Donald, is a professor emeritus in economics at Stanford. Her sister, Maya Harris West, until recently was the executive director of the American Civil Liberties Union's northern California chapter. Breakthrough achievement was never the problem in this family. "When I grew up, my parents were actively involved in civil rights. That's how they met and got married," she says. "They were protesting, and I was protesting too. I was in a stroller, but I was there."

A graduate of Howard University and Hastings College of Law, Harris has confounded expectations at every turn in her career, including in her effort to transform the district attorney's office in San Francisco. When she took over, there wasn't e-mail, voice mail, or caller ID. Computers and telephones were shared. There was one copy machine for two hundred people.[2] But the bigger hurdle, she discovered, was changing attitudes about getting tough on crime. "We've got to get out of this dynamic of simply asking the criminal justice system two questions—'Are you tough on crime?' or 'Are you soft on crime?'" she says. "Instead we have to ask, 'Are you smart on crime?'"

The key, she said, has been to speak to her community in a manner that redefined what law enforcement's role should be for urban dwellers who were as likely to be victims as criminals. "They are poor. They are people of color. They are vulnerable people who need a voice that treats them with dignity in the system."

"We do want law enforcement; we just don't want excessive force," she tells her audiences. "We don't want racial profiling. We do want public safety; we just want proportionality and fairness, because the way that the African American community talks about the criminal justice system, it gives the impression that we just want to open up the jail doors and let everybody out."

As the first public official in California to endorse Obama in 2007, she was also cochair of his California campaign and a member of its national leadership team. "There is something about who he is and what he does—and how he has done it," she said. "But the other part is our country and how it has come along."[3]

Harris, who was unopposed in her 2007 reelection bid, doesn't mind being called a "first," and she minds only slightly being branded a female Obama. Such labels, she concedes, come with the territory, even though San Francisco also has women in charge of its police and fire departments.

"There is something to be said for being the first in terms of breaking the stereotype of who can do what," said Harris. "It's not because you're the first person that could do it, at all. It's just everyone's ability to imagine who should, or can, do what."

At the same time, Harris has come up with a handy answer to one of the most common questions she received when she took over as district attorney. "They would ask me, 'Well, what does it feel like to be the first woman?'" she said, laughing over lunch at her regular table at the Four Seasons. "I said, 'Well, you know I've always been a woman, so I don't really know.' But then I would say, 'But I'm sure a man could do it just as well, right?'" At that moment, she sounded just like Colin Powell.

Not all rising stars choose elective politics for themselves. Harris' own family provides as good an example as any. Her sister's husband, Tony West, the prosecutor-turned-defense-attorney, ran for office eight years ago and lost—"the best candidate to have never won a race," in his words.[4] Now he is content to work the levers of political power from the sidelines.

All three traveled to Iowa to campaign for Obama, spending their New

Year's holiday canvassing for votes. West watched his sister-in-law try to convince elderly black citizens to come out and vote. "It was almost heartbreaking to watch Kamala talk to this woman through the crack of her door trying to convince her that this is possible," he recounted. "And the woman just saying, 'You know, baby, that's not going to happen. You know he can't get elected. No black man can get elected.' It was unbelievable."

Well, believe it.

CALIFORNIA ASSEMBLY SPEAKER KAREN BASS

Karen Bass never planned to run for elective office. Like Barack Obama, the Los Angeles Democrat started as an inner-city community organizer. Unlike him, she says, she harbored no unrealized political ambitions.

But politics found the fifty-five-year-old Bass, perhaps as early as the age of fourteen, when she started knocking on doors for Bobby Kennedy. Now, as the first African American woman to become Speaker of the California state assembly, Bass sees her life as a full circle.

"There's a whole group of us in the L.A. area, around the same age range, who have all been activists since we were teenagers," she told me. "All of us came out of the Vietnam War time, out of the black studies time. It was post–civil rights, but we were influenced and our values were set by the civil rights movement."

Only four years after winning her first elective office, representing Los Angeles in Sacramento, the former physician's assistant rose to become one of the state's most powerful lawmakers. Republican California governor Arnold Schwarzenegger, who is married to Bobby Kennedy's niece Maria Shriver, joked at Bass' inauguration that they had something in common: "Both of us were told by Kennedys what to do."[5]

The only other woman to lead either house of the state legislature, Republican Doris Allen, was recalled from office after only three months in 1995, so Bass has already exceeded that record. The most famous African American breakthrough in California was, of course, Willie Brown, who was elected Speaker of the assembly in 1980 before going on to become mayor of San Francisco in 1996.

Brown, in his book *Basic Brown: My Life and Our Times,* summed up the challenge for African American politicians as well as anyone. "The fact of the matter is that as a black politician, you're constantly having to spend energy to integrate yourself into the minds of white power brokers as a real, pure force of politics," he wrote. "You also have to spend as much time reintegrating yourself into the black community."[6]

Bass and Brown are not that much alike. As flamboyant as he was skilled, Brown spent the bulk of his political career creating and maintaining his northern California power base. Bass only arrived in the state capitol in 2004, after founding a nonprofit group, the Community Coalition, designed to address the crack epidemic that ravaged families in her L.A. neighborhood in the 1980s.

Term limits will force her to give up her seat in 2010. In the meantime, she is using her perch to wrestle the state's budget—and it's $26.3 billion deficit—into shape. Governor Arnold Schwarzenegger, in an interview with a newspaper columnist, decried term limits. "Look at Karen," he said. "As leader, it's her first budget. I mean, poor girl. She gets thrown into this. . . . It makes it very, very difficult when people start from scratch all the time."[7]

But Bass has built a career working on causes large and small—from limiting the number of liquor stores in South L.A. to establishing protections for the state's eighty thousand foster children.[8] Perhaps she will run for Congress when term limits force her to leave Sacramento. Perhaps she will not.

Bass threw her ardent and early support to Obama, appearing onstage with Oprah Winfrey and Caroline Kennedy on the day Shriver made her own surprise Obama endorsement.[9] And when Obama returned to California for a glittery Hollywood fund-raiser designed to bring Hillary Clinton's disappointed stars back into the fold, it was Bass who introduced him.

Although Obama is younger than she, Bass says she feels a kinship with him, one rooted in the statistical improbability of their respective achievements. "I feel bad for him in a way, although it's the same position I was in," she said shortly before Obama won the general election. "Twenty-four hours after I was sworn in, I had to jump into the middle of this economic crisis, which a few months ago felt like it was just California. Now it turns out it's an international meltdown."

Bass, like many women who rise to power, has found gender to be a greater hindrance than race. Her male colleagues, she said, were "really knee deep in questioning my ability to be strong. But I'm used to that, and I'm used to being a woman in leadership dealing with sexism. It annoys you, but you know what it is, so you don't allow it to confuse you, or create doubts, or compromise your confidence."

By all accounts, she has charmed her colleagues with competence. But race, she hastens to acknowledge, presents its own challenge. When I asked her whether Obama's success meant the country had arrived at a new race-neutral plateau, she replied: "I don't believe there is a race-neutral moment in the United States."

On the day she took office, Bass told the celebratory crowd, "We have to respond to the current economic crisis the way we would a natural disaster. But the Golden State's excruciatingly difficult budget crisis has made Bass's job ever more difficult, sparking friction with Schwarzenegger's office and earning her critics within her own Democratic caucus. It is possible term limits never looked so good.

HEAD-TO-HEAD IN ATLANTA

There is probably no other state, county, or city in America where black politics runs as wide or as deep as it does in Atlanta, Georgia. The city's connection to the civil rights movement is so deep and tight that it is nearly impossible to find a black elected official today who does not claim a political lineage full of figures from the history books.

City council president Lisa Borders, fifty-one, keeps her history on the wall of her city hall office in the form of a huge blown-up photograph from her baptism. The presiding cleric is her grandfather, the Reverend William Holmes Borders, who pastored the city's historic Wheat Street Baptist Church for more than fifty years. It was at her grandfather's church that she first met Maynard Jackson, later Atlanta's first black mayor. And it was then, at the age of eleven, that she decided that she too would be mayor someday. "Maynard was my inspiration to politics," she says now. "My grandfather was my motivation."

Her ambition places her on a collision course with another rising star of Atlanta politics. State Senator Kasim Reed won his first election to the state house of representatives ten years ago at the age of twenty-eight, and has since moved on to the state senate. He managed both of Atlanta mayor Shirley Franklin's campaigns and, last year, played a part in persuading Franklin to break with Atlanta's black political establishment to endorse Barack Obama. He too has acquired the bug for municipal politics.

Each is a first. Each longs to break through once again. The 2009 race for the open mayor's seat will be the test.

In spite of her grandfather's accomplishments, Borders was discouraged from running for office. "It was my community, our community, who said, 'You can't win. What are you doing? You're not in the machine,'" she told me after chairing a council session on water rates. "When I asked permission, I didn't think they'd say no," said Borders, who won the special election and then a full term the following year. "And even when they said no, it was kind of like, 'I don't care. I'm going to do it anyway.' The expectation was that I would fail."

After first pursuing a corporate career in real estate development, Borders turned to politics in 2004, when she ran in a special election for the recently vacated city council presidency. She declared her intention to run for mayor a scant three years later.

Her corporate background, she said, shapes her thinking as much as the civil rights history she grew up with. "It's not that there's still not a room and a place for protests in the street, because there absolutely is," she said. "But I think that the venue primarily has moved from the streets to the suites. And I think those of us who have been blessed and are beneficiaries of the civil rights movement now have not only a responsibility but an obligation to figure out now what's the next platform."

But before she can get to the next platform, Borders has had to cope with suspicions within her own community. Because her storied grandfather was a Republican, opponents have suggested she is as well—not a good thing in overwhelmingly Democratic black Atlanta. (She is a Democrat.) Because she is single, some have questioned her sexual orientation. (She is straight and the divorced mother of a son.) But most of all, Borders fights against the notion that she is an outsider. With her private-school education and fair skin, she finds that white people tell her she is "not really black." But black people do too.

"Let me have my Cosby moment right here," she says, getting worked up as we talk about the questions raised about her in her own community. "'You told me to go to school, get my education. You told me to pay my bills in full and on time. You told me to give back to the community. You told me to raise my child. I did everything you told me to do, and I not only did it, I didn't meet but exceeded your expectations. Exactly where did I lose my blackness?'"

She leans back in her chair. "And I said it in a debate. You could have heard a pin drop."

Kasim Reed, who earned his undergraduate and law degrees at historically black Howard University in Washington, is a partner at a big Atlanta law firm. Perhaps because he is dark-skinned where Borders is fair, he is more sanguine about the identity question. "Every serious public figure that I know is going to go through some form of hazing on, and test of, their blackness," he told me. "I go through it. But the community, I think, brings you home."

Reed says he was almost "brought home" in 2002. He was riding high after Mayor Franklin's election, helped run her transition team, and had been elected legislator of the year. The last thing on his mind was that he would have to worry about his own reelection. But then he ran into a constituent at a grocery store in his southwest Atlanta neighborhood who scolded him for failing to spend enough time in the community. "She told me that if I didn't start going to baptisms and ball fields and sitting with people, they were going to bring me home," he said.

He plans to apply the lesson he learned then to the next mayor's race. In a city that elected its first two African American mayors—Maynard Jackson and Andrew Young—by driving up the black vote, the formula has shifted, and it is not only because white voters have returned to the city. It is also because the civil rights babies are planning to follow the path established by the presidential candidate both Borders and Reed crossed the old guard to endorse: Barack Obama.

"You build coalitions," Borders says. "You have to build coalitions and have enough ambassadors on your behalf that can be in all of the different spheres of influence across the city—white, black, short, tall, gay, straight . . . Jewish, Muslim, Christian, whatever."

Reed agrees. "I'm not going to be the mayor of the black community," he says. "I'm going to be the mayor of the whole city or I would just go and do something else."

But this is still Atlanta, and both would-be mayors are careful to pay their respects to the ones who paved the way. Reed, for example, says his ambition would not have allowed him to run against Representative John Lewis, the black Democrat who easily turned back a generational challenge in 2008. "I would not dream of doing that," he said. "Because to me, that would just be so disrespectful. I would not want to be the congressman who beat John Lewis." Also, judging by Lewis' substantial margin of victory, Reed probably would have lost.

Borders, who also considers herself the popular mayor's close ally, sees the clash with Reed coming, and has decided to plunge in even though

Franklin tried to encourage her to run for Congress or Georgia secretary of state instead. "I'm only going to do what I want to do, and it's this tiny little thing called mayor," she said. "That's all I ever wanted to do."

Like many breakthrough politicians, Borders and Reed care about more than just their own political futures. Borders, the mother of a twenty-six-year-old son, has come to realize that the generation that follows her has little use for traditional politics, something she hopes Obama's success will change. "We've got to make sure that everyone gets a bite of the apple," she says. "That's the bottom line, whether it's women, people of color, people that are physically challenged, whatever—everyone gets a bite of the apple."

And Reed is concerned about a gap he sees growing between successful African Americans, such as Obama and himself, and those who are still struggling. "I am worried that there is a cadre of black people that are being taken and rocketed into a new place and that we're too distant from the rest of black people," he said. "It scares me."

STATE REPRESENTATIVE BAKARI SELLERS

When Bakari Sellers decided to run for office in 2006, it never occurred to him to try for school board or city hall first. He set his eye on the South Carolina House instead, and started knocking on doors of houses where black people lived as well as on those where Confederate flags graced the stoop.

This would have been bold enough for any black candidate, but it was an especially ambitious undertaking for a twenty-one-year-old law student. A veteran black lawmaker took him aside to warn him he might be reaching too far, too fast. Run for school board instead, he was told.

"It's kind of like your daughter coming up to you and saying that she wants to be a doctor, and you tell her, 'No, you can't be a doctor, be a nurse instead,'" Sellers told me as he took a break from studying for the bar exam. "Now, there's nothing wrong with being a nurse, but you always teach people you don't want to dash their dreams. I just kind of took it as a chip on my shoulder and wanted to prove him wrong."

Sellers did prove him wrong, defeating Thomas Rhoad, an eighty-two-year-old incumbent who had held the seat longer than Sellers had been alive. In defeating Rhoad, the oldest member of the House, Sellers became the youngest.

Sellers came by his ambition honestly. His father, Cleveland Sellers Jr., was a confidant of Martin Luther King Jr. as well as a leader of the Student Nonviolent Coordinating Committee, and served time in jail for his role in a protest that would come to be known as the Orangeburg Massacre. The elder Sellers was nineteen years old when he spent the summer in Holly Springs, Mississippi, organizing with Fannie Lou Hamer's Mississippi Freedom Summer voting rights project.

To him, it is only natural that his son should choose politics as a path to the kind of activism he sought out in spite of his own father's disapproval back in 1964. "He grew up in an environment in which politics was front and center," Cleveland Sellers told me. "He was in a household in which all of the young people were always encouraged to be involved in political action and political movement."

In Cleveland and Gwen Sellers' household, it was not unusual for one of the three children to pick up the phone and find "Uncle Julian" Bond or "Aunt Kathleen" Cleaver on the other end. By stepping immediately into politics, young Bakari set out to reap the whirlwind his father had sowed.

"Having the opportunity to learn from those types of heroes and sheroes has put me on this path," he says.

Sellers was raised on breakthrough politics. Cleveland Sellers supported both of Jesse Jackson's presidential runs and takes pride in the notion that the second and third generations of black activists and politicians—including Obama—are walking through the doors he and his cohorts knocked down.

"Well, they are supposed to," he said. "They are on our shoulders, and that's the way the process evolves. If I had to talk about whose shoulders I might have been on, then I would have been talking about Roy Wilkins and Du Bois, who kind of set the stage, and made it possible for us to engage in the 1960s."

But at the age of twenty-four, Sellers sees the world through a prism different from the one that shaped his father's experiences. Although he believes the sit-ins and protests of his father's era were essential to African American progress, race, he says, is no longer at the root of the problems facing American society.

"During the forties, fifties, sixties, and seventies they basically stemmed around Jim Crow and segregation," he says. "Whereas now I think the argument, especially here in South Carolina, is if you're poor and black in South Carolina or poor and white in South Carolina, you face basically the same issues." Those issues, he says, are inequities in health care and education. "If we talk about issues that are near and dear to us on a fundamental level, I really don't think it matters if you're black or white. People will respond."

In choosing to pursue elective politics, Sellers cut his teeth interning for Representative Jim Clyburn and Atlanta mayor Shirley Franklin. It seemed a natural leap for him to throw himself into the Obama campaign in 2008, especially during the competitive South Carolina primary. He likes to think of both himself and Obama as "skinny guys with funny names."

But politically, he says, that's where the similarity ends. "I want to serve South Carolina," he says. "We have such a very, very long way to catch up with the rest of the Union, and I want to fit in whatever capacity that might be."

What form might that take? "I'm not a huge fan of D.C.," he says mischievously. "But the governor has a nice house."

GEORGIA ATTORNEY GENERAL THURBERT BAKER

One of Thurbert Baker's earliest memories is watching a Ku Klux Klan rally in his hometown of Rocky Mount, North Carolina, when he was six years old. It was the first time he discovered that there were people out there who might hate him simply because of the color of his skin. Somehow, neither this incident nor the time he spent picking tobacco and cotton as he was growing up scarred him. In fact, it may have spurred his incentive to get away.

"We were all sharecroppers back in those days," he said. "But I knew we could do something better."

About that time, he told his mother he wanted to be a lawyer, not because he wanted to beat the Klan but because he liked watching Perry Mason on television. As would happen throughout the rest of his life and career, he was affected by the racial upheaval that surrounded him, but not necessarily a part of it.

Along the way, Baker, now fifty-five, began to challenge the naysayers, winning admission to the University of North Carolina and turning himself into a top-fifty all-American fencer (of all things). He moved to Georgia to attend Emory Law School, made the right connections, and began climbing the rungs of state politics, which culminated in his 1997 appointment and subsequent election as the only African American state attorney general in the country.

"I think the easy way out sometimes is to tell people what they can't do simply because it hasn't been done," he says now, sitting in his office near the state capitol in Atlanta. "I wasn't going to follow those people. I simply wanted to do better. I had to do better. I was tired of the tobacco fields of North Carolina."

"Things were changing," he adds. "And I had that opportunity to prove people a little bit wrong about their perceptions, the myths that surround who we are and what we do."

Baker was the first in his family to go to college, and he followed through with a vengeance. It was when he got to law school in Atlanta that he attracted the attention of his first powerful political mentor, former Atlanta mayor Maynard Jackson. And that was when he started to consider politics for himself. People like to complain about government, he noticed, but few seem to want to do anything about it.

He made his first run for political office in 1988 at the age of thirty-six by setting his eye on a suburban statehouse seat from majority-white DeKalb County. Predictably, he was warned it was too soon. "I had a great desire to go do it, and I thought I could," he remembers now. "That was sort of the bottom line. I've never lacked confidence in what I could do. And so I ran, and got elected."

Baker served five terms in the state legislature, rising to floor leader. "It was a lot of fun just showing the people who said you couldn't do it that we could do it if there was a plan to do it," he said, still chuckling at the victory twenty years later.

But he did not win his promotion to attorney general the first time by beating electoral odds. He did it by catching the eye of another powerful Georgia political player, former Democratic governor Zell Miller. Miller appointed Baker to serve the unexpired term of Mike Bowers when Bowers quit to run for governor. Baker had only a matter of months to mount a 1998 campaign to win election to the job he had been handed. No one necessarily thought he would be able to pull it off.

"Not a lot of people thought that an African American could be the attorney general of Georgia, a Deep South state," Baker said. "We have never had an African American run statewide and get elected for a four-year term. And we certainly hadn't had one to be the attorney general."

Baker, however, was certain he could do it. "Call me crazy, call me stupid, I just never thought I couldn't get elected. It just never occurred to me." And once again, he was right.

Since he has been in office, Baker, whose Web site trumpets that he is "tough as nails," has assumed the role of legal insider, not legal crusader. This has sometimes rubbed veteran civil rights activists the wrong way. He received blistering criticism when he refused to release Genarlow Wilson, who was sentenced to ten years in prison in 2005 for engaging in consensual oral sex with a fifteen-year-old when he was seventeen. Wilson's had become a celebrated case in the activist community, and Baker enraged many when he appealed a judge's decision to release him in 2007. (Wilson was ultimately released, and subsequently received a scholarship to attend Atlanta's Morehouse College.) But Baker said he was merely upholding the law as written.[10]

"How many times did I hear the story, or the request, 'Just ignore the law, Thurbert'?" Baker told me in his defense. "I mean, I heard that more times than you can imagine. I'm sitting here, the attorney general of the state. Now, I can't ignore the law. But what you have to do in those cases is you have to prod from the inside out."

Baker stands by his decision to pursue his unpopular position on this and other cases. "I figure the best way for you to help is not to treat somebody differently on the back end if they've gone out and robbed somebody," he told me. Rather, he says, the better approach is "to catch them on the front end."

Like almost every other black elected official, he spent 2008 measuring his own considerable political expectations against Barack Obama's success. Obama, he believed, would have a "cascading effect" on black officials at every level.

"I believe when people take off the shackles of history and believe something like that is possible, it is not so difficult for them to believe that Thurbert Baker can be the attorney general of Georgia or that Thurbert Baker can be a governor or a senator."

Governor? Senator? It is clear even in casual conversation that Baker's ambitions do not end at the attorney general's office.

LOUISIANA HOUSE SPEAKER PRO TEMPORE KAREN CARTER PETERSON

Karen Carter Peterson always planned for public service. The daughter of a tax assessor, she started campaigning door-to-door for her father when she was seven years old, and essentially never stopped. And in New Orleans, politics is a blood sport.

Like many black politicians of her age and experience, the thirty-nine-year-old Peterson jumped on the Obama bandwagon early, choosing not to follow the lead of more entrenched elected officials who signed up with Hillary Clinton. But for Carter, going against the tide was nothing new. In 2006, she ran against incumbent New Orleans congressman William Jefferson, who was under investigation, and later indicted, on federal bribery charges. Her challenge won national attention and support, but she lost to Jefferson 57 percent to 43 percent. "I guess the people are happy with the status quo," she said.[11] Peterson was thirty-seven, Jefferson fifty-eight, but he had the distinction of being the first African American elected to Congress from Louisiana since Reconstruction, and he won support from other elected officials, including New Orleans mayor Ray Nagin.

Now, as New Orleans still struggles to right itself in the wake of 2005's Hurricane Katrina and 2008's Hurricane Gustav, Peterson believes there may yet be another chance. "There are needs that can't be met, quite bluntly, by state government or local government," she said. "And federal assistance is the only way that we're going to resolve some of the problems that we have."

Peterson signed up with Obama early and says she struggled to get other state officials to join her. She even had trouble talking her mother into it.

"That is absolutely a generational thing from the women's perspective," Peterson told me. "I think there are a lot of women like my mother who were going to have a dilemma between the opportunity for an African American and the opportunity for a woman. It was that basic."

Peterson also shares similar policy goals with other breakthrough candidates. Like Washington, D.C., mayor Adrian Fenty and Cory Booker in Newark, she believes improving public education requires going up against an entrenched establishment often made up of constituencies that have formed the backbone of black political support—teachers, unions, and school boards. "Many have failed our children," she told me. "Unfortunately, we have gotten complacent. And I guess many people had thought, maybe because we got into these positions, that we arrived. And we just began to accept that because we had African Americans in position, for example, in the school board, that things would be okay. We stopped judging people to some extent on the content of their character."

Peterson did get to Washington once, but as an intern for former U.S. senator John Breaux when she was a student at Howard University. She still is thinking of giving it another try, but at thirty-nine years of age and with a new husband, her own ambitions give her pause.

"Certainly my husband and I are talking about kids," she said. "Am I going to be a pregnant congresswoman? How does that impact a new marriage? And so there are a lot of realities that I think that men do not have."

Mayors

If there are any places that have seen breakthroughs in African American leadership before, they are the nation's cities. In the late sixties and seventies, in the wake of urban riots, economic distress, and other tension, a number of African American mayors rose to power. Richard Hatcher in Gary, Indiana; Kenneth Gibson in Newark; and Carl Stokes in Cleveland all were seasoned urban leaders who owed their political rise almost entirely to minority voter support. Some, such as Detroit's Coleman Young, became political institutions in their own right, inspiring succeeding generations in turn.

Mayors are executives who must manage politics as well as they fill potholes. The newest generation of city executives is staking their success on spurning old machines and building new relationships with the business community, which has the resources to revitalize tired old downtowns, stem crime, and rebuild schools. As their cities struggle, they have little choice but to carve new paths.

PHILADELPHIA: MICHAEL NUTTER

Michael Nutter probably sealed his reputation as a black maverick the day he decided to endorse a white woman for president. At a time when it looked like a black man might be a serious candidate for the first time, this was a politically courageous feat.

Nutter was not shy about his decision. Although he was aligned safely in the shadow of one of the state's most powerful politicians— former Philadelphia mayor and now governor Ed Rendell—Nutter broke with much of his city's black establishment when he decided not to back Obama. When Clinton dropped out and Nutter shifted his allegiance to the apparent party nominee, there was nary a ripple.

It turned out the people who elected him to do more important things than endorse other politicians were not all that upset with his choice. "It was kind of like, 'We really like the job you're doing, kind of disagree with this decision over here, but yeah, that's politics,'" he told me later. "'So you're a politician, you deal with that. Make our streets safe. Do your job.'" Obama did win the majority of votes in Philadelphia, but Hillary Clinton did better than expected. For that, she would have Michael Nutter to thank.

Politicians, of course, always deal in politics. One of Obama's chief backers was Representative Chaka Fattah, who had run against Nutter for the city's top job in 2007 and been endorsed by Obama. But barely a hundred days into his new job, Nutter had more urgent things on his mind than national politics.

Philadelphia, once one of the nation's largest cities and its first capital, was a troubled city. Shiny glass-encased skyscrapers were sprouting up downtown, within a stone's throw of Nutter's city hall office. But you didn't have to go far to come upon all of the traditional signs of urban decline: blocks of dilapidated and vacant buildings, struggling schools, and, most potently, searing street violence.

Nutter's first big challenge arrived on the spring night police sergeant Stephen Liczbinski was shot. The police officer was responding to a routine call when he was killed in the line of duty. In the wake of the shooting, officers on the hunt for the cop-killers pulled over a car carrying three young black men, dragged them into the street, and proceeded to kick and beat them in full view of a hovering news helicopter. Four of the officers were later fired.[12]

Both incidents were shocking. Only the latter—with its visual echoes of Los Angeles' 1992 Rodney King assault—got national attention. In Philadelphia itself, the greater trauma seemed to center on the shooting of the officer, who was buried on a gray and rainy day after a service in a landmark downtown basilica with thousands of uniformed officers in attendance.

When the manhunt for Liczbinski's killer turned up one of three suspects in an abandoned row house the day before the funeral, Nutter himself showed up to witness the arrest. "I stood two feet away from him and said, 'You know, I'm really disappointed in you,'" he told me the next day as we sat in his city hall office. "To his face. I'm standing here in the garage, no cameras around. There were no other people. It was just, 'As a black man, I am disappointed in what you have done.' I can get away with saying that. We're just two guys standing here in a garage."

Nutter is convinced he can get away with a lot. After all, he was not even supposed to have this job.

Nutter's victory in the 2007 mayoral election was a shock to the system of Philadelphia's black political establishment. After fifteen years on the city council, he decided to leap into a five-way competition to succeed tarnished outgoing mayor John Street. "I love this place," Nutter said of the city council at the time. "But it is time for me to leave."[13] When he announced his candidacy for mayor, he promptly dropped to fifth place in the polls, where he languished for months. Three months before the primary, Nutter was still polling at 8 percent. Even with a reputation as a reformer—on ethics, same-sex partner benefits, and municipal smoking bans—Nutter was politically overshadowed by a field that included a multimillionaire insurance executive, Tom Knox (who at one point led the polls two to one), and two well-known members of Congress, Chaka Fattah, who is black, and Bob Brady, who is white and chairman of the city's Democratic Party.

But, armed with Nutter Butter cookies, which he doled out on the campaign trail, and a canny campaign that caught fire at the last minute, the forty-nine-year-old Wharton School graduate confounded conventional wisdom. He beat all comers in the primary and won the general election by the largest margin in seventy-five years.[14]

Along the way, he fought off—or shrugged off—the same perceptions that seem to dog every African American shooting star: Exactly who was he? Fattah took it up another notch after Nutter proposed a plan to reduce violent crime by allowing police to "stop, question, and frisk" people suspected of carrying concealed weapons. Nutter, Fattah said, might want "to remind himself that he's an African American."

That approach did not work for Fattah, perhaps because Philadelphia's new mayor would have bigger fish to fry: a soaring homicide rate, a desperately underfunded retirement system for city employees, and fleeing taxpayers (a hundred thousand had left since 1990).

And as the winter of 2008 approached and the national economic meltdown hit home, it only got worse, as the mayor announced plans to close eleven libraries, cut jobs, and take a 10 percent cut in his own $185,000 annual paycheck. "We must batten down the hatches and prepare for the worst," he said in making the painful cuts. "And that means reshaping government for leaner times."[15]

COLUMBUS: MICHAEL COLEMAN

Michael Coleman is used to keeping his balance when it comes to the tightrope of heightened expectations. In 1980, when he graduated from the University of Dayton Law School, he snagged a job in the office of the Ohio attorney general. Immediately, everyone else had plans for his career, he recalls. Black lawyers, people said, always went to work in the civil rights division.

"I said I didn't want to go to the civil rights section," the fifty-four-year-old Coleman recounts. "They said, 'Why not?' I said, 'Because I want to learn about business. Sit me in the antitrust section.'" And that's where he went.

Coleman did not have anything against civil rights. He "adored" Martin Luther King Jr., and watched with awe from his hometown of Toledo when Cleveland elected its first black mayor, Carl Stokes, in 1967. But he grew up the son of a physician and attended private schools, a relatively privileged upbringing that exposed him to all of the options available to middle-class black children raised after the turmoil of the 1960s ended. "I played on the playground in the 'hood in the morning, and in the evening I went to the art museum," he said.

But even though he appreciated the accomplishments of Stokes and King, he did not aspire to be a civil rights leader. He thought of himself as a future businessman. It was not until 1999, after a career in law and seven years spent first as a member of the Columbus city council and then as president of the council, that he began to eye the city's top job. He won the Democratic primary by beating State Senator Ben Espy, a former boss and another African American. He then went on to defeat Republican county commissioner Dorothy Teater, a white woman, becoming the first Democrat to lead the city in more than a quarter century.

"We beat her by twenty-one points," Coleman said. "In doing that I made a conscious effort to reach out into neighborhoods that were not my base, in the minority community. It was in parts of Columbus that didn't have a strong record of voting for Democrats, much less African Americans, for much of anything."

By working from the outside in, Coleman followed a pattern that has become a familiar one for African American breakthrough candidates seeking election in majority-white districts: Woo the white voters first, "not as someone who is waving the civil rights flag," as Coleman describes it, then come home to the base later.

There is a certain trickle-down sensibility to this political approach, one that assumes that catering to the majority eventually benefits the minority. "We have to branch out and talk about issues for all people," Coleman said, linking himself to political leaders such as Obama, whom he endorsed, and Newark mayor Cory Booker. "Our goal is to represent all the people. I'm African American, proud of it. I was born black, going to die black, going to be black, and that's the way it is. And I'm very proud of that fact, but as a mayor, I have to represent everybody."

But Coleman could not escape his history-making turn as the first black mayor of Ohio's largest city if he wanted to.

"When I was elected, the biggest thing that the press talked about was being the first African American mayor of this city—I mean, for a whole year," he told me, still exasperated about it nine years later. "My response always was, and still is, I'm proud to be an African American, I'm proud to be a mayor, but if my legacy is to be the first, then I would have failed as a mayor. I want my legacy to be, 'He's the best mayor that ever has been in the city of Columbus.'"

To achieve that, Coleman has staked his reputation on a plan to boost the city's economic base while tackling its problems—enforcing a citywide curfew for teenagers out after midnight, installing safety cameras, demolishing abandoned houses, and building eighty-six miles of off-road bike paths by 2012.

These are race-neutral solutions familiar to anyone involved in municipal government. "'Coleman-isms' is what we call it in Columbus," the mayor told me. "Grow outward with the plan, grow inward with the passion. What that means is you redevelop the central city. Now, that doesn't have the stamp of race on it. But what it does, what that policy says, is rebuild the inner city. Bring it back.

"We have this big hole in this donut," he continued. "The hole in the donut is where a lot of people live. Many of them happen to be African American. But I'm not saying, 'Let's help black folks'; what I'm saying is, 'Let's fill this hole.'"

Coleman says he cried the night Barack Obama won the Iowa caucuses, and he became one of the Illinois senator's most enthusiastic supporters. Their experiences as breakthrough leaders, he said, are fated to be similar. "The day after the election, black communities are going to be saying, 'All right—now we have a black president, now I want mine,' right?" Coleman predicted. "That's what's going to happen. It happened to me. But Barack has to resist being remembered as being the first black president. Although that's important, he has to be remembered as one of the best presidents this nation's ever had. That's what his legacy ought to be."

WASHINGTON, D.C.: ADRIAN FENTY

An avid athlete, Adrian Fenty, thirty-seven, recently waved away an ambulance after he tumbled head-over-handlebars off his bike near a city freeway. He ran the twenty-six miles of the Marine Corps Marathon in three hours and thirty-seven minutes. But those are not the toughest things Washington, D.C.'s young mayor has tackled.

Fenty has a Zelig-like ability to appear wherever cameras are rolling—whether at crime scenes or at neighborhood block parties. "What's tried and true about electoral politics is staying out in the community," he says. "Being omnipresent and visible."

The nation's capital is a famously divided city: Democrats versus Republicans, insiders versus outsiders, natives versus carpetbaggers. What most Americans fail to realize is that Washington also is home to one of the country's most dramatic racial divides. Rock Creek Park winds its way through the heart of the nation's capital, providing a pastoral escape, as well as the setting for a 1975 Blackbyrds hit that heralded the joys of "doing it after dark" there. To the west of the park lie the city's richest neighborhoods and most prestigious addresses, including Georgetown, Cleveland Park, and Chevy Chase. To the east and south are the city's poorest, blackest, most crime-ridden neighborhoods. Property values plummet as travelers move west to east.

The city is largely African American, so ever since it elected its first mayor in 1975, its mayors have been black, beginning with Walter E.

Washington, two scandal-scarred terms with Marion Barry, a placid one under Sharon Pratt Kelly, and another under business-minded Anthony Williams.

Fenty's 2006 election represented a different type of breakthrough, a generational one that promised to bridge a long-standing chasm. For something remarkable occurred on election day: Fenty won everywhere—in black neighborhoods and white, north and south, east and west. He won in every single precinct, the first time any mayor had done so.

"During the campaign, I thought a lot about a kind of a new way of running cities and also maybe a new way of doing politics," Fenty tells me as we sit in the glass-walled conference room of his mayoral command center. "Substituting the politics of patronage with the politics of performance."

For all of its federal trappings, the city of Washington, D.C., is no different from most American cities, Fenty said. "Whether it's the eighty-five-year-old woman who has lived in Washington, D.C., her whole life, or the twentysomething [Capitol] Hill staffer who's moved into the city—people really just want to see the city work, whether it's the police department, the schools, or anything else."

Fenty's biggest nonathletic challenge has been his decision to seize control of the city's struggling schools. He hired a no-nonsense outsider, Michelle Rhee, to reform the crumbling system even though she had no previous administrative experience. As the greatest test of whether Fenty or any other mayor can make the city work, the school makeover is critical. Fenty and Rhee have set out to close nearly two dozen schools, replace dozens of teachers and administrators, and expand school choice for the system's seventy-three thousand students. Rhee told John Merrow, the special correspondent for *The NewsHour with Jim Lehrer,* that Fenty has never said no to her.[16] "I was willing to stake everything on us shaking things up and trying to make this system as best as it could be for the children of the District of Columbia," Fenty said.[17]

The verdict is out on Fenty's takeover of the schools, but he is convinced the key to turning around the schools—and the city—lies in a businesslike approach. He cites models such as Baltimore mayor Martin O'Malley, San Francisco's Gavin Newsom, Atlanta mayor Shirley Franklin, Cory Booker of Newark, and Buffalo's Byron Brown. These role models, he said, have one thing in common: "being more of a CEO mayor than a politician mayor."

"When you start talking a lot of prose or verbiage or speechify-ing—whatever you want to call it—eyes start to glaze over," Fenty told me confidently. "But when you say, 'This is broken; this is how I'm go-ing to fix it, and this is who I'm going to hold accountable,' it's a clarity that hasn't existed in politics for a while."

Casting aside politics is a tough standard for a leader who relies on the prospect of reelection to do his job, but Fenty at least gives the appear-ance of being supremely unconcerned with all that. As *Washington Post* columnist Marc Fisher summed it up: "If they are viewed with suspicion by older voters, both black and white, they don't much care. Their focus is on their own generation and those who come behind them. When they speak of a new America—and they all do—they see the colorblind friendships so common among their children, and they think of their colleagues from college and beyond, believing that they can populate government with top-shelf thinkers and doers like themselves."[18]

Fenty imagines that Obama, whom he endorsed and supported, would be the same type of president—visible, hands-on, and uncon-cerned with the pressure that inevitably is brought to bear from within the community he represents.

"When I'm out in the community . . . people don't ask me about the race or gender of the people I appoint," he says, noting one early criti-cism of his time in office. "Most people are telling me that they want officers walking the beat, more aggressive community policing and reductions in crime. Nine out of ten people I meet want the schools fixed. They are not asking for one type of person for the job—the issue is getting the job done."[19]

But getting the job done is a complex task in any city. Fenty fired six social workers after four girls who slipped through the city's social safety net were murdered by their mother and not missed for months. People hissed at him at community meetings. But, for now, Fenty has held his ground in the face of the criticism.

"If you campaign for your base, then you're going to administer for your base. Because you'll always be thinking about your next election and all you'll be caring about is satisfying that small group of people you know who got you elected or who you hope will get you elected."

Fenty grew up in a household where he was exposed to the value of public activism. But he sees himself as a different kind of change agent. Fixing the troubled schools, he believes, qualifies as a modern-day civil rights movement.

"Just saying, 'This is wrong, it has to change, and we're willing to in a very big public way change it and do something about it,'" he told me. "I think the civil rights movement was about much more than the leaders. I think it was about the people being ready for the change and pushing for the change. I think that's the case now."

BUFFALO: BYRON BROWN

When Byron Brown was elected Buffalo's first African American mayor in 2005, he achieved a milestone. Then he focused on trying to get past it.

"I don't think you can necessarily dwell on being first, because in a strange way, it can detract from your ability to be successful," Brown told me. "The focus for me was what I could bring to the community for all people—the training, the education, my vision for the future, and being able to paint a picture that resonated with everyone, as opposed to my own specific racial group."

Brown, like many other breakthrough candidates, discovered there was no easy path to satisfied political ambition. Like others, he was forced to learn his political home truths the hard way.

Home truth number one: The powerful seldom invite you to the party.

Brown moved to Buffalo from Queens, New York, when he was seventeen years old, to enter his freshman year at Buffalo State College. He learned the ropes in politics through internships with various local officials, including George K. Arthur, the president of Buffalo's city legislature, the Common Council, who had, in 1985, run for mayor and lost. Shortly after graduation, Brown returned to Arthur's office, this time as chief of staff. After working his way through various levels of local and state government in staff positions, Brown decided to try for elective office himself.

It was not an easy leap. When he decided to take on an eighteen-year incumbent in his first try, for a seat on the county legislature, he was pointedly discouraged. Years later, when he decided to run for mayor, he remembers one powerful black official taking him aside with a warning.

"I have another candidate for that office," the official said. "And if you go ahead and run for that office, I'm going to destroy you. I'm going to destroy your career, and you'll never be able to even work in Buffalo again, let alone run for office."

Brown recalls that he replied, "Well, sir, thank you for taking the time to meet with me. And your response convinces me why I do have to run for this office. Thank you and have a good day."

Home truth number two: Losing teaches you how to win.

Brown lost that first county legislature's race by 167 votes. "I was the upstart," Brown remembers now. "Everybody trained their guns on me. Everybody attacked me."

The second time he ran for office, this time for Buffalo Common Council, he won by two hundred votes. "I knew exactly some of the adjustments I needed to make to be in a better position next time around," he said. So he raised more money, recruited more volunteers, and collected more signatures than the African American incumbent. "Very early on I began to show that the machine could be beaten," he said.

Brown spent three terms on the council before deciding to run for state senate, an effort many political observers assumed would spell the end of his political career. But he became one of only two people to defeat an incumbent that year, and one of only two African Americans elected to the state legislature from outside New York City.

Five years later, he turned his ambitions back to Buffalo city hall, and this time he won the mayor's office easily, collecting 64 percent of the vote. The man who had initially urged Brown not to run later called him to tell him he was doing a good job.

Home truth number three: The hard part starts *after* you win.

Brown, bespectacled and soft-spoken, in no way fits the image of a typical machine politician. For some of the community's longtime leaders, that has taken some getting used to.

"My style is still a little—different," Brown admits. "When things occur, I'm not calling for marches. I'm not calling for protests. I'm not calling for demonstrations. I'm not screaming in public meetings and getting emotional and banging my fist on the table. I mean, I can give fiery speeches, but on different topics and for different reasons. They see me as calm, cool, collected, and because of that, slick."

But Brown has bigger concerns at hand. Buffalo is the second-poorest big city in the United States, with a poverty rate that increased from 26.6 percent in 2005 to 29.9 percent in 2006 at the same time as the national poverty rate was sliding down to 12.3 percent.[20] There are ten thousand vacant structures in the city—eyesores that undercut the new mayor's plan to revive its economy. In order to succeed, Brown has to be the man who can turn the struggling city around. That does not have a lot to do with race. It has more to do with a reduction in the city's crime rate—down 7 percent since he took office—and $1 billion in new economic development. Those trend lines, he says, transcend race.

As a member of New York State's political leadership, Brown endorsed his state's U.S. senator, Hillary Clinton, during the 2008 presidential primaries. But he also said he was "awestruck" at Obama's success.

"The question that I still have is, how much does it really say about how far America has come and how much we have really changed as a nation?" Brown said. "Does this really signal that we are a more united, more tolerant country than we have ever been?

"I think the jury is still out."

CONCLUSION

If there is anyone out there who still doubts that America is a place where all things are possible; who still wonders if the dream of our founders is alive in our time; who still questions the power of our democracy, tonight is your answer.

—PRESIDENT-ELECT BARACK OBAMA,
NOVEMBER 4, 2008

WHEN I WAS A CHILD, IT WAS POPULAR TO BELIEVE THAT IF YOU OWNED a sturdy enough shovel, you could dig a hole from your backyard straight through to China. No one ever seemed to discuss what was supposed to happen once we arrived at the other end.

In many respects, this is the same open-ended dilemma faced by many of the accomplished African Americans we have met in these pages. The air that must be breathed on the plateau at the end of the big dig is often mighty thin.

That has never been truer than now, as America and the world contemplate the single-generation leap we have accomplished with the election of Barack Obama. Surely my parents, who took part in the March on Washington, are spinning in their graves. Sometimes I feel like I am spinning on dry land. But then I think of the challenges ahead for any new president, and sober right up.

There has been extensive discussion about what Obama's election has meant for black political participation, but much less attention paid to what his ascendance tells us about the nation's majority population. For decades, black voters have consistently demonstrated their willingness to vote across racial lines; white voters, not so much.

The dozens of people I interviewed for this book have spent years wrestling with this and related issues, in most cases long before they first heard the name Barack Obama. They are optimistic and cynical, future-oriented and past-obsessed. But they share a general sense of expectation that falls into three rapidly collapsing categories: the past, the present, and the future. Barack Obama, now perched at the top of the electoral heap, represents all three categories, so his victory tells us much.

It turns out the Obama phenomenon was about race, but not in simple black and white. We know that race pride helped fuel black turnout, but less explored is the question of how the *white* voters who control the franchise went from resistance to acceptance in a single generation. How were Latino voters moved to speak so forcefully on Election Day, delivering two-thirds of their votes to Obama? What do those shifts tell us about the health of the nation? What predictions can they help us make about the future for the diverse collection of Obama wannabes moving to take the reins at every level of government?

Some activists such as Al Sharpton, who have been on the scene for decades, say there is nothing new here. Black leaders have broken through before, and then fallen by the wayside. "I remember when I was a kid, we first elected a black mayor," Sharpton said. "And then we discovered black mayors weren't going to solve just black problems and in some cases weren't even going to address them. I'm not here with amnesia. I've seen this before."

Indeed, the writer Philip Dray notes that during Reconstruction there were as many as sixteen black members of Congress, but by 1901, "black Southerners had been virtually expunged from politics, even as voters."[1] The next breakthrough on a federal level did not occur until 1929, when Oscar Stanton De Priest of Illinois arrived. He served only five years, and it took eleven years for the next real wave of black political representation to arrive.[2] That's when Harlem elected the flamboyant Adam Clayton Powell Jr., a one-man political bulldozer, to Congress. The only other black member of Congress at the time, William Dawson of Illinois, ultimately spent twenty-seven years in Washington.[3]

Powell's was an interesting case. He was immensely charismatic and popular within the black community and eventually rose to chair the influential House Education and Labor Committee. Powell remained in Congress as a powerful civil rights advocate until, hobbled and diminished by indictment and scandal, he was defeated for reelection by Charles Rangel in 1970.

Rangel would later break through in 2006, becoming the first African American to head the House Ways and Means Committee. This, however, did not happen until he was seventy-six years old.

By contrast, today's breakthroughs are seizing power at every level of government, and stepping up to the plate at much younger ages. Although we as a nation have become somewhat addicted to rejecting the old when we embrace the new, the twenty-first-century breakthroughs feel different, more enduring.

"Something is happening," John Lewis, the Georgia congressman, told me long before Obama's eventual rise seemed plausible. "There are people who say, 'I want to be an engineer. I want to be a firefighter. I want to be a police officer.' But you hear more and more, 'I want to be governor. I want to be mayor. I want to be president.' That's a good thing."

Much as I pressed, I could not ultimately settle on a single, generic definition of what constitutes a breakthrough leader. Certainly most have reaped the fruits of the civil rights movement to attend Ivy League schools and gain white acceptance, but after that it gets complicated. Even among those who embrace this new generation's approach, an emotional attachment to the 1960s civil rights protest ethic remains. Michael Eric Dyson, the Georgetown sociology professor, worried aloud to me about the consequences of what he called "new-breed Negro politics." How much of what was good about the movement would be lost along the way?

Still, even some of the movement's original agitators believe a tactical reevaluation may be in order. "Forty years later we're still singing 'We Shall Overcome,'" Oakland mayor Ron Dellums told me as we sat in his high-ceilinged and lavishly paneled office. "It's a beautiful hymn. We've just been singing it too damn long."

That reevaluation is clearly already under way, as black politicians elected to represent a more diverse electorate balance conservative solutions such as school vouchers and tougher sentencing against more liberal priorities, including affirmative action and reducing recidivism. They are more likely to cater to white voters and assume that black supporters will understand. At the same time, they are establishing a respectful, but arm's-length, distance from the traditional civil rights movement.

At risk in all this is the gerrymandering strategy that got black lawmakers elected in the first place. If whites will vote for blacks, the need for elaborately drawn congressional districts that maximize the black vote declines accordingly. If white voters have grown more willing to reach out, why shouldn't black candidates reach back?

"At some point we may have to reexamine the kinds of things we had to do in order to get the Corys and the Obamas," said Julius Chambers, who, as head of the NAACP Legal Defense and Education Fund, once championed these methods. "I think that if the people we believe are getting into these positions are as committed as I believe many of them are, we can see the same kinds of achievements five years down the road that we saw back in the sixties—perhaps more effectively."

But there is this worry: Could African American political power slip away if the old guard's successors are too busy looking ahead to pay proper respect to the past? Who will hold this new breed accountable to communities still struggling with disparities in education, health care, and employment opportunity?

That argument, which Obama's election only fueled, rages unabated among the activists, elected officials, and future politicians.

"Do you need a specific black politics today to address that, or can you do it in a larger sphere of postracial politics?" pollster Cornell Belcher said. "There's a larger back-and-forth debate that's going on right now that's either going to completely destroy what we know as black politics or reinforce it. And I don't know how that debate is going to play out."

The Reverend Joseph E. Lowery, cofounder of the Southern Christian Leadership Conference, left his polling place on Election Day shouting "Hallelujah!" after he voted for Obama. But he does not believe the struggle ends there. "We haven't spent half as much energy holding them accountable as getting them elected," he said of African American political leadership.

But there is far less room for error for guests who have just received their first invitation to the ball. The same qualities that make new faces fresh and appealing can also render them vulnerable. Detroit's Kwame Kilpatrick was the nation's first hip-hop big-city mayor when he was elected at the age of thirty-one, but he never quite seemed to know when the party stopped and governing began.

Most of the elected officials who talked to me are well aware of this extra scrutiny. "I feel like I'm supposed to try to solve . . . to pay a special kind of attention to the mayhem in poor communities, in communities of color," Deval Patrick, the Massachusetts governor, said. "And fortunately I want to. But I also feel that pressure. I feel that special expectation."

So, you might ask, what else is new? Extraordinary achievers are typically subject to extraordinary expectations. Joe Reed, the Alabama power broker, says that's why civil rights veterans insist on their right to play the outside game, even when African Americans become the insiders. "What black folks have got to understand is, if you were a warrior by training and a warrior by philosophy, you can't all of a sudden not be a warrior," he told me.

But the warriors are fading. The Reverend Jesse Jackson, who endorsed Obama, made his ambivalence abundantly clear by veering drastically off message—repeatedly—throughout the 2008 campaign. In the end, however, one of the more poignant images on election night was of Jackson, with his forefinger pressed tightly against his lips, crying with apparent joy (or regret) as he watched Obama take the Grant Park stage.

"You can't separate what's happening today from Selma, the Democratic convention in '64 from the Democratic convention in '08," Jackson told me weeks before. "It's a series of several martyrs and marches which begin to result in several changes in the broader culture."

The old guard still envisions a vital role for itself in this broader culture, perhaps especially in the age of a black president. Like Alabama's Joe Reed, they believe the present must take cues from the past. "Only a charlatan or a fool would say we haven't made progress as a race," said Basil Paterson, whose son is New York's governor. "But only a fool would think it's enough."

Still, there is an eager and growing audience among citizens of every race ready to embrace the notion that the end of race-based politics is near. Retired general Colin Powell, who crossed party lines to support Obama toward the end of the campaign, is perhaps its chief proponent. "We can no longer afford to put ourselves in a box so that only an Al Sharpton—and I don't want to be critical of Al—but only an Al Sharpton or a Jesse Jackson can, quote, *speak* for the black community," he told me long before Obama won. "I don't think Jesse can turn out the black vote any more than I think Al Sharpton can turn out the black vote. I don't think there's anybody left like that."

That leaves the future. Do these new leaders represent a fundamental shift in the way race politics has played out in the years since the Voting Rights Act took full root? Or are they merely the latest stage in a political evolution that has yet to fully unfold? Is the air up there still thin?

"What makes the hip-hop generation great is our improvisation, our innovation," Cory Booker said. "Even though we'll sample from the old, we need to write our own beats and rhythms and move forward."

This is a deeply threatening notion for some African Americans, especially the ones still more strongly attuned to Ella than Eminem. But those who are ready for the change see little choice.

That change is more likely than ever to remain confined to the Democratic Party. The Joint Center for Political and Economic Studies found that black identification with the GOP dropped 60 percent between 2004 and 2008. Only 4 percent of African Americans polled in October 2008 identified themselves as Republican.[4]

Former Maryland lieutenant governor Michael Steele, a black Republican who led his party's nominating convention in chants of "Drill, baby, drill," worries that the GOP's relationship with the black community has reached a low point.

"Heck, even Giuliani—even though most blacks in New York can't stand him—he did get a certain level of vote that was higher than most of the Republicans got," he told me. For Steele and others within his party, new future-oriented rhythms may be required.

"The civil rights moment—that central moment in August of 1963 when Dr. King gave that famous speech—he wasn't speaking to the people in front of him," Steele said. "He was speaking to this generation. He was giving them the blueprint that they would need in order to realize the fulfillment of the American dream."

Shannon Reeves, who has the unenviable task of rebuilding the Republican Party brand in the black community, sees a ray of hope in Obama's success. The Illinois senator, he argues, built a winning coalition independent of civil rights politics. "Democrat or Republican, it's time for generational change," Reeves told me. "I'm forty years old, and I'm just vowing my generation's legacy will not be hip-hop music. It's got to be bigger than that. Our parents and grandparents had the civil rights movement, and opened up all these doors. We've got to be able to take it to the next level."

Such coalition building, when done carefully, can expand an African American candidate's voter base, and also free him or her from conventional definitions of black leadership. Politicians such as Barack Obama, Deval Patrick, Artur Davis, and Cory Booker are staking their futures on such broadened horizons. "The diversity of the black community is such that, these days, having one black leader is offensive, frankly," Booker told me. "There's not one white leader. There's not one Latino leader. So we are evolving as a larger community."

But there is danger in embracing a whole lot of change all at once. The breakthrough generation may have different backgrounds and have achieved new levels of political success. But then what?

"They are different because they have to negotiate a range of constituencies in ways that past folks haven't," Eddie Glaude Jr. said. "But we also have to look at the deliverables. What are they doing? How are they positioning themselves? What are they putting forward? And how are they impacting black communities, substantively, as they emerge on the national stage?"

In the end, the outstanding question revolves around definitions of leadership. Some of the leaders of a generation ago readily admit that making a difference now may depend on their ability to hand over the reins with a measure of grace. "Along the way some people get confused," veteran civil rights activist Cleveland Sellers said. "They think that they have positions for life."

"One guy said to me, 'You're the only civil rights leader I know who didn't get embalmed in office,'" Vernon Jordan, the power lawyer and former Urban League chief, told me. "I said, 'That's true, because I believe if it's worth having, it's worth giving up. Pass the baton.'"

For the breakthrough leaders of the present, including Obama, leadership means setting the correct example. California House Speaker Karen Bass said that when she leaves office, she does not plan to return to the Los Angeles community organization she built. Instead, she has cultivated a new set of leaders to pick up where she left off. Obama's campaign may have done the same. Campaign manager David Plouffe predicted that his candidate's success "will breed a new generation of activists, people who become candidates and operatives."

The future of black politics—however it is now defined—could well depend on it. The NAACP's Ben Jealous says the new leaders must close the gap that separates the political elite from the concerns of the people they compete to represent. "The grassroots of this country are so far from the glass ceiling," he told me. "There is a lot of work to do to build ladders and staircases, and generally decrease the distance between the grassroots and the glass ceiling."

This optimism wars with pessimism in much of the politically aware black community. Days before the election, one friend told me that if Obama lost, he would sink into despair and leave the country. No other African American, he predicted, would get an opportunity like this for another hundred years. I started to agree with him, but then stopped myself. I thought back to the people I'd met while working on this book, and I was reminded that the bench is deep—crammed elbow to elbow with mayors, state lawmakers, and other rising stars poised to grab at the next brass ring.

Barack Obama's success is an achievement that goes broad and deep. It has changed attitudes as well as electoral possibility, and not just for politicians. A majority of all voters said in a postelection survey that the Obama victory would lead to improved race relations overall.[5] This is all the more remarkable given how fresh so many of the nation's racial scars still remain. In four southern states—Alabama, Mississippi, Louisiana, and Arkansas—Obama did more poorly than John Kerry did four years ago. "Given the political environment of 2008, those declines can only be attributed to race," political scientist David Bositis wrote in a separate report.[6]

Perhaps a wholesale shift in racial understanding was too much to hope for in a single electoral cycle. But then again, what did happen was no small thing. Americans were willing to place a widespread acceptance of African American culture, previously limited to arts, letters, sports, and entertainment, into a broad political context.

"This certainly doesn't wipe that bloody slate clean," historian Henry Louis Gates Jr. wrote the day after the election. "His victory is not redemption for all of this suffering; rather, it is the symbolic culmination of the black freedom struggle, the grand achievement of a great, collective dream."

Hopeful signs abound that the sandpaper friction that brought us to this new place is already smoothing over. The Pew research organization found that American voters—even those who supported John McCain—were feeling extraordinarily good about themselves and hopeful about Obama after the election. Interestingly, the black voters who were so pessimistic at the beginning of Obama's campaign are the ones who are the most optimistic now that it has ended.

"The world as we knew it before November 4 is no more," said Corey Ealons, the Obama campaign's liaison to African American media outlets. "We're living in a new world now, and African American leaders are going to have to accept that."

CHARLAYNE HUNTER-GAULT, THE journalist who in 1961 became the first black student at the University of Georgia, wrote shortly after Obama's victory of encountering a white man in a business suit on an Atlanta street the day after the election. "Congratulations," the man said, extending his hand. "For what?" she replied. "For Obama," he replied. She demurred. "But I didn't have anything to do with it." "Oh yes," he replied. "You're an American and this is an American victory."

"I have watched the ranks of young and not-so-young professionals like these swell as they took their places in a world since the days of our movement—not totally free of barriers, but barriers no longer insurmountable," she wrote later, describing what she saw in her hometown on election night. Hunter-Gault now lives and works in South Africa, so she has borne witness to what happens when sandpaper politics occurs on a dramatic scale. She has seen what happens when leaders excel, and also when they stumble out of the gate. Governing is complicated, so merely winning an election does not constitute the end of the battle. But there is little question that we in this country may be reaching the end of the "firsts." Perhaps breakthroughs are on the verge of becoming enough of a part of the national political landscape that at some point we will cease noticing them altogether.

AFTERWORD
TO THE ANCHOR BOOKS EDITION

ON AN EARLY SPRING EVENING IN THE NATION'S CAPITAL, ALL OF THE
lights were ablaze at 1600 Pennsylvania Avenue. In the ornate East
Room, Barack Obama—just a little over two months into his young
presidency—was commanding roadblock network coverage for his
second prime-time news conference.

After spending forty-five minutes on a series of predictable questions about war, peace, deficits, bank bailouts, and the generally abys-
mal state of the national economy, the president suddenly called on
ABC News radio correspondent Ann Compton.

Compton, seated in the fourth row, was caught off guard. She had
prepared six different questions to ask the president—just in case—but
decided instead to follow up on a question about homelessness posed
by Kevin Chappell of *Ebony* magazine.

"Could I ask you about race?" she said, popping to her feet.

"You may," the president responded, sounding resigned and expectant.

"Yours is a rather historic presidency," she began. "And I'm just won-
dering whether, in any of the policy debates that you've had within the
White House, the issue of race has come up, or whether it has in the way
you feel you've been perceived by other leaders or by the American people. Or have the last sixty-four days been a relatively color-blind time?"

There had been a lot on the president's plate in those first few months. But, remarkably, until Compton asked that question, there had been very little discussion about race or the breakthrough nature of this presidency. And that was just the way Obama and his inner circle liked it.

"I think that the last sixty-four days have been dominated by me trying to figure out how we're going to fix the economy," he responded. "And that affects black, brown, and white.

"Obviously at the inauguration," he continued, "I think that there was justifiable pride on the part of the country that we had taken a step to move us beyond some of the searing legacies of racial discrimination in this country."

Obama appeared to be thinking aloud, riffing on a topic clearly not part of his advance briefing.

"But that lasted about a day," he said with a half smile as the room erupted in chuckles. "And, you know, right now the American people are judging me exactly the way I should be judged, and that is, are we taking the steps to improve liquidity in the financial markets, create jobs, get businesses to reopen, keep America safe? And that's what I've been spending my time thinking about."

Nearly four months passed before the president spoke specifically about race in a public forum again. The occasion was the centennial celebration of the nation's oldest civil rights organization, the National Association for the Advancement of Colored People, where he agreed to deliver the keynote speech on the convention's final night.

Aides said Obama fretted over the speech, much as he had over the turning point race speech he'd delivered in Philadelphia a year before. A lot had come to pass since then. Obama-the-beleaguered-candidate had by now given way to Obama-the-preoccupied-president.

When he and I spoke hours before he delivered the NAACP speech, he had just returned from a week of summitry and symbolism in Russia, Italy, and Ghana. "I thought it was important, against the backdrop of G8 summits and trips to Russia, just to remind people that Africa is not separate and apart," he told me.

This was how Obama liked to take note of the historic nature of his presidency—by noting the distinctions but leaving it up to the listener to connect the dots.

He would tease former NBA great (now Detroit mayor) Dave Bing about the giant Afro he wore in his youth—something no white president could have gotten away with. Or he and Michelle would invite Stevie Wonder and Earth, Wind & Fire to play at the White House. He even swapped out the bust of Winston Churchill in the Oval Office for one of Martin Luther King Jr.

"Oh, absolutely!" the president told me when I asked if he sent these signals on purpose. "Look, I don't just have a bust of Martin Luther King. I've got an original program that a friend gave me, framed, of the March on Washington. That has a place of honor in the White House, because I think it's important to remember the incredible battles that were fought that allow me to occupy that office.

"I don't think that Michelle has any qualms about letting people know where she's from and what her history is," he added. Indeed, when schoolchildren came to visit the White House, the first lady thought nothing of pointing out that the building had been constructed, in part, by slaves. And when she traveled the short mile to the Capitol to unveil a new statue, the face under the drape was that of Sojourner Truth, the black feminist and abolitionist.

"The more we are delivering those messages," the president told me, "without beating people over the head, the more the culture as a whole—not just black folks but white folks as well—are going to be engaged in a shift in perceptions that is healthy for the country."

Not beating people over the head. On race and other matters, this would come to be an Obama trademark. And no one who had been watching the former Illinois senator's life and career as he steered around racial potholes (without pretending to be something he was not) should have been surprised.

It would not be overstating it to say Obama owed his election to black and brown voters. A U.S. Census Bureau study released nine months after the election confirmed that two million more African Americans, two million more Latinos, and 600,000 more Asians turned out to vote in 2008. In the same election, the white vote declined slightly.[1]

But Obama prizes his subtlety. When civil rights lightning rod Al Sharpton was invited to the White House, he came in the company of Republican firebrand Newt Gingrich and Michael Bloomberg, the liberal Republican mayor of New York. Black magazines like *Essence*, *Ebony*, and *Jet*, and Hispanic outlets like Univision were accorded pride of place at White House news conferences and invited on board Air Force One. But while the president fielded their racially coded questions about immigration, homelessness, and black unemployment, he doggedly scrubbed overt references to race from his answers.

For black audiences, he did not have to be explicit. The standing-room-only crowd at the NAACP meeting was like a Sunday church meeting—hot, emotional, and joyously reciprocal. When his voice rose, so did theirs. When he talked about how he benefited from their sacrifices, it was all anyone wanted to hear.

"I think people have a good realistic sense of what's taking place in the country," he told me before the NAACP speech, which turned into a passionate call-and-response sermon about racial disparities and responsibility. "They understand that my election represented a broader shift than had taken place previously, in which the American people are more interested in judging people by results than they are by the color of their skin. I think people also have a realistic assessment that racism hasn't entirely gone away, and there are a whole bunch of structural barriers out there that still prevent too large a percentage of African Americans from achieving their piece of the American dream. I think people have a good, solid, clear-eyed view of what's going on out there. They understand we have made progress, but that we still have more work to do."

Exactly one week later, the nation was suddenly plunged into one of those unforeseen moments that proved the president's words to be more than true. Arriving home from a trip spent shooting a documentary in China, prominent Harvard historian Henry Louis Gates Jr. was arrested on the front porch of his home in Cambridge. The ensuing high-decibel debate would lay to rest any lingering notion that Obama's election had catapulted America into racial nirvana.

Gates was a friend of the president and at the least an acquaintance of probably every other high-profile black person in America. His arrest—which at first blush appeared to be a blatant case of racial profiling—commanded immediate attention.

It soon emerged that Gates and another man had forced their way into the home because his key somehow did not work. Once inside, the esteemed professor was on the phone when he noticed Sergeant James Crowley, a white policeman, standing on his front porch. A bypasser had called to report seeing the two men (Gates and his driver, as it turned out) breaking in.

What happens next is subject to some dispute. Gates produced identification to prove he was in his own home. Words were exchanged. The officer's badge number was demanded. Voices were raised, after which Gates was handcuffed, hauled away, and spent four hours in jail.

"In some ways this is every black man's nightmare and a reality for many black men," Deval Patrick said.[2]

"I think it's fair to say, number one, any of us would be pretty angry," the president said when he was asked about the incident at the very end of a prime-time news conference nearly a full week later. "Number two, that the Cambridge police acted *stupidly* in arresting somebody when there was already proof that they were in their own home. And number three—what I think we know separate and apart from this incident—is that there is a long history in this country of African Americans and Latinos being stopped by law enforcement disproportionately, and that's just a fact."

Almost instantly, the president's statement eclipsed all else on his crowded agenda. In part because the normally cautious and race-neutral black politician used the vivid word "stupidly," the discussion

quickly boiled down to whether Obama had attacked law enforcement. Lost in the cable television– and blog-fueled whirl that followed was the nuance of what the president had acknowledged—that
this sort of thing happens all the time. Obama had acknowledged in
his second book, in fact, that it had happened to him.

Talking Points Memo, a liberal blog, offered its tongue-in-cheek
headline: "Breaking: President is Black Guy."

The Gates incident forced the president to veer from the breakthrough script. By sympathizing with his friend, he managed to remind lots of folks invested in the idea of Obama as a race-neutral black
man that he viewed the world through a fundamentally different lens
than they did.

"The fact that this has become such a big issue I think is indicative
of the fact that race is still a troubling aspect of our society," Obama
said when he subsequently tried to tamp down the uproar over the
Gates arrest and his comment. "Whether I were black or white, I think
that me commenting on this and hopefully contributing to construc-
tive—as opposed to negative—understandings about the issue, is part
of my portfolio."

The debate died down only once Gates, Crowley, the president,
and vice president agreed to meet at the White House for a supremely
awkward blue-collar-friendly photo opportunity—the "beer summit,"
it came to be called. Each man drank a different brand of beer fifty feet
away from the cameras, and—more important—away from the micro-
phones ushered onto the White House lawn to record the moment.

There was no way this highly choreographed moment of camara-
derie—with Obama and Biden in shirtsleeves, and their guests in suit
coats—could signal the end of racial conflict in America. Certainly
the scab would reopen, if not with these players, then with others.

Race would have to be part of the first black president's portfolio—
and it would always run the risk of causing a distraction from other urgent matters at hand. Two cable networks flashed countdown clocks
on the screen in the hours leading up to the meeting. "I have to say

I'm fascinated with the fascination about this evening," the president observed beforehand.

America, it turns out, was not practiced in the idea of treating race as anything other than a source of conflict. Even with a black man now standing behind the White House podium, old tensions remained.

The same week the Gates arrest was dominating headlines, a white Florida doctor was circulating an e-mail with the subject line, "Coming Soon to Health Care Facilities." The image embedded in the e-mail was labeled "Obama Care" (the "C" rendered as a hammer and sickle), and the president was portrayed wearing a bone through his nose, a feathered headdress, and a loincloth.[3]

This was some distance from the "postracial" ideal.

White people were not the only ones trafficking in troubling behavior. Obama's former pastor Jeremiah Wright briefly resurfaced a few months into his presidency, grousing to a reporter that "them Jews" were keeping him away from Obama.

"They will not let him talk to somebody who calls a spade what it is," he said as he was leaving an ecumenical preachers' meeting in Hampton, Virginia. "I said from the beginning: He's a politician; I'm a pastor. He's got to do what politicians do."[4]

And when Obama nominated U.S. district judge Sonia Sotomayor, who was born in Puerto Rico, to be the nation's first Hispanic Supreme Court justice, it took virtual nanoseconds for opponents to brand her a racist based on her work on behalf of the Puerto Rican Legal Defense and Education Fund—now known as LatinoJustice PRLDEF.

"I think that a lot of Republicans are trying to fight culture wars, and reengage in the kind of identity politics that was all the rage back in the eighties and nineties that just isn't really relevant to people's lives right now," the president told me just before Sotomayor was confirmed. "And there was, I think, a period of time, of excess, when everybody spent an awful lot of time trying to read the cultural symbols of race into every aspect of our lives. The overwhelming majority of

Americans at this point recognize that race is still an issue, but it's not the only issue."

Many Americans were poised to agree, and breakthrough politicians carefully studied Obama's efforts to neutralize—or at least minimize—race. Some considered his optimism overstated, but they also seemed to understand he was communicating a message on this, the touchiest of debates, in a way many Americans wanted to hear.

But people of different races often don't seem to hear the same thing the same way, as the Gates arrest showcased. As I toured the country speaking about politics and race and this book, I lost count of the number of times people—most of them white—asked me, brightly, whether Obama's election meant the advent of a new color-blind world. If I demurred, many would argue the point with me, often with passion.

At the same time, I encountered any number of skeptical African Americans who would praise Obama, and then lapse into a recitation of the hurdles they still face. "See what I mean?" was the collective cry after Gates's arrest.

A NEW CONVERSATION

Yet I became convinced that many Americans have embarked on an interesting journey. It turns out that Obama's election may have served as a key in the lock that guards our nation's racial psyche.

All of a sudden, many people seem to have claimed permission—even an imperative—to talk about racial taboos. Because television had brought me into many of their homes, I discovered audiences who felt they knew me well enough to ask me awkward questions without fear of insult.

Why, one man in Maryland wanted to know, weren't more black people "articulate" like Barack Obama? Wouldn't that solve our problems?

Why, another woman in Oakland wanted to know, couldn't we stop talking about race? Didn't this election prove we were past all that? One PBS viewer wrote to ask why we couldn't just *forget* that Obama is black altogether.

Phone callers jammed the lines on a radio talk show in Minneapolis to debate whether Obama's success proved affirmative action obsolete. The outcry to my fairly neutral response ("Well, uh, not necessarily.") was so great, the host immediately booked a separate program focusing on that single topic.

In Mountain View, California, a white woman who described herself as an "old hippie" said Obama "was what I've been waiting for." She was convinced he was not a politician in the old-fashioned sense, and that race had absolutely nothing to do with it. "I can't say I feel represented because he is so intelligent," she mused, "because that would be egotistical."

Another man at the same event, held at Google headquarters, confessed his disappointment that the conversation we were having turned on race instead of class. He too wanted to erase color from the debate. Why, another man asked, did identity politics—framing debates in the context of race—still seem to play such a role in the national conversation?

Race confusion made its way into the conversation most often when the questioners were self-declared liberals who believed in racial transcendence.

On one occasion, when I spoke at a liberal-minded private school in Washington, D.C., an older, bearded white man began a question to me, mere days after Obama was inaugurated, by mentioning his activist bona fides up front. He had marched in Selma, he wanted me to know. He had traveled to Mississippi during Freedom Summer in 1964. So why, he wanted to know, hadn't Obama done more in office by now?

Give the president another week, I suggested, as the audience burst into laughter. But what really stuck with me was why the questioner felt he had to provide evidence of his own racial enlightenment before he could offer even a mild criticism of the black president.

In San Antonio, a young African American schoolteacher in town from Chicago for a convention asked me what she should say to students who felt she injected race into too many classroom discussions.

My response: Why would we want to forget race, unless we consider it a negative? I discovered this answer rapidly silenced entire ballrooms full of people. Was it conceivable one's racial identity could be a good thing? Part, but not all, of who we are?

What is it about race that pushes our buttons so? I am not sure of the answer, but I have a few theories.

Like clogged arteries, we have allowed our apprehension about race to slow and obstruct healthy conversation. Especially for white people, the very idea of alluding to race often feels threatening. I cannot tell you the number of times I've had a white acquaintance attempt to describe the only other African American standing in a room by every other identifying characteristic except race. ("It's the guy in the blue blazer and khakis with the short hair." "Oh, you mean the black guy?" "Um . . . yes, now that you mention it.")

But I discovered that once the pressure valve is released, people are desperate to talk about race—as long as the conversation is leached of accusation, guilt, and blame. Unfortunately, this is seldom the case.

BREAKING THROUGH: THE OTHER SIDE

Since this book was published on inauguration day, many of the people profiled in it have reached for new brass rings. And many have seen their careers and ambitions boosted by Obama's rise.

Several were tapped to serve in the Obama administration. Ron Sims, the executive of Washington state's King County, moved to Washington to become deputy secretary of the Department of Housing and Urban Development. San Francisco attorney Tony West was appointed Attorney General Eric Holder's deputy at the Department of Justice's civil division. Michael Steele won election as the first African American chairman of the Republican National Committee.

Steele, who often rattled many of his membership by lacing his rhetoric with hip-hop-style references, immediately became a lightning rod within and outside of his own party.

When Steele went on a minority recruiting mission at a conference of Young Republicans meeting in Indianapolis, one blogger asked him how he planned to recruit "diverse populations" to the GOP.

"My plan is to say, 'Y'all come,'" Steele responded eagerly. The questioner shot back, "I'll bring the collard greens!" and Steele, unfortunately, replied, "I got the fried chicken and potato salad!"

It was a joke, but it did not look so good on YouTube, and liberal critics were all over it. (President Obama had even mocked Steele at the annual White House Correspondents' dinner, saying he understood Steele was in the house—"or, as he would say, 'in the *heezy*.'" The black folks in that crowd—astounded that they were witnessing any U.S. president appropriating such street slang, especially to mock another black man—laughed harder than most.

"Michael, for the last time," the Democratic president added as Steele sat smiling in the audience, "the Republican Party does not qualify for a bailout."

For most other would-be breakthroughs, pure politics governed their futures. In Georgia, when Atlanta city council president Lisa Borders dropped out—and then back into—the mayor's race, she found herself, along with Georgia state senator Kasim Reed, as part of a five-candidate primary field.

This was a sign of Atlanta's robust and deep black political bench. But there was also the chance that a divided black electorate—already declining as the city's demographics shifted—might benefit the lone white candidate, city councilwoman Mary Norwood. If she were to win, she would be Atlanta's first white mayor in more than thirty-five years.

But the White House Project, an advocacy group that trains women to run for office, noted that Georgia has failed to break through on another front. Even with Atlanta mayor Shirley Franklin and Lisa Borders in place, no woman represents the state in Congress, and only seven of its fifty-six state senators are women. Among states with women in office, Georgia fell from thirty-first to thirty-seventh in 2008.

Meanwhile at the state level, after a dozen years as attorney general, Thurbert Baker followed through on his blunt hint to me that he would run for governor. He raised more than $700,000 in six months.

U.S. representative Kendrick Meek declared his candidacy for the U.S. Senate seat being vacated by Florida's Mel Martinez, only to find himself competing for the Democratic nomination with Corrine Brown, another member of Congress from Florida. At sixty-two years old, Brown also happened to be one of his mother's best friends. (Brown, Meek, and Alcee Hastings were Florida's first African Americans in Congress since Reconstruction when they were elected together in 1992.)

But even if Meek—who almost immediately won endorsements from the Democratic establishment—bested Brown in a primary contest, he would survive to face a near certain general election showdown in 2010 against one of the state's most popular politicians—Republican governor Charlie Crist.

The governor's fundraising prowess—he raised more than $4 million in just seven weeks—was such that he threatened to swamp both his GOP primary opponent, former state house speaker Marco Rubio, and any Democratic nominee. (Meek raised $2.6 million in six *months*.) Polls also showed Crist with a formidable advantage, in part because he came into the race with a statewide and even national political profile.

Also hoping to build on Obama's success in 2010 were U.S. representative Artur Davis, who followed through on his pledge to run for Alabama governor, and San Francisco district attorney Kamala Harris, who launched an expensive race for California attorney general. Each was an early Obama supporter. But winning in California and winning in Alabama required different approaches.

Davis almost immediately set about distinguishing himself both from the state's black political leadership and from the president he helped elect. Predictably, the aging black leaders he'd feuded with since he first ran for Congress spent the spring shopping around for an alternative candidate. Davis, they said, was unelectable. They did not have to say why they thought so. Headline after headline continued to pose the question: Was Alabama ready for a black governor?

But a succession of other well-known potential candidates considered—and then decided against—challenging Davis. These included Jim Folsom, the lieutenant governor, and Sue Bell Cobb, the chief justice of the state Supreme Court. The only Democrat left standing was Ron Sparks, the state's agriculture commissioner.

At the same time, Davis searched for the political sweet spot that would allow him to link himself to a popular president without alienating the conservative Alabama voters he would need to win.

So, although he was a frequent White House guest, he also thought nothing of voting against the president's energy bill and openly opposing the House version of a costly health care bill the president desperately wanted. "Is the state of Alabama ready for a liberal black governor?" a Davis campaign political adviser asked. "Probably not. Are they ready for Artur Davis? I believe so."[5]

In California, the Obama connection was considerably more helpful for Kamala Harris. She announced her statewide run for attorney general shortly after Obama was elected, and within eight months had raised $1.3 million—in part by tapping into a nationwide fundraising network cultivated during Obama '08. But along the way, she learned how complicated it can be for candidates based in the liberal Bay Area to overcome suspicions in other more conservative parts of the state.

Her first test came on the touchy issue of immigration. As San Francisco's top prosecutor, she created and championed a program designed to prevent nonviolent, first-time drug offenders from returning to jail. She dubbed it "Back on Track." But a half dozen of the offend-ers who emerged from the program turned out to be undocumented immigrants. One was subsequently arrested for robbery and assault.[6]

Harris subsequently tightened the rules for the program, defend-ing it as a solution for recidivism. Ten percent of the Back on Track graduates, she said, commit new crimes. The statewide average is 54 percent.[7]

Still, this was an early stumble in a state where illegal immigration remains a sensitive topic. At least six candidates are competing for the attorney general's post.

Harris hoped to offset this controversy with more positive news—a 23 percent drop in elementary school truancy as a result of an aggres-sive campaign launched on her watch.

THE CRITICS

Harris, Davis, and every other breakthrough candidate I've talked to in the past several years freely admit that erasing race is easier said than done. And often the harshest criticism comes from within the black community.

There was some uneasiness in the air as President Obama arrived to speak at the NAACP in July. The president had gained a reputation during the campaign for scolding black audiences—albeit usually to warm applause—on matters of responsibility. Obama actively resists the notion that this is *all* he has to say to African American audiences, and in that he is correct.

At the NAACP address, he spent far more time talking about racial disparities in crime and education than he did preaching the message of by-your-own-bootstraps responsibility. The next day's newspapers, however, showed how different people can hear the same thing and come away with different conclusions. The *New York Times* empha-sized the personal responsibility message. The *Washington Post* focused on the disparity piece. The *Times* reporter is white; the *Post* reporter black.

"I think what is absolutely true is if I'm going to speak honestly to the African American people, the way we talk around the kitchen table, then we're going to acknowledge that when you have the majority of African American children growing up not knowing their father, that that's a problem, and that our fathers need to step up," Obama told me when I spoke with him hours before the speech. "I make no apologies for making that statement, because everybody knows it's true.

"Maybe nobody else wants to say it," he added. "But I think it's clear."

But if there was one entirely predictable event in the first months of Barack Obama's presidency, it was that the barely tamped down unhappiness simmering among some in the African American academic left would resurface. Notable among those critics was Georgetown professor Michael Eric Dyson, an early Obama supporter who had harsh words for the president after he took office.

On *Davey D's Hip-Hop Corner*, a radio program taped in Oakland that popped up on YouTube in May, Dyson said he had yet to be invited to the White House. Why? "I'm not an uncritical, celebratory figure," he said. "I don't just cosign what's going on.

"I tell you, it seems to be an *incapacity* of Mr. Obama to explicitly embrace blackness," he said, his voice rising on the tape as he complained that Obama failed to mention Martin Luther King Jr. by name during his inauguration address.

"He is willing to sacrifice the interests of African Americans in deference to a conception of universalism, because it won't offend white people," he said.

Dyson muted his criticism after the Gates incident, praising the president for defending the Harvard professor, while reserving his right to fault him for other shortcomings. But others, who'd held their tongues months after Obama was elected, remained vocal and bit-ing. By and large, they declared, the president would not speak up for black issues. Cornel West, the Princeton professor who was lured into the Obama fold for the duration of the campaign but also relegated to the sidelines after inauguration, told liberal radio host Amy Goodman on *Democracy Now!* that he, too, had not spoken with Obama since inauguration day.

"I think he holds me at arm's length," West said. "And for good reason. Because he knows that there's a sense in which I would rather be in a crack house than a White House that promotes neoimperial policies abroad and neoliberal policies at home."[8]

Obama, he told a Sunday-morning church service at Howard University, was a "cracked vessel, like anybody else."

"We love you Barack," he cried as the congregation laughed, "but you're not Jesus."

I asked Obama about comments like these.

"First of all, I think that if I was spending all my time worrying about critics, I'd be a basket case right now," he told me, chuckling. "Taking criticism is part of the job. The other thing, I think, is that I spend a lot more time thinking about what the teacher, the bus driver, or the barber are saying than I do with what intellectuals are saying."

Benjamin Jealous, the young new president of the NAACP, enthusiastically supports Obama but says holding the president's feet to the fire is essential.

"The best thing that we can do for him is to come to bear with all the pressure we can bring to live up to the promises that he made," he told me when I spoke with him for PBS's *NewsHour*. "On January 20, he was the first black president and we celebrated him. That's what that day was all about. But January 21, he became the forty-fourth president. Full stop. End of story. If we want to see civil rights advance, if we want to see human rights advance, then we have to push him just as hard as we can."

There was plenty of precedent for this squabbling within the fraternity. There is scarcely a black politician alive who has not had to face down severe criticism from within his or her own community. In Massachusetts, Deval Patrick came in for withering verbal assault from the Reverend Eugene Rivers, an outspoken clergyman and activist.

In a 1,300-word letter delivered to the governor's office, Rivers wrote, "Where is the promised opportunity for poor, urban blacks? Where are the benefits for the black community from President Obama's economic stimulus package?" Other black clergy in the Bay State, however, declined to support Rivers.

But such disagreement paled in the face of the nitty-gritty work of balancing a state budget in the midst of a dramatic economic downturn. Patrick had to sign off on more than $1 billion in tax increases, abandon cherished priorities, and embrace the kinds of revenue solutions that make reelection a dicey prospect. It got so bad at one point that when Patrick announced he would cut funding for two Boston-area zoos, he was promptly accused of forcing the zoo to euthanize cute animals.

By midsummer, Patrick's popularity was taking a significant political hit. A *Boston Globe* poll found 56 percent of voters disapproved of his job performance. Only 35 percent approved, and 61 percent said the state was on the wrong track. As recently as the previous December, 64 percent viewed him favorably, and the precipitous plunge did not bode well for the governor's 2010 reelection prospects.[9]

In addition to Republican Charlie Baker, Patrick also faced a likely challenge from Tim Cahill, who quit the Democratic Party, presumably to run for governor as an independent. "It's almost like blood in the water," University of Massachusetts political science professor Paul Watanabe told the *Boston Globe*.[10]

Perhaps. But Patrick was entering his reelection campaign prepared, hiring Obama campaign manager David Plouffe—who also worked for Patrick in 2006—to come back on board.

In Newark, Cory Booker's dogged optimism basically wore his natural opponents down. "We've gained some incredible ground in three years," he boasted to The Daily Beast Web site in the spring. "I think with another five years, we could just blow people away."

Booker could have moved on by now. He was asked to join the Obama administration as director of the new Office of Urban Affairs, but declined. "That's not playing to my sense of purpose," he loftily told *Time* magazine. He'd also resisted New Jersey governor Jon Corzine's offer to run as his lieutenant governor, even when four Democratic heavyweights, including U.S. senator Robert Menendez, made a personal appeal. (This decision, however, could not have been difficult, since Corzine's popularity was cratering at the time.)

Instead, Booker stuck to his promise to run for reelection in 2010, even though his most stubborn municipal critics never went away. "I give him credit. The homicide rate has gone down," said poet, activist, and author Amiri Baraka. "But I don't know if you can judge the quality of life in a city by just the homicide rate. Where is the employment? Where is the education? What is in it for the residents?"[11]

Because Obama's profile was so much higher, the critique was correspondingly more pointed, and more heated. As a result, it was not hard to see signs of some White House sensitivity when it came to matters of race. When controversial pop icon Michael Jackson died suddenly, it took Obama days—and repeated questions from reporters—to issue a routine statement of regret.

On Memorial Day, he sent flowers to a Confederate soldiers' monument—a White House tradition—but he also sent flowers to a Washington, D.C., memorial honoring African Americans who fought on behalf of the Union in the Civil War.[12]

Eric Holder, the nation's first African American attorney general, made clear that he believed the Obama breakthrough took the nation only part of the way. He made headlines early on when he declared in a Black History Month speech that America is "a nation of cowards" when it comes to talking about race (a statement that caused the White House no small amount of heartburn). But in a less noticed speech delivered to the NAACP the same week Obama appeared, Holder warned the crowd to "resist the temptation to conclude that our nation has fulfilled its promise of full equality based on one moment or on one election. We know better than that."[13]

NEW OPTIMISM

Still, Americans seem to be inordinately proud of themselves for the breakthrough they engineered in 2008, and there is some reason to believe they have cause for that pride. The electorate that sent Barack Obama to the White House was the most diverse in history.

Regionally, the greatest strength was demonstrated in the old Confederacy, with a surge in black voting in Mississippi, North Carolina, and Louisiana.

Obama was not the only one to benefit. In May 2009, an extraordinary thing happened in the small town where three civil-rights workers—James Chaney, Andrew Goodman, and Michael Schwerner—were famously murdered by the Ku Klux Klan in 1964. Philadelphia, Mississippi, elected its first black mayor, James Young.

It cannot be overstated what a symbolic turnaround this was. Philadelphia is still 60 percent white, so to win election, Young almost certainly had to have won support from the children of people who had more in common with the Klan than the SCLC.

At fifty-three, the new mayor was only a little older than the president. But he was old enough to have integrated his elementary school. "The places where we were locked out, I'm going to have the key," Young exulted. "The places we couldn't go, I've got the key. No better way to say it than that."[14]

President Obama's election did not completely change America's mind on race. I've found as many bright spots as depressing ones as we as a nation continue to wrestle with what we say we believe and how we act on it.

But forty years after affirmative action transformed college campuses and workplaces, public accommodations laws continue to allow people of color to walk through previously closed doors, while successive generations of ambitious black politicians have claimed seats at the table. The NAACP's Benjamin Jealous describes the "transformative possibility" of the moment.

But possibility requires patience. And so do breakthroughs.

NOTES

All quotes from the following individuals, unless otherwise noted, are from author interviews: Steve Adubato Sr., Steve Adubato Jr., John Anzalone, David Axelrod, Charlie Baker, Thurbert Baker, Karen Bass, Cornell Belcher, Julian Bond, Carolyn Booker, Cary Booker, Cory Booker, Lisa Borders, David Bositis, Donna Brazile, Edward W. Brooke, Byron Brown, Wayne Budd, Diane Bystrom, Karen Carter Peterson, Diahann Carroll, Julius L. Chambers, William Lacy Clay Jr., William Jelani Cobb, Michael Coleman, Stephen Crosby, Mildred Crump, Wayne Curry, Natalie Davis, Artur Davis, Ron Dellums, Steve DeMicco, Sheila Dixon, Michael Eric Dyson, Corey Ealons, Christopher Edley Jr., Adrian Fenty, Rev. Floyd Flake, Harold Ford Sr., Shirley Franklin, Eddie Glaude Jr., Lani Guinier, Kamala Harris, Carol Hardy Fanta, Kerry Healey, Wade Henderson, Eleanor Holmes Norton, Charlayne Hunter-Gault, Jesse Jackson Sr., Jesse Jackson Jr., Benjamin Jealous, Elaine Jones, Vernon Jordan, John Knight, John Lewis, Reginald Lindsay, Rev. Joseph E. Lowery, Mark Mallory, William Mallory, Roland Martin, Carrie Meek, Kendrick Meek, Michael Nutter, Barack Obama, Michelle Obama, Diane Patrick, Deval Patrick, Basil Paterson, David Paterson, David Plouffe, Colin Powell, Joe Reed, Kasim Reed, Shannon Reeves, Ron Rice Jr., Doug Rubin, Sharon Sayles Belton, Kurt Schmoke, Bakari T. Sellars, Cleveland Sellars Jr., Al Sharpton, Michael Steele, David Tuerck, Joan Wallace Benjamin, Tony West, Douglas Wilder, Dianne Wilkerson, Roger Wilkins, Andrew Young.

INTRODUCTION

1. "Busing in Boston: Looking Back at the History and Legacy," *Harvard Graduate School of Education News,* September 1, 2000.
2. Gwen Ifill and Bob Keeley, "16 Hurt in Wild Melee at South Boston High," *Boston Herald American,* October 3, 1980.

3. Yvonne Abraham and Francie Latour, "School Study Finds Deep Racial Divide," *Boston Globe,* September 2, 2003.

4. United States Census Bureau, *Baltimore, Maryland: Census 2000 Demographic Profile Highlights,* Summary File 1 and Summary File 3.

5. Richard Ben Cramer, "Can the Best Mayor Win?" *Esquire,* October 1984.

6. Michael Shultz and Michael Hymowitz, "Why Murphy Lost: Black Vote Was Split," *Evening Sun* (Baltimore), September 14, 1983.

7. Gwen Ifill, "Mayor Looks Ahead, Even Past 1987," *Evening Sun,* September 15, 1983.

8. "First Black Mayor of Baltimore Dies," *Baltimore Sun,* January 13, 2003.

9. United States Census Bureau, *Comparison of Population and Housing Characteristics from the 1990 and 1980 Censuses,* Summary Tape File 1A, May 14, 1991.

10. United States Census Bureau, *Median Household Income by County,* 1979, 1989.

11. United States Census Bureau, *Prince George's County, Maryland: Population and Housing Narrative Profile: 2005,* 1.

12. George J. Church, "What Does Jesse Really Want?" *Time,* April 16, 1984.

13. Gwen Ifill, "Jackson Visits Link Biblical, Political Issues," *Washington Post,* April 4, 1988.

14. "Jesse!?" *Time,* April 11, 1988.

15. Haynes Johnson and Gwen Ifill, "Jackson Stirs White Underdogs," *Washington Post,* April 2, 1988.

16. Gwen Ifill, "The Victor: Jackson Still Battling the Skeptics," *Washington Post,* March 27, 1988.

17. Gwen Ifill, "Letter from the Jackson Campaign," *Washington Post,* April 11, 1988.

18. Gwen Ifill, "The Victor: Jackson Still Battling the Skeptics," *Washington Post,* March 27, 1988.

19. Gwen Ifill, "Declaring He Can Still Win, Jackson Blasts Foes and Aides," *Washington Post,* April 29, 1988.

20. Pew Research Center, "Can You Trust What Polls Say About Obama's Electoral Prospects?" July 2, 2007.

21. V. Lance Tarrance Jr., "The Bradley Effect—Selective Memory," RealClearPolitics.com, October 13, 2008.

22. Barack Obama, interview by Katie Couric, *CBS Evening News,* November 3, 2008.

23. Pew Research Center, "Can You Trust What Polls Say About Obama's Electoral Prospects?" July 2, 2007.

24. King County executive Ron Sims, official bio, September 29, 2008.

25. David Bositis, "The Political Intermediation Process in the United States: How the American Party System Segregates African American Interests," paper presented at The Integration Debate: Competing Futures for American Cities Conference, John Marshall School of Law, September 5, 2008.

26. Frederic J. Frommer, "Black Conservatives Conflicted on Obama Campaign," Associated Press, June 14, 2008.

Chapter One: BREAKING THROUGH

1. George Horace Gallup Jr., *The Gallup Poll Book: Public Opinion 2003* (Lanham, Md.: Rowman and Littlefield, 2004).

2. *Newsweek* poll, July 6, 2007.

3. National exit polls, CNN, 2004, 2008.

4. Zoltan Hajnal, "Obama's Extra Hurdle?" *Wall Street Journal*, July 13, 2007.

5. Joan Vennochi, "Hoping for Change," *Boston Globe*, October 25, 2007.

6. Gallup Poll, August 6, 2007.

7. Center for the Study of the American Electorate, November 6, 2008.

8. Speech in Canandaigua, New York, August 4, 1857, in *Frederick Douglass: Selected Speeches and Writings*, edited by Philip S. Foner, abridged and adapted by Yuval Taylor (Chicago: Lawrence Hill Books, 1999), 367.

9. Kay Mills, *This Little Light of Mine: The Life of Fannie Lou Hamer* (Lexington: University Press of Kentucky, 2007).

10. Ibid., 315.

11. Pew Research Center and National Public Radio, "Optimism About Black Progress Declines," November 13, 2007.

12. Ibid.

13. Harris Poll, "Denzel Washington Remains America's Favorite Movie Star," January 15, 2008.

14. Institute for Research in African-American Studies, *The Political Orientation of Young African Americans* (New York: Columbia University, 2004).

15. Colin Powell, *My American Journey* (New York: Ballantine Books, 1996), 600.

16. Ibid., 601.

17. Francis X. Clines, "The Powell Decision," *New York Times*, November 9, 1995.

18. Jim VandeHei and Josh Kraushaar, "GOP Fails to Recruit Minorities," *Politico*, May 20, 2008.

19. William L. Clay, *Just Permanent Interests* (New York: Amistad Press, 1993), 222.

20. Kevin Merida, "The Steepest Climb," *Washington Post*, December 27, 2007.

21. Powell, *My American Journey*, 61.

22. Joint Center for Political and Economic Studies, *Changing of the Guard: Generational Differences Among Black Elected Officials* (Washington, D.C.: Joint Center for Political and Economic Studies, 2001).

23. National exit polls, CNN, 2008.

Chapter Two: THE GENERATIONAL DIVIDE

1. Rhonda Cook and Bill Rankin, "Former Atlanta Mayor Bill Campbell Goes Free Friday," *Atlanta Journal-Constitution,* October 23, 2008.

2. Geoff Mulvihill, "Newark's Mayor Booker Among Politicians Boosted by Obama's Rise," *Newsday,* March 16, 2008.

3. National exit polls, 2008.

4. Jonathan Kaufman, "Republicans Falter in Outreach to Blacks, Hispanics," *Wall Street Journal,* September 5, 2008.

5. Teresa Wiltz, "Obama Has Jay-Z on His iPod and the Moves to Prove It," *Washington Post,* April 19, 2008.

6. Michael Dawson, "He's Black and We're Proud," TheRoot.com, February 27, 2008.

7. The Center for Information and Research on Civic Learning and Engagement Youth Voter Turnout Study, www.civicyouth.org.

8. Pew Research Center exit poll analysis, "Inside Obama's Sweeping Victory," November 5, 2008.

9. John Lewis and Michael D'Orso, *Walking with the Wind* (New York: Simon and Schuster, 1998).

10. Andrew Jacobs, "Black Ohioans Backing Clinton Feel the Pressure to Switch," *New York Times,* February 28, 2008.

11. Cobb quoted in Shannon McCaffrey, "Black Voters Generations Apart," Associated Press, January 18, 2008; William Jelani Cobb, "Civil Rights Leaders Aloof from Obama," *Atlanta Journal-Constitution,* January 16, 2008.

12. Shailagh Murray, "For Black Superdelegates, Pressure to Back Obama," *Washington Post,* March 3, 2008.

13. Ben Smith, "Two Democrats Give Longtime Congressman Rare Reelection Fight," *Atlanta Journal-Constitution,* May 13, 2008.

14. ABC News election night coverage, November 4, 2008.

15. Logan Hill, "How I Made It: Spike Lee on 'Do the Right Thing,'" *New York,* April 7, 2008.

16. Nedra Pickler, "Obama Gets Big Welcome," Associated Press, May 8, 2008.

17. George E. Curry, "NAACP Process Rankles Its Board," *Philadelphia Inquirer,* June 9, 2008.

18. Eddie S. Glaude Jr., *In a Shade of Blue: Pragmatism and the Politics of Black America* (Chicago: University of Chicago Press, 2007).

19. Ronald S. Sullivan and Eddie S. Glaude Jr., "Rethinking the NAACP," *Washington Post,* March 21, 2007.

20. *The NewsHour with Jim Lehrer,* August 28, 2008, http://www.pbs.org/newshour/bb/politics/july-dec08/jjackson_08-28.html.

21. Michael Wilson, "In Alabama Politics, How New Kid Won the Bloc," *New York Times,* July 3, 2002.

22. "Reverend Dr. Calvin O. Butts III Endorses Hillary Clinton for President," press release, January 20, 2008, http://www.hillaryclinton.com/news/release/view/?id=5346.

23. Abigail Thernstrom and Stephan Thernstrom, "Is Race Out of the Race?" *Los Angeles Times,* March 2, 2008.

24. "Affirmative Action Opponents Turn in Petition Signatures," Associated Press, March 11, 2008; Peter Slevin, "Affirmative Action Foes Push Ballot Initiatives: Activists, with Eyes on November, Focus on Five States," *Washington Post,* March 26, 2008; Colleen Slevin, "Colorado Voters Reject Affirmative Action Ban," Associated Press, November 7, 2008.

25. Tim Murphy, "Powell's Kid Backs Obama," *New York,* March 24, 2008.

Chapter Three: BARACK OBAMA

1. Barack Obama, *Dreams from My Father* (New York: Three Rivers Press, 1995).

2. Ashley Parker, "What Would Obama Say," *New York Times,* January 20, 2008.

3. Audie Cornish, "Race Matters Emerge Ahead of South Carolina Primary," National Public Radio, January 14, 2008.

4. *Meet the Press,* NBC, January 13, 2008.

5. Obama conference call with reporters, January 13, 2008.

6. *Barack Obama Answers Your Questions,* MTV, November 2, 2008.

7. Glen Johnson and Dan Sewell, "Obama Tells NAACP Blacks Must Take Responsibility," Associated Press, July 14, 2008.

8. Obama speech in Selma, Alabama, text as delivered, *Chicago Sun-Times,* March 4, 2007.

9. "GOP Lawmaker Apologized for Referring to Obama as 'Boy,'" Associated Press, April 14, 2008.

10. Charles Babington, "Obama Braces for Race-Based Ads," Associated Press, June 23, 2008.

11. Joan Lowy, "Forum Sells 'Obama Waffles' with Racial Stereotype," Associated Press, September 13, 2008.

12. "Club President Who Sent Image of Obama Quits Post," Associated Press, October 23, 2008.

13. George Will, "Misstep in a Liberal Minefield," *Washington Post,* January 17, 2008.

14. Frank Ahrens, "BET Founder Johnson Defends His Recent Criticisms of Obama," *Washington Post,* January 15, 2008.

15. Alexandra Berzon and Michael Mishak, "Tackling Race to Negate It," *Las Vegas Sun,* September 10, 2008.

16. Barack Obama interview on *The NewsHour with Jim Lehrer,* March 17, 2008.

17. Transcript of Rev. Jeremiah Wright speech to National Press Club, *Los Angeles Times,* April 28, 2008.

18. Lynn Sweet, "Obama Woos Black—and White—Voters on Basis of What He Can Get Done," *Chicago Sun-Times,* January 24, 2008.

19. Barack Obama, T*he Audacity of Hope: Thoughts on Reclaiming the American Dream* (New York: Crown) p 233.

20. Barbara Jordan, Democratic National Convention keynote address, July 12, 1976.

21. Barack Obama, victory speech after South Carolina primary, *New York Times,* January 26, 2008.

22. Charles Kaiser, "Full Court Press," Radar.com, February 13, 2008.

23. NBC News/*Wall Street Journal* poll, October 2008.

24. Ben Smith, "How Obama Quietly Targets Blacks," *Politico,* October 7, 2008.

Chapter Four: THE RACE-GENDER CLASH

1. Donna Brazile, St. John's University keynote speech, September 27, 2008.

2. Roger Simon, "Jackson to Dems: Play Nice," *Politico,* February 20, 2008.

3. Annette John-Hall, "Black Women's Clinton Problem," *Philadelphia Inquirer,* March 7, 2008.

4. Niall Stanage, "Stumping for Clinton, Steinem Says McCain's POW Cred Is Overrated," *New York Observer,* March 2, 2008.

5. John Gibson, "The Real Deal," February 26, 2008, www.foxnews.com/radio/johngibsonradio.

6. "Playing the Gender Card," Election 2008 in Brief, University of Southern California, March 7, 2008, http://election2008.usc.edu/2008/03/clinton-gender.html.

7. Robin Morgan e-mail, forwarded to author February 8, 2008.

8. *Washington Post*/ABC News poll, September 5–7, 2008.

9. *This Week with George Stephanopoulos,* ABC, September 14, 2008.

10. National exit polls, *New York Times,* November 4, 2008.

11. David Paul Kuhn, "White Women Cold Toward Obama," *Politico,* May 30, 2008.

12. Jonathan Kaufman, "White Men Hold Key for Democrats," *Wall Street Journal,* February 19, 2008.

13. Charles Babington, "Clinton Says Misogyny's Role in Campaign Is Unclear," Associated Press, April 10, 2008.

14. WKYT Kentucky poll, May 7–9, 2008.

15. "Obama Apologizes for Calling TV Reporter 'Sweetie,'" *Newsday,* May 15, 2008.

16. Lois Romano, "Clinton Puts Up a New Fight," *Washington Post,* May 20, 2008.

17. South Carolina primary exit poll, CBS News, January 26, 2008.

18. Pennsylvania primary exit poll, *New York Times,* April 22, 2008.

19. Melissa Harris-Lacewell, "Hillary's Scarlett O'Hara Act," TheRoot.com, February 8, 2008.

20. Alice Walker, "Lest We Forget: An Open Letter to My Sisters Who Are Brave," TheRoot.com, March 27, 2008.

21. Tim Wise, "Your Whiteness Is Showing," TimWise.org, June 6, 2008.

22. Kelly Brewington, "A New Type of African American Politician," *Baltimore Sun,* February 3, 2008.

23. *New York Times*/CBS News poll, February 26, 2008.

24. Sara Kugler, "Clinton, in Mississippi, Again Raises Possibility of Ticket with Obama," Associated Press, March 7, 2008.

25. Peter Wallsten, "It's One Issue That Remains a Focus," *Los Angeles Times,* March 13, 2008.

26. Betsy Reed, "Race to the Bottom," *Nation,* May 19, 2008.

27. Gregory S. Parks and Jeffery J. Rachlinksi, "A Better Metric: The Role of Unconscious Race and Gender Bias in the 2008 Presidential Election," Cornell Legal Studies Research Paper No. 08-007, March 4, 2008.

28. *Nightline,* ABC, February 28, 2008.

29. "Women Win the Right to Vote," *Historical Gazette* (Portland, Ore.) vol. 3, no. 5 (1995), http://www.aracnet.com/~histgaz/hgv3n5.htm.

30. Joan Vennochi, "Still, No Satisfaction for Clinton's Sisterhood," *Boston Globe,* April 17, 2008.

31. *Wall Street Journal*/NBC News poll, June 6, 2009.

32. Frank Rich, "Angry Clinton Women ♥ McCain?" *New York Times,* June 15, 2008.

33. Gerda Lerner, *Black Women in White America* (New York: Vintage Books, 1973), 356.

34. "Women of Color in Elective Office 2008," Center for American Women in Politics fact sheet.

35. Madeleine M. Kunin, *Pearls, Politics and Power* (White River Junction, Vt.: Chelsea Green Publishing, 2008), 151.

36. Sophia Nelson, "Black. Female. Accomplished. Attacked," *Washington Post,* July 20, 2008.

37. Jennifer L. Lawless and Richard L. Fox, "Why Are Women Still Not Running for Public Office?" Issues in Governance Studies no. 16, Brookings Institution, Washington, D.C., May 2008.

38. Kelsey Volkmann and Sara Michael, "Four Black Women Hold Senior Posts," Examiner.com, November 11, 2007.

39. Sheila Dixon, inaugural address, *Baltimore Sun,* December 5, 2007.

40. Tanika White, "Mayor Sparkles at Diversity Gala," *Baltimore Sun,* December 5, 2007.

Chapter Five: ARTUR DAVIS

1. Jay Reeves, "Davis Is Son of a Schoolteacher," Associated Press, June 25, 2002.

2. Jay Reeves, "Five Term Ala. Congressman Loses," Associated Press, June 26, 2002.

3. Mary Orndorff, "Congressional Runoffs' Price Tag," *Birmingham News,* July 17, 2002.

4. Laura Whittington, "Ala. Races Nasty at Finish," *Roll Call,* June 20, 2002.

5. Michael Wilson, "In Alabama Politics, How New Kid Won the Bloc," *New York Times,* July 3, 2002.

6. Jonathan Allen, "Alabama Rep. Hilliard Falls to Challenger Davis," *Congressional Quarterly Daily Monitor,* June 26, 2002.

7. Barry Saunders, "Troubling Tactic in Black vs. Black Races," *Raleigh News and Observer,* June 8, 2002.

8. Toby Harnden, "Dream Coming True for Gifted Black Politician," *London Daily Telegraph,* June 25, 2002.

9. Mary Orndorff, "Sharpton Begins Blitz for Hilliard," *Birmingham News,* June 21, 2002.

10. Juliet Eilperin, "Davis Ousts Hilliard in Alabama Runoff," *Washington Post,* June 26, 2002.

11. Jeffrey McMurray, "Hilliard: Runoff Loss Just the Beginning of Black, Jewish Conflict," Associated Press, June 28, 2002.

12. National 2008 exit polls, *New York Times,* November 4, 2008.

13. Dana Beyerle, "Davis May Face Uphill Battle," *Gadsden* (Ala.) *Times,* November 9, 2008.

14. Nicole Duran, "The New Kid on the Block," *Campaigns and Elections,* June 1, 2007.

15. *This Week with George Stephanopoulos,* ABC, April 27, 2008.

16. Matt Bai, "Is Obama the End of Black Politics?" *New York Times Magazine,* August 10, 2008.

17. Mary Orndorff, "Davis Finds Friends on Hilliard's DC Turf," *Birmingham News,* September 14, 2002.

18. Rick Harmon, "Pollster Methods Flawed, Obama Supporters Believe," *Montgomery Advertiser,* January 30, 2008.

19. Eddie Land, "Will This Be Breakthrough Year in Alabama as Well?" *Birmingham News,* June 8, 2008.

20. Charles J. Dean, "The Rise and Stall of Politico Joe Reed," *Birmingham News,* June 22, 2008.

21. Ibid.

22. Jessica Brady, "Sweet Home Alabama," *Roll Call,* May 22, 2008.

23. Hastings Wyman, "Artur Davis, Barack Obama and the Alabama Governorship," *Southern Political Report,* June 18, 2008.

24. Anzalone-Lizst Research, Alabama statewide trend polling presentation July 14–17, 2008.

25. Larry Copeland, "Southern Towns Shrink, Economic Woes Grow," *USA Today,* June 17, 2008.

26. Michael Melia, "Davis, One of Youngest New Members, Gets Adjusted to Congress," States News Service, November 13, 2002.

27. Jonetta Rose Barras, "Shifting Ground," *Blueprint,* April 15, 2003.

28. House Judiciary Committee hearing, October 30, 2007, video and transcript available at http://speaker.house.gov/blog/?p=893.

29. Artur Davis, "Results Matter," *Blueprint,* January 4, 2007.

30. Editorial, "Obama Win a Plus for Artur Davis," *Birmingham News,* January 6, 2008.

31. Charles J. Dean, "Obama Victory Enhances Davis," *Birmingham News,* February 8, 2008.

32. "Catfish Disaster Funds Distributed," WSFA-TV (Montgomery, Ala.), February 21, 2008.

33. Rick Harmon, "Alabamians Need to Help Less Fortunate, Congressman Says," *Montgomery Advertiser,* March 26, 2008.

34. "Not Just About Obama," *Press Register* (Mobile, Ala.), February 11, 2008.

35. Bobby Matthews, "Congressman Holds Town Hall Meeting," *Demopolis* (Ala.) *Times,* May 27, 2008.

Chapter Six: LEGACY POLITICS

1. Jesse Jackson Sr., "Most Democratic Candidates Are Ignoring African Americans," *Chicago Sun-Times,* November 27, 2007.

2. Jesse Jackson Jr., "Jesse Jr. to Jesse Sr.: You're Wrong on Obama, Dad," *Chicago Sun-Times,* December 3, 2007.

3. Don Frederick, "Top of the Ticket," *Los Angeles Times,* January 18, 2008.

4. "Remarks by Rep. Jesse Jackson, Jr. (D-IL) at the 2008 Democratic National Convention," Federal News Service, August 25, 2008.

5. Danny Hakim, "Patterson's Reflections on Projecting Strength Despite the Obstacles," *New York Times,* March 11, 2008.

6. Michael Cooper and Mike McIntire, "Studying the Footprints of a Governor-to-Be," *New York Times,* March 16, 2008.

7. Tom Humphrey, "Middle or First Name?" *Knoxville News,* March 30, 2008.

8. Ibid.

9. William L. Clay, *Just Permanent Interests: Black Americans in Congress* (Amistad Press, 1992).

10. Richard Locker, "Judge Sentences John Ford to Another 14 Years in Prison," *Memphis Commercial Appeal,* September 29, 2008.

11. "A Rude Start to Jake Ford's Campaign," *Memphis Commercial Appeal,* April 5, 2008.

12. Gwen Ifill, "Candidates Battle to Fill Frist's Senate Seat," *The NewsHour with Jim Lehrer,* October 6, 2006.

13. Daniel Libit, "Why Poll Numbers Skewed: Race Effect?" *Politico,* May 16, 2008.

14. Jessica Brady, "Sweet Home Alabama," *Roll Call,* May 22, 2008.

15. National exit polls, CNN, 2006.

16. Harold Ford Jr., speech, Clinton School of Public Service, University of Arkansas, September 24, 2007.

17. Ibid.

18. Harold Ford Jr., "Go Meet Them, Senator," *Newsweek,* June 2, 2008.

19. *The Charlie Rose Show,* PBS, February 4, 2008.

20. Chris Haliskoe, "Congressman Ford Speaks at Open VISIONS," *Fairfield Mirror,* February 21, 2008.

21. Clint Brewer, "Harold Ford Jr.'s Complicated Future," *City Paper* (Nashville, Tenn.), April 30, 2008.

22. Ford, speech, Clinton School of Public Service.

23. William L. Clay, *Just Permanent Interests* (New York: Amistad Press, 1992).

24. Jonathan Weisman and Matthew Mosk, "Party Fears Racial Divide," *Washington Post,* April 26, 2008.

25. Royse, "Affirmative Action Sit-In Ends."

26. Adam C. Smith, "Princes of Politics Have a Lot in Common," *St. Petersburg Times,* July 14, 2002.

27. David Royse, "Affirmative Action Sit-In Ends," Associated Press, January 20, 2000.

28. Ellen January Kleineman, "Mayor–Super Delegate Endorses Obama," *Cleveland Plain Dealer,* February 26, 2008.

29. Jonathan Casiano, "Black Politicians' Legacies Inspire Sons," *Star-Ledger* (Newark, N.J.), March 20, 2006.

30. Kathy Barks Hoffman, "Obama Can't Be Too Cozy with Detroit Mayor," Associated Press, June 1, 2008.

Chapter Seven: CORY BOOKER

1. Jonathan Schuppe, "TV Show Based on Newark Shootings Troubles Victims' Families," *Star-Ledger* (Newark, N.J.), December 13, 2007.

2. Janet Frankston Lorin, "Shootings Renew Mayor's Sense of Purpose," Associated Press, August 18, 2007.

3. Brad Parks, "Booker Orders Flags Flown at Half-Staff Through July 17," *Star-Ledger*, July 12, 2007.

4. Mark DiIonno, "So Their Deaths Won't Be in Vain," *Star-Ledger*, August 12, 2007.

5. Andrew Jacobs, "Booker Comes Under Siege After Bloodshed," *New York Times*, August 7, 2007.

6. Andrew Jacobs, "A Pivotal Moment for Booker," *New York Times*, August 12, 2007.

7. Cory Booker, Harvard Class Day speech, June 4, 2008.

8. Katie Wang and Claire Heininger, "Sharpe James Shows; Says He'd Make a Good Goalie," *Star-Ledger*, October 25, 2007.

9. Damien Cave, "Pledging to Revive Newark and Reduce Crime, a New Mayor Goes to Work," *New York Times*, July 2, 2006.

10. Andrew Jacobs, "Battling the Old Guard and the Rumor Mill," *New York Times*, July 3, 2007.

11. Jeffery C. Mays, "Into the Penalty Box for 'Ignorance': ESPN's Melrose on the ice for disparaging Newark," *Star-Ledger*, November 7, 2007.

12. Jonathan D. Tepperman, "Complicating the Race," *New York Times*, April 28, 2002.

13. Walter Dawkins, "Cory Booker Comes Home to Applause," *Record*, June 19, 2007.

14. Susan Headden, "The Guy in the Thick of It," *U.S. News & World Report*, April 16, 2006.

15. Andrew Jacobs, "On the Streets and in the Police Stations," *New York Times*, December 29, 2007.

16. Cory Booker, Harvard Class Day speech, June 4, 2008.

17. Katie Wang, "Obama Campaign Taps N.J. Director," *Star-Ledger*, August 21, 2008.

18. Cory Booker, "The Reformer," *Esquire*, December 2002.

19. Headden, "The Guy in the Thick of It."

20. Jeffery C. Mays, "Newark's Brick Towers Comes Down Today," *Star-Ledger*, December 12, 2007.

21. Andrew Jacobs, "Cheers in Newark for a Housing Project's Downfall," *New York Times*, December 13, 2007.

22. Howard Witt, "A Civil Rights Phenomenon," *Star-Ledger*, September 20, 2007.

23. Booker, "The Reformer."

24. City of Newark 100-Day-Plan Report, October 2006.

25. Jonathan Schuppe, "Newark Applauds Big Drop in Crime," *Star-Ledger,* July 7, 2007.

26. Spencer E. Ante, "Newark and the Future of Crime Fighting," *BusinessWeek,* August 25, 2008.

27. Anthony Faiola, "Newark's Revival: It's No Joke," *Washington Post,* December 31, 2007.

28. Editorial, "Newark's Upbeat Numbers," *Star-Ledger,* August 30, 2007.

29. Cory Booker, Harvard Class Day speech, June 4, 2008.

30. Text of teleconference between former New Jersey governors Brendan Byrne and Tom Kean, "Blame the Whole City for Street Violence," *Star-Ledger,* August 12, 2007.

31. U.S. Census Bureau, 2006 American Community Survey.

32. Andrew Jacobs, "Seeking the Key to Employment for Ex-Cons," *New York Times,* April 27, 2008.

33. Louise Roug, "New Jersey Finds Itself an Unlikely Political Battleground," *Los Angeles Times,* February 4, 2008.

34. Ibid.

35. Jeffery C. Mays and Katie Wang, "Booker, Adubato Seeking a Truce," *Star-Ledger,* February 17, 2008.

36. Jeffery C. Mays, "Booker Sees Slate of District Leaders Fall Short," *Star-Ledger,* June 5, 2008.

37. Jeffery C. Mays and Katie Wang, "Adubato Stepping Down as Newark Center Head," *Star-Ledger,* August 29, 2008.

38. Katie Wang, "Newark Council, Mayor Booker at Odds over Police Department," *Star-Ledger,* April 1, 2008.

39. Jonathan Schuppe and Jeffery C. Mays, "Booker to Appoint Acting Chief to the Post," *Star-Ledger,* August 14, 2007.

40. Andrew Jacobs, "Battling the Old Guard and the Rumor Mill," *New York Times,* July 3, 2007.

41. Jeffery C. Mays and Jonathan Schuppe, "A Break in Form in Newark Police Appointment," *Star-Ledger,* August 19, 2007.

42. Jeffery C. Mays and Katie Wang, "Booker Sorry for Offensive Remarks—Housing Leader's Survivors Outraged," *Star-Ledger,* August 3, 2007.

43. Jeffery C. Mays and Katie Wang, "For Booker, Often-Told Tales Turn into Trouble," *Star Ledger,* August 6, 2007.

44. Joan Whitlow, "Verdict Not Yet in on Booker's First Year in Office," *Star-Ledger,* July 1, 2007.

45. Jeffery C. Mays, "For Tiki, Shaq and Others, Newark's a Hot Investment," *Star Ledger,* December 7, 2007.

46. Jeffery C. Mays and Katie Wang, "Plan to Aid Ex-cons Stumbles," *Star-Ledger,* December 2, 2007.

47. Scott Raab, "The Battle of Newark, Starring Cory Booker," *Esquire,* July 2008.

48. Booker letter to Mark Warren, *Esquire* editor, June 11, 2008.

49. Katie Wang and Jeffery C. Mays, "Shootings Refocused Booker on Mission," *Star-Ledger,* August 28, 2007.

50. Tom Moran, "In Jersey, Politics Is a Game for Everyone," *Star-Ledger,* January 2, 2008.

Chapter Eight: THE POLITICS OF IDENTITY

1. Thomas Dyja, *Walter White: The Dilemma of Black Identity in America* (Ivan R. Dee, 2008).

2. Edward W. Brooke, *Bridging the Divide: My Life* (Rutgers University Press, 2007).

3. Michael Weisskopf, "Obama: How He Learned to Win," *Time,* May 8, 2008.

4. Barack Obama, *The Audacity of Hope* (New York: Crown, 2006).

5. David Mendell, *Obama: From Promise to Power* (New York: Amistad Press, 2007), 138.

6. Leonard Pitts Jr., "Concentrate on Obama's Record, Not His Color," *Miami Herald,* August 15, 2007.

7. Matt Bai, "Working for the Working Class Vote," *New York Times Magazine,* October 19, 2008.

8. *Real Sports with Bryant Gumbel,* HBO, April 5, 2008.

9. Bomani Armah, "Okay, Barack. Now Show 'Em Your White Side," *Washington Post,* March 23, 2008.

10. Alec MacGillis, "The Obamas Are Tired of the Blackness Question," *Washington Post,* August 14, 2007.

11. Christi Parsons, Bruce Japsen, and Bob Secter, "Barack's Rock," *Chicago Tribune,* April 22, 2007.

12. Barack Obama, *Dreams from My Father* (New York: Three Rivers Press, 2004).

13. Dave Davies, "Leading Black Clergy Group Backing Obama," *Philadelphia Daily News,* March 13, 2008.

14. Mark Warren, "Cracking the Racial Code," *Esquire,* June 2008.

15. Linda B. Blackford, "Will Obama Fight for Rural Voters?" *Lexington Herald Leader,* May 25, 2008.

16. Andrew Greeley, "Obama vs. McCain: Race Permeates Society," *Chicago Sun-Times,* June 11, 2008.

17. David Goldstein, "Sebelius Says GOP Will Try to Use Obama's Race to 'Frighten' Voters," *Kansas City Star,* June 26, 2008.

18. Adam Nagourney, "For Obama, a Struggle to Win over Key Blocs," *New York Times,* April 24, 2008.

19. *An Evening with Diahann Carroll,* PBS, May 7, 2005.

20. Abdon M. Pallasch, "Obama Rips Nader's 'Talking White,'" *Chicago Sun-Times*, June 26, 2008.

21. Mireya Navarro, "Who Are We? New Dialogue on Mixed Race," *New York Times*, March 31, 2008.

22. Mark J. Bonamo, "Booker Honors History as He Makes It," *Hackensack Chronicle*, February 20, 2008.

23. Rachel Kapochunas, "Black Caucus Members Endorse Challenger to White Memphis Incumbent," CQ Today Online News, April 17, 2008.

24. Pamela Perkins, "Harold Sr., Jr. Speak Out Against Family Members," *Memphis Commercial Appeal*, April 6, 2008.

25. Trey Popp, "The Man Who Would Never Be Mayor," *Pennsylvania Gazette*, January/February 2008.

26. Karen Tumulty, "Obama's Bitter Lesson," *Time*, April 17, 2008.

27. Charles J. Dean, "Obama Victory Enhances Davis," *Birmingham News*, February 9, 2008.

28. Mike Allen and John F. Harris, "Obama Supported by Wilder," *Politico*, August 28, 2007.

29. Beth Fouhy, "Obama Says Clinton Criticism Not Racially Motivated," Associated Press, April 15, 2008.

30. "Bill Clinton Says Obama Campaign Played 'Race Card' on Him," *Los Angeles Times*, April 23, 2008.

31. Editorial, "Mr. Obama's Profile in Courage," *New York Times*, March 19, 2008.

32. Jim Belshaw, "Obama's Offering of Grown-up Words Welcome," *Albuquerque Journal*, March 23, 2008.

33. Navarro, "Who Are We?"

34. Nicholas Kralev, "Rice Hits U.S. 'Birth Defect,'" *Washington Times*, March 28, 2008.

35. Marcus Mabry, *Twice as Good: Condoleezza Rice and Her Path to Power* (New York: Modern Times, 2007).

36. Associated Press, "Congressman Emanuel Cleaver: Whites Like 'Articulate' Barack Obama," *Chicago Sun-Times*, April 1, 2008.

37. ABC News/*USA Today*/Columbia University Poll, "Blacks, Politics, and Society," September 23, 2008.

Chapter Nine: DEVAL PATRICK

1. Andrea Estes and Frank Phillips, "New Healey Ad Again Links Patrick, LaGuer," *Boston Globe*, October 6, 2006.

2. Frank Phillips, "'Inmates' Take Protests to Patrick," *Boston Globe*, October 21, 2006.

3. Wil Haygood, "A Long Way from Home," *Washington Post,* October 25, 2006.

4. Lynne Duke, "Civil Rights Is Familiar Terrain for Clinton's Justice Choice," *Washington Post,* February 14, 1994.

5. Wil Haygood, "Partners in Power," *Boston Globe,* September 23, 1993.

6. Ibid.

7. Pierre Thomas, "Deval Patrick and the 'Great Moral Imperative,'" *Washington Post,* October 26, 1994.

8. Haygood, "Partners in Power."

9. Chaz Firestone, "Deval Patrick on the Jena Six and Gay Marriage," *Brown Daily Herald,* October 3, 2007.

10. Lani Guinier, *Lift Every Voice* (New York: Simon and Schuster, 1998), 204.

11. Ibid., 54.

12. Pierre Thomas, "Justice Dept. Civil Rights Chief Pledges Activism," *Washington Post,* April 15, 1994.

13. Pierre Thomas, "Deval Patrick and the 'Great Moral Imperative,'" *Washington Post,* October 26, 1994.

14. Sharon Walsh, "Deval Patrick to Head Texaco Task Force," *Washington Post,* June 24, 1997.

15. Brian C. Mooney, "Patrick's Path from Courtroom to Boardroom," *Boston Globe,* August 13, 2006.

16. Deval Patrick, Profile of Barack Obama in "Leaders and Revolutionaries" section, *Time,* April 29, 2008.

17. Martha T. Moore, "Obama Fights to Overcome View He's Inexperienced," *USA Today,* October 25, 2007.

18. Frank Phillips, "Reilly Leads, Patrick Gains in New Poll," *Boston Globe,* March 12, 2006.

19. Laura Kirtsy, "With Love and Pride, Governor Deval Patrick's Daughter Comes Out Publicly," *Bay Windows,* June 12, 2008; "Mass Gov. Marches with Daughter in Gay Pride Parade," Associated Press, June 14, 2008.

20. Scot Helman, "Patrick Faces Challenge in Black Community," *Boston Globe,* January 15, 2006.

21. Matt Viser, Frank Philips, and Andrew Ryan, "Senate Asks Wilkerson to Immediately Resign," *Boston Globe,* October 3, 2008.

22. Transcript of Deval Patrick's acceptance address, *Boston Globe,* November 7, 2006.

23. Lisa Wangsness, "Higher Expectations," *Boston Globe,* October 17, 2007.

24. Glen Johnson, "Patrick Upgrades State Vehicle from Ford to Cadillac," Associated Press, February 16, 2007.

25. HubPolitics.com; CoupeDeval.com, February 16, 2007.

26. Willie Brown, *Basic Brown: My Life and Our Times* (New York: Simon and Schuster, 2008), 284.

27. Governor's news release, February 21, 2007.

28. Frank Phillips and Andrea Estes, "Patrick to Repay Taxpayers for Décor," *Boston Globe,* February 21, 2007.

29. Frank Phillips, "Patrick Says He Erred in Call to Firm," *Boston Globe,* March 7, 2007.

30. Lisa Wangsness, "Patrick Urges Iowa to Put Hope in Obama," *Boston Globe,* December 30, 2007.

31. Ken Maguire, "Obama Fashions Playbook in Part on Patrick's Successful Campaign," Associated Press, January 12, 2008.

32. Lisa Wangsness, "Patrick to Target Obama Doubters," *Boston Globe,* January 12, 2008.

33. Deval Patrick, *Boston Globe,* January 5, 2008.

34. John J. Monahan, "Patrick to Stump Campaign Trail for Obama," *Worcester Telegram and Gazette,* December 15, 2007.

35. Matt Viser, "DiMasi Slams Obama, Patrick," *Boston Globe,* January 23, 2008.

36. Charles Cheippo and Jim Stergios, "The Politics of Hope," *Weekly Standard,* April 14, 2008.

37. Tammy Daniels, "Patrick Describes Her Fall and Rise," iBerkshires.com, September 10, 2008.

38. Ken Maguire, "Patrick Cites Accomplishments," Associated Press, December 19, 2007.

39. Matt Viser, "Patrick to Cut 1,000 Jobs from State Payroll," *Boston Globe,* October 16, 2008.

40. Robert Gavin, "Governor Faces Big Test in Jobs Plan," *Boston Globe,* March 7, 2008.

41. Transcript, "State of the Commonwealth Address," January 24, 2008.

42. Patrick testimony to the Joint Legislative Committee on Bonding, Capital Expenditures, and State Assets, December 18, 2007.

43. "Patrick: DiMasi 'Fix' in Early Against Casino Bill," Associated Press, March 24, 2008.

44. Andrea Estes, "53% in Poll Back Patrick Casinos Plan," *Boston Globe,* September 30, 2007.

45. Matt Visser, "Patrick Fights Odds on Casinos," *Boston Globe,* March 19, 2008.

46. "Patrick: DiMasi 'Fix' in Early Against Casino Bill."

47. Andrea Estes and Frank Phillips, "Liberal Gaming Critics Feel Betrayed by Patrick Plan," *Boston Globe,* September 29, 2007.

48. Steve Bailey, "Governor Slots?" *Boston Globe,* September 14, 2007.

49. Letter to the editor from John Harding of Westwood, Mass., *Boston Globe,* January 16, 2008.

50. Frank Phillips and Matt Viser, "How Leaders Warmed a State House Chill," *Boston Globe,* August 22, 2008.

51. Matt Visser, "Patrick Is in a Bind with His Base," *Boston Globe,* April 2, 2008.

52. Howie Carr, "Bio Hazard: Gov's Book Exposes Him as an Author-tunist," *Boston Herald,* March 8, 2008.

53. Rasmussen Reports, April 23, 2008.

54. Dean Barnett, "Checking in on Obama's Role Model," *Weekly Standard,* April 1, 2008.

55. Jon Keller, "President Obama: The Preview?" *Wall Street Journal,* May 3, 2008.

56. Michael Levenson, "Study of Traffic Stops Is Derailed," *Boston Globe,* September 9, 2007.

57. Chaz Firestone, "Deval Patrick on the Jena Six and Gay Marriage," *Brown Daily Herald,* October 3, 2007.

58. Steve Bailey, "Deval's Bad Timing," *Boston Globe,* January 23, 2008.

59. "Governor Patrick's First Year," editorial, *Boston Globe,* January 4, 2008.

Chapter Ten: THE NEXT WAVE

1. "The State of the Black Union 2006," OnePeoplesProject.com, March 5, 2006.

2. Nina Martin, "Why Kamala Matters," *San Francisco Magazine,* August 2007.

3. Carla Marinucci, "Can Obama Do for U.S. Politics What Tiger Woods Did for Golf?" *San Francisco Chronicle,* November 13, 2007.

4. Joe Garofoli, "Obama Power Broker New Face of Black Politics," *San Francisco Chronicle,* March 1, 2008.

5. Samantha Young, "LA Democrat Sworn In as First Black Woman to Lead Assembly," Associated Press, May 13, 2008.

6. Willie Brown, *Basic Brown: My Life and Our Times* (New York: Simon and Schuster, 2008), 47.

7. George Skelton, "Gerrymandering a Key Culprit in California Budget Mess," *Los Angeles Times,* August 28, 2008.

8. Nancy Vogel, "Karen Bass Sworn In as California Assembly Speaker," *Los Angeles Times,* May 14, 2008.

9. Nancy Vogel, "Next Speaker Enjoys Broad Support," *Los Angeles Times,* March 2, 2008.

10. Jim Wooten, "Genarlow Gambled and Lost," *Atlanta Journal-Constitution,* June 12, 2007.

11. Associated Press, "Louisiana Democrat Wins House Runoff, Despite Bribery Scandal," *USA Today,* December 10, 2006.

12. Steve Scully, "Philly's Cop Beating, No Rodney King," Time.com, May 14, 2008.

13. Trey Popp, "The Man Who Would Never Be Mayor," *Pennsylvania Gazette,* January/February 2008.

14. Ibid.

15. Jon Hurdle, "Philadelphia Making Cuts to Help Close a Budget Gap," *New York Times,* November 7, 2008.

16. John Merrow, "DC School Chancellor Targets Teachers, Angering Union," *The NewsHour with Jim Lehrer,* PBS, September 18, 2008.

17. John Merrow, "Schools Chief Comes Under Fire," *The NewsHour with Jim Lehrer,* PBS, February 7, 2008.

18. Marc Fisher, "Funny, Haven't DC Voters Heard This Before?" WashingtonPost. com, January 8, 2008.

19. Courtland Milloy, "In City Brimming with Black Talent, Fenty's Cabinet Lacks Color," *Washington Post,* June 20, 2007.

20. Brian Meyer, "Mayor Brown Says Buffalo Is 'Turning a Corner' in Fight Against Poverty," *Buffalo News,* August 31, 2007.

CONCLUSION

1. Philip Dray, *Capitol Men* (New York: Houghton Mifflin, 2008), x.

2. Kwame Anthony Appiah and Henry Louis Gates Jr., eds., *Africana: The Encyclopedia of the African and African American Experience* (New York: Basic Books, 1999).

3. William L. Clay, *Just Permanent Interests* (New York: Amistad Press, 1992), 77.

4. David Bositis, national opinion poll, Joint Center for Political and Economic Studies, October 21, 2008.

5. Andrew Kohut, "High Marks for Campaign, a High Bar for Obama," Pew Research Center for the People and the Press, November 13, 2008.

6. David A. Bositis, "Blacks and the 2008 Elections: A Preliminary Analysis," November 13, 2008.

AFTERWORD TO THE ANCHOR BOOKS EDITION

1. Sam Roberts, "2008 Surge in Black Voters Nearly Erased Racial Gap," *New York Times,* July 20, 2009.

2. Matt Viser and Andrew Ryan, "Gov. Patrick: Arrest 'Every Black Man's Nightmare,'" *Boston Globe,* July 23, 2009.

3. Zachary Roth, "Conservative Activist Forwards Racist Pic Showing Obama as Witch Doctor," Talking Points Memo, July 23, 2009,

http://tpmmuckraker.talkingpointsmemo.com/2009/07/conservative_activist_forwards_racist_pic_showing.php?ref=fpa.

4. David Squires, "Rev. Jeremiah Wright Says 'Jews' Are Keeping Him from President Obama," *The Daily Press*, June 10, 2009.

5. Patricia Murphy, "Can Artur Davis Win in Alabama?" *Politics Daily*, July 10, 2009.

6. Juliana Barbassa, "Immigrant Law Loopholes Threaten S.F. Mayor's Bid," Associated Press, June 27, 2009.

7. Kamala Harris, "San Francisco D.A.: 'Back on Track' Saves Money and Reduces Crime," *Los Angeles Times*, June 26, 2009.

8. Amy Goodman, *Democracy Now!* July 22, 2009.

9. Frank Phillips and Matt Viser, "Patrick Support Plummets, Poll Finds," *Boston Globe*, July 26, 2009.

10. Matt Viser and Andrea Estes, "Politicians Ready to Party Like It's 1990," *Boston Globe*, July 9, 2009.

11. Sean Gregory, "Cory Booker Is (Still) Optimistic That He Can Save Newark," *Time*, July 27, 2009.

12. Darlene Superville, "Obama Heads to Arlington Cemetery for Memorial Day," Associated Press, May 25, 2009.

13. "Remarks by Eric Holder at the NAACP's Clarence M. Mitchell Jr. Memorial Lecture Luncheon," July 13, 2009.

14. Ed Lavandera, "Black Mayor of Mississippi Town Brings 'Atomic Bomb of Change,'" CNN.com, June 1, 2009.

ACKNOWLEDGMENTS

Nobody believes me now, but when Doubleday first approached me to write a book about Barack Obama, on the off chance that he might become America's first black president, I turned them down. Only two years ago, the idea still seemed just short of preposterous.

But thanks to Janet Hill, I got the chance to dig even deeper than that and write the book I've been carrying around in my head all these years. Neither she nor Christian Nwachukwu was with the project at its end, but they were there at the beginning, which made all the difference.

I could not have done it without the steadfast encouragement of my editor, Gerald Howard, the loyalty of my book agent, Robert Barnett—who has been after me for a decade to write a book—or the patience of my colleagues at *The NewsHour with Jim Lehrer* and *Washington Week*. I am not quite sure how I managed to write this book during a momentous election year while keeping two jobs going, but I think it had something to do with having the wit to be employed by PBS.

I owe a special debt to all of my author friends who held my hand on this maiden voyage into long-form writing, and on whose work mine came to rely.

Colette Rhoney, my friend and researcher, was a happy find. She knows more about politics in her pinky finger than most do in their entire bodies. This project would have been completely impossible without her. Kathryn Lynch, my assistant producer and calendar juggler, was always cheerful, efficient, and fast. Roberto Ifill brought his economist's eye and artist's gift to reading and rereading disjointed chapters, helping to craft them into a workable whole.

At a critical time, during the run-up to the vice presidential debate, a host of angels descended on me to tend to a broken ankle and keep me on track in life and in work. Michele Norris; Desiree Hicks; Athelia Knight; Maria Ifill Philip; Sandra and Journey Gregg; Broderick, Aja, and Norris Johnson—I love you all.

Most of all, however, I have to thank the lawmakers, agitators, and academics who have kept me guessing about the direction our nation will take. Without a vibrant and ever-changing national political debate, I would not have a story to tell.

INDEX

43, 44, 47–48; Orangeburg Massacre, 217; politics and, 19–20; reenactment of "Bloody Sunday," 58; role of women and, 84–85; Selma-to-Montgomery march, 1965, 9, 21, 41, 58, 101; violence against leaders, 195

Clarke, Yvette, 42

Clay, William Lacy, Jr., 40, 125–28, 167

Clay, William Lacy, Sr., 24, 125–28

Cleaver, Emanuel, II, 176–77

Cleaver, Kathleen, 217

Cleveland, Ohio, 114, 223, 227

Clinton, Bill, 8, 18, 35, 52, 55, 79, 103, 117, 119, 124, 165–66, 173, 184, 185, 192; black loyalty to, 34, 39, 40, 41–42, 131; South Carolina gaffes, 97, 130

Clinton, Hillary, 84, 117, 186; Al Sharpton and, 26; black endorsements, 34, 39, 40, 41, 42, 47, 49–50, 59, 88, 94, 100, 118–19, 130, 145, 167, 172, 177, 222, 224, 234; debates with Obama, 55–56, 68; defeat of, effect, 82; gender issues, 40, 55, 56, 61, 70–83, 167; Kennedy supporters, 113; male voters for, 79; Obama and, 58, 212; primaries, 7, 52, 64, 75–76, 77, 79, 96–97, 98, 172, 194, 195; Vernon Jordan and, 31

Clyburn, Jim, 218

Clyburn, William, 40

Coalition politics, 30, 181, 215, 242

Cobb, Sue Bell, 259

Cobb, William Jelani, 40–41

Cohen, Steve, 121, 168

Colbert, Stephen, 149

Coleman, Michael, 226–29

Colorado, 8

Color blindness, 17, 55, 64, 194

Columbus, Ohio, 226–29

Compton, Ann, 247–48

Conservative Christians, 8

Conyers, John, 127, 168

CORE (Congress of Racial Equality), 85

Corker, Bob, 120, 121

Corzine, Jon, 264

Cosby, Bill, 21, 22

Cosell, Howard, 3

Crosby, Stephen, 193, 203

Crowley, James, 257–52

Crump, Mildred, 139, 149, 151, 153, 157

Cunningham, Dayna, 183

Curry, George, 43

Curry, Wayne, 6–7, 28

Davis, Artur, 15, 88, 89–109, 243; in Congress, 89–109; defeat of Hilliard, 46, 91–94, 96, 101; governor try, 90, 104–9, 172; identity politics and, 172; Obama and, 94–98, 103, 104, 106, 258–59

Davis, Geoff, 59

Davis, Natalie, 92, 107, 108

Dawson, Michael, 37, 238

Dayton, Ohio, 35–50

Dellums, Ron, 24–25, 29, 36, 49–50, 68, 239

DeMicco, Steve, 140–41, 145

Democratic Leadership Council (DLC), 27, 103, 105, 123–24

Democratic National Convention: 1964, 85, 116, 241; 1984, 113; 1988, 9; 1992, 20; 2004, 64; 2008, 7, 20, 113–14

Democratic Party: in Alabama, 97–99; Al Gore campaign and, 48; black identification with, 241; black mayors and, 4; gains in the South, 100–101, 105–6; Jesse Jackson presidential campaign, 7–10; John Kerry presidential campaign, 11; Shirley Chisholm's presidential try, 1972, 24–25; voter turnout, 2008, 19

Demographics, 2, 3–7